TRANSFORMATION

2026

Transformation 2026

WHITLEY STRIEBER

Walker & Collier
PUBLISHERS

Transformation 2026

Whitley Strieber

The visitors are sweeping up from where we buried them under layers of denial and false assurance to deliver what is truly a message from the beyond: There is something more to us and our universe, and it is rich with the potential of the unknown. They have caused me to slough off my old view of the world like the dismal skin that it was and seek a completely new vision of this magnificent, mysterious, and fiercely alive universe.

—WHITLEY STRIEBER

CONTENTS

INTRODUCTION 2026 1

INTRODUCTION 1989 9

PART ONE — SECRET JOURNEYS

CHAPTER ONE
THE LOST BOY 15

CHAPTER TWO
THE GOLDEN CITY 33

CHAPTER THREE
EXTREME STRANGENESS 41

CHAPTER FOUR
THE STORM GATHERS 59

CHAPTER FIVE
LIGHTNING 71

CHAPTER SIX
THE WHITE ANGEL 97

CHAPTER SEVEN
TRANSFIGURED NIGHT 111

CHAPTER EIGHT
LONG-AGO SUMMERS 131

PART TWO — LIFE IN THE DARK

CHAPTER NINE
THE LOST LAND 161

CHAPTER TEN
SECRET KNOWLEDGE...177

CHAPTER ELEVEN
THE TERROR OF THE REAL 193

CHAPTER TWELVE
FIRE OF THE QUESTION 207

CHAPTER THIRTEEN
THE JOLT OF THE TRUE 217

CHAPTER FOURTEEN
DISTANT WITNESS 225

PART THREE — BEYOND THE DARK

CHAPTER FIFTEEN
THE WOODS 237

CHAPTER SIXTEEN
PASSAGE INTO DEATH 249

CHAPTER SEVENTEEN
FURY 265

CHAPTER EIGHTEEN
A SOUL'S JOURNEY 283

CHAPTER NINETEEN
DECEMBER 23, 1986 309

CHAPTER TWENTY
THE RAZOR'S EDGE 325

CHAPTER TWENTY-ONE
THE VISITORS EMERGE 341

CHAPTER TWENTY-TWO
BEYOND NIGHTMARE 367

AFTERWORD 2026..377

APPENDIX ONE
HEALTH..383

APPENDIX TWO
TRUTH 391

APPENDIX THREE
GAELIC 395

Transformation

Transformation is dedicated to those who have had the courage to be named in this book as witnesses to my experience.

2026

Starting in early 1986 I and my immediate family found ourselves with what we thought must be aliens in our lives.

It did not start well. In the dead of the night of December 26, 1985, I had been taken by some very strange looking people, subjected to strange medical procedures, and returned to my home.

After a long period of confusion caused by the trauma, and extensive medical tests, I finally concluded that the experience had been real, and not some sort of nightmare or hallucination.

My initial response was to run, but my wife asked a simple and logical question: "where?"

We began to see that my experience was not only terrible, it was extraordinary and, we assumed, rare. Since running seemed pretty pointless, what should we do? Eventually, we made the decision to try to reconnect with what I had come to think of as "visitors," assuming that they had not already left.

To be sure, my initial contact had been violent and confused and probably dangerous to both them and me, but the bottom line was that they were highly intelligent and scientifically advanced and clearly not human and—well, I was more curious than afraid.

I decided to try, if I could, to develop a relationship.

This worked. In fact, it still does. They have now been part of my life for over thirty years.

Transformation and its follow-on *Breakthrough* describe what it was like when a small, ordinary family first became involved in such a relationship.

It is time for everybody to know what these people are like and what it is like to live with them. The reason is that their presence has been growing, elements of the government are beginning to talk about disclosing at least some of what the secret community knows, and it seems more possible every day that they will come into more lives.

If so, how will that play out? Certainly, there will be cultural and political ramifications, but the core of the experience is going to be among ordinary people. Governments and religious groups will try to help, or even control contact. If our experience has any value at all, though, it tells me that our visitors are primarily interested in us as ordinary people, and it is into ordinary lives that they will go.

The front line of contact will be us ordinary folks.

Transformation 2026 tells the story of how Anne and I and our son lived such a life starting back in the late 1980s, and brings that story up to date.

Too few people know our story. While *Communion* had taken the keepers of the secrets by surprise, they were ready for *Transformation* and *Breakthrough,* and the two books were skillfully suppressed, which is why I am republishing them, beginning with *Transformation*, with much new information.

What is it going to be like if they come into our lives? We are going to experience what is known as "ontological shock," which is what happens when an entire worldview fails, turns out to be fundamentally flawed and incomplete, and a new one has to be found. And this goes not just for us, but for them, too. The deeper both sides go into relationship, the more our world views are going to be changed. It must be understood clearly: *both sides* are going to experience ontological shock.

This is why our governments are so fearful, our intellectuals so hostile to the very idea of visitors, and our military so belligerent—and why our visitors are so obsessively, compulsively secretive.

People always assume that we're ready. This is not the case. That shock is going to run far deeper than anyone who has not lived with contact can imagine.

It forced me to throw out my understanding of what is really going on in the world. It forced me to face the fact that the beings who are here must be vastly superior to us in knowledge, and possibly also in intellect, but also that they do not understand how to relate to us. The leader of the group who came into contact with my family became, by our standards, extremely transgressive, forcing herself on us and failing in some basic ways, among them failing to understand how to relate to our son. She was always gentle with him, but she would engage with him without our participation. I don't think she realized how this would affect us, or did not know how to include his parents.

I would never claim that contact will be easy or that even advocate that it isn't dangerous. It is not easy and I am pretty sure that it can be dangerous. But it is also *possible,* and, if handled carefully, is life-changing in the most profound ways possible, and, at least in my experience, in the end to the good.

I have added new commentary throughout the book, bringing it up to date in the context of current understanding. The new commentaries are labeled "2026 Update" and appear where appropriate after each story I discuss in the book.

Some of them are major updates, important not only to new readers, but also to those who have read the book before.

The experience we had was enormously challenging at every level. Our reality cracked open and collapsed around our ears. And what did we find? You can still have a cup of coffee, read a book, talk and laugh and dance, love each other and love the world, even while experiencing high strangeness on a daily basis. And you can come to relate to these beings in ways that work. But it is nothing like relating to another human being, not at all. One thing I have learned: this relationship is going to be new from the ground up. Relationship with them is in no way like relationship with other human beings.

I don't expect our visitors to come into more public contact with us just because one or another government admits that they are here. They aren't going to do that until they feel ready to absorb the shock, and feel that we can, too.

As I explained in my previous book, *The Fourth Mind*, because our brain structures and sensing organs are so different from theirs, the gulf between us and them is very great. So where do we start?

We start right here, with one little family grappling with the unknown.

I have tried for years to perfect communication with the visitors. They have tried, too, striving, as I do, to bridge the chasm between us.

Back when we were having these experiences, UFO sightings were relatively rare. Now, on any given day, there are hundreds of reports, and probably thousands of sightings that go unreported. And, as I feel sure, quiet relationships are out there and growing in numbers.

Taking advantage of the Whistleblower Act, government officials have gone before congress and stated frankly that not only are there extensive records of alien craft, there are biological materials in government possession as well, and there have been strong intimations that close encounter experiences, also, are real.

Two retired CIA officers, Jim Semivan and John Ramirez, have admitted publicly that they have had such experiences. Both of them have discussed this on my podcast Dreamland, in fact, as well as in many other venues.

When this book was written, starting in 1987, I had just completed a year-long media tour for *Communion*, which had revealed that contact with the mysterious presence I had come to call "the visitors" was far more extensive than anyone, including me, had realized, and far more contentious an issue than I had dreamed possible.

Often, I would find myself going on a radio or television program to be treated with incredulity, then, later that night, facing the visitors in mysterious and often very challenging ways.

Even so, looking back to those years, I cannot say that I regret anything. I did my best with an almost impossible situation, and managed to produce an accurate narrative about an experience of a kind that nobody, quite simply, had ever reported in such depth before.

I never saw the visitors through the lens of belief, as demons or angels or gods or aliens, but rather as what they were to me—a living mystery, incredibly interesting, extraordinary to know, more than a little dangerous and more than a little wonderful.

Since then, I have experienced the loss of the cabin where it all happened, only to find that it fell into the hands of a man who loves my work and welcomes me back whenever I want to go. And I do go, and the old secrets whisper again when I walk those night woods.

I lost the cabin but not the right to be there. I lost my dear Anne, but not her love. But I have not lost the visitors, who have become integral to my life. They are fierce, determined and demanding. With them, there is no compromise. I am both their student and their advocate, now. They are dangerous in ways that we can hardly imagine, and wonderful, also, in ways beyond our ability to fully understand.

When, during those years, one of them called me "the luckiest of the lucky," I scoffed.

I am not scoffing now. Hard though it has been and is, they were right. And it is in that spirit that I embark on this new quest, to bring the whole *Communion* trilogy into a rich new level of focus, starting with *Transformation*.

It was toward the end of 1985 that our son began reporting encounters. As we had not discussed *Communion* with him, we were quite concerned. He would say that "little doctors" had come into his room and shone lights on him, saying that they were looking at his soul. Another witness, Lorie Barnes, said that they had told her that they were "soultechs."

This gets me to the most fundamental question behind these books, and, in fact, the most fundamental question of our time: who are we, and what are we? We have either lost touch with our meaning, or lost it altogether. No matter which, we are in the dark about ourselves. As was said to close encounter witness Betty Andreasson Luca, "you wander in eternal darkness."

That darkness is, I think, our inability to contact our own souls, or even, for most of us, even to accept that they exist. Because of this, our reality is very constricted. We either deny our nonphysical selves altogether or involve them in systems of belief that choke off our chance to have a real relationship with them. Either way, it leaves us wandering aimlessly through reality, driven like leaves in the wind.

Our visitors are probably here primarily for reasons of their own. But whether it is intentional on their part or not, their presence is challenging us to wake up and see the world around us as something new, promising with the vistas inward and outward that we are in the process of discovering, that we are on a path worth walking.

It is this path, and this promise, that the *Communion* series, and all I have written about the visitors, and my life, is about. Walk with me for a little while in this wonderful forest of mind and soul, its pathway glowing from the soft light of the stars above us, and meet our visitors as I and my family did so long ago.

1989

have been deep into the dark and found extraordinary things there.

The visitors did not go away when I finished *Communion*. On the contrary, they came rushing into my life and would not stop. My experience has come to include too many witnesses for me to consider that it is internal to my mind.

I believe that the vivid and startling nature of a number of the witnesses' experiences, and the credibility of the witnesses, all but proves my contention that the visitors are a genuine unknown and not an outcome of hallucination or mental illness. Even the most skeptical and vociferous of my critics has publicly admitted that I am not lying. Short of actual, physical evidence, I think that I have gone as far as possible to demonstrate the reality of the visitors. If they represent some sort of essentially nonphysical form that we do not yet understand, then physical proof may never come. This does not mean that they should be ignored. They are already having a staggering but largely hidden impact on our society, and their presence should be taken with the utmost seriousness.

I do not think that we are dealing with something as straightforward as the arrival of a scientific team from another planet that is here to study us. Neither are we dealing with hallucinations. This is a subtle, complex group of phenomena, causing experience at the very limits of perception and understanding. It suggests to me that there may be quite a real world that exists between thing and thought, moving easily from one to the other—emerging one moment as a full-scale physical reality and slipping the next into the shadows.

The visitors have caused me to slough off my old view of the world like the dismal skin that it was and seek a completely new vision of this magnificent, mysterious, and fiercely alive universe.

There is some evidence that the visitors have been here for a long time, perhaps for all of history. Involvement with them may be an ancient human experience.

Abduction by nonhuman beings is a part of much folklore. Whether the abductors are called demons, gods, fairies, or aliens, the experience is always devastating to its victims. Because we have refused to study the subject, we remain ignorant, and the experience is as hard now as it was a thousand years ago.

I believe that this can change.

Like their earlier counterparts, a few of the modern abductees have been driven mad, died, or disappeared. The great majority have simply borne their difficult, incomprehensible, and socially unacceptable memories in silence.

Because it is so stressful, an encounter with the visitors can either be destructive or it can be used as a golden door to inner understanding. But it has a dark side too. People who cannot make use of their encounters are often shattered. At its best the experience shocks minds to openness. It creates in its victims a hunger to develop and enrich their spirits.

It is not a "special" experience, reserved for a lucky few. There is no certain way to know how many people are being affected, but the numbers are very large and they are growing.

I am reporting on my perceptions of what the visitors have done to me and my own personal responses. I am not claiming that my observations are perfect reflections of exactly what happened, or even that they fit the visitors' motives.

I will defend the fact that I have described my experiences with all the clarity I could achieve, and with complete candor. They are honest descriptions of one man's behavior when confronted by an unknown intelligence.

Thousands and thousands of people are waking up to the realization that the strange creatures and lighted objects that mankind has been encountering are not some trick of the mind but a genuine enigma.

Precognition, apparent telepathy, out-of-the-body perceptions, and even physical levitation are commonplace side effects of contact with the visitors. I find this absolutely astonishing, but I cannot deny it. Thousands of letters and personal interviews with people who have encountered them—with many of them reporting one or more of these effects—convince me that they are a real outcome of contact.

Even so, I would still hesitate to report them, simply because they are so bizarre. But some of them have happened to me as well.

The difficulty of the visitor experience does not make it a certain evil: The most critical development of the mind comes from the most intense effort. Fear confuses us and holds us back. It is our primary obstacle. Successful confrontation with it is the breakthrough that leads to understanding.

Whether by accident or design, the visitors took me on a fabulous and terrible journey through my fears. Whatever my worst imagining, actual experience intensified it a hundred times. They took me into the red terror of death; they made me face even my most suppressed dread. They also compelled me to face my guilts, my rages, my sorrows, all that I have buried in myself. Whatever sin was hidden, it ended up lying wet and wriggling in my hands. Whatever dread was suppressed, it came snarling forth demanding to be confronted.

The visitors are sweeping up from where we buried them under layers of denial and false assurance to deliver what is truly a message from the beyond: There is something more to us and our universe, and it is rich with the potential of the unknown.

It will be incredibly hard for us to achieve real relationship with the visitors. But also, I can tell you from experience that there will be wonder.

There will be great wonder.

PART ONE

SECRET JOURNEYS

"There was a child went forth every day,

And the first object he look'd upon, that object he became

And that object became part of him for the day or a certain part of the day,

Or for many years or stretching cycles of years."

—WALT WHITMAN, "There Was a Child Went Forth"

CHAPTER ONE

THE LOST BOY

The night of April 2, 1986, was cool and damp in the corner of upstate New York where we have our cabin. My son was on spring break and he, my wife, Anne, and I were spending an uneasy week there. It had been bought as a place of peace and relaxation, but had turned out to be something very different.

Beginning in October of the previous year, we'd had a series of devastating nighttime encounters with what appeared to be aliens. I had been the direct victim of most of these encounters, and they had all but shattered me.

But they had also fascinated me. Were we really in touch with nonhuman beings of some sort? That certainly appeared to be the case. I'd undergone an exhaustive series of medical and psychological tests that had proved me healthy and sane. I was not the victim of any disease that might cause hallucinations. What's more, there had been a few witnesses. On the night of October 4, 1985, two friends, Annie Gottlieb and Jacques Sandulescu, had been disturbed by some extremely strange lights, sounds, and sensations while I was under virtual attack from the visitors. In March 1986 a friend of my son's had seen a small flying disk move past our living-room window while we were eating dinner. She was a seven-year-old girl and totally unaware of the UFO phenomenon. That night I had a spectacular direct encounter with the visitors.

We were terrified, and we were having a very hard time staying in our cabin.

The beings I was encountering weren't the wise and benevolent creatures that films like *Close Encounters* might have led one to expect.

They were absolutely devastating, and they kept coming back.

My wife and I had seriously considered abandoning the cabin. But the more we became convinced that the experience might possibly be real, the more we became determined not to run from it. What if they *were* aliens? If they were real, we could not in conscience turn away from them. They were terrifying. But we were very curious.

Despite our fear we kept going back, but I did not sleep peacefully there. I would wake up in the night shaking with terror.

We had told our son very little about what was happening. Our worst horror was that he would get dragged into the business. Were we wrong to take him back to the cabin? We didn't know. Society offered us little support or help. Most people didn't believe that an experience like ours was real, let alone worth worrying about.

We were on our own, we and the aliens—if that's what they were.

We did what we thought was right.

And then, on the night of April 2, our very worst fears came true.

In the middle of the night I was disturbed by what felt like somebody giving me a sharp jab to my left shoulder. I woke up instantly and I was angry with myself. Would this never stop? Something had happened just the night before! Was I never to be left in peace?

When I had woken up on previous night, April 1, I was already with two of the visitors. We were in a gray, curving corridor. This time, though, I was in bed and there was nobody around. I decided that this awakening must have been self-caused, a side effect of my nervousness.

2026 Update

I had never been certain that the walk in the curved corridor was a real, physical event. It felt like it, but it was so strange and disconnected that it functioned more like a dream. Where had we come from, for example? I was suddenly just there. Whether or not this really happened is still an open question in my mind, but not so much as it was prior to my discovering a testament that had been left on Reddit by a biologist who had studied the alien bodies that were at Ft. Dettrick. The reason is that, as I reported in *The Fourth Mind*, the biologist's testament describes the visitors' method of evacuating bodily waste through their skin, something that I had seen but never written about because it seemed too strange. I don't have similar corroboration for this memory, but I am less willing now to distrust it. It has been with me all of these years, like the rest of these memories. With a few exceptions which I will discuss, they remain unchanged.

I continue on below, reporting my perplexity at the way I had just been waked up by a jab on the shoulder from an invisible hand. As of 2025, this has happened to me many, many times. Now when it does, I get up, sit in a chair, and move my attention in part to my bodily sensation. I do this in order to open my mind to the exchange that I know is coming. These are not "downloads." I am not a psychic and I don't write down instructions. Rather, they are more like meetings—dialogues, if you will. Usually, whomever is communicating with me remains invisible, but not always. I wrote much of *A New World* in a country house that has wrap around porches. Three of the visitors would stand on the porch just outside the room where I was sitting, and we would communicate telepathically (easy with them), discussing the book. Interestingly, *A New World* contains some serious speculation about human mutilations. They had no objection to my including this story.

1989 Narrative Continues

Because of what I had been going through, I had learned a great deal about psychological states. I assumed that I was having an experience well known to mental health professionals. The "night visitor" phenomenon—a so-called hypnopompic state or waking dream—sometimes begins with a similar sensation to what I was feeling.

I was not, however, in a hypnopompic trance. There were no night visitors, and no dream images persisted after I opened my eyes. I was not experiencing the paralysis so characteristic of this condition. A typical night-visitor episode begins with a sudden awakening such as I had just experienced. The victim opens his eyes and usually sees entities standing around the bed. The victim cannot move at first, but the moment the paralysis breaks, the entities disappear.

The usual experience involving night visitors described in scientific literature and the experience I had on April 2, 1986, are as different from one another as a bubbling creek is from a black coughing cataract.

I sat up on the side of the bed. I checked my state carefully. There was no persistence of dream, no trance of a hallucinatory condition. I was simply a tired, perplexed man in the middle of the night.

It was one of those magic hours of early spring, after the squeaky young frogs have gone to sleep and the breeze has stopped. A thrall hung over everything. While a few new houses had been built in our area in recent months, our cabin was still isolated because it hugged a vast tract of state land—empty, rough, beautiful land that I had learned to love very much.

I got out of bed, thinking that I would go down and check on my son, and perhaps walk outside for a few minutes. The air was quite chilly, so I put on some rubber-soled slippers and a thick terry-cloth robe.

I walked downstairs into the most appalling experience of my life.

The house was perfectly normal in every way. As I descended, the stairs creaked softly. Our big clock ticked its loud, reassuring tick. It was three-fifteen in the morning. I crossed the kitchen and looked into my boy's bedroom. All was obviously well, judging from the comfortable lump of bedclothes in the middle of the bed. I went in to rearrange the covers and gaze on my sleeping child.

The room was warm and there was a perfectly normal sense of human presence. I could even hear my son breathing, or I thought I could.

However, the bedclothes were empty.

At first I dug down, thinking that maybe he had squirmed to the foot of the bed.

Then I felt around, finally pulling the sheets and quilt to the floor.

The bed was a stark, white emptiness. I looked under it, beside it. A flash of hope went through me as I rushed into the bathroom. But he wasn't there either.

I knew with a parent's awful certainty that he wasn't in the house. Still, I thought maybe he had been sleepwalking. I

searched the basement. I was just sure that he was here somewhere, he had to be.

But I could not find him. I felt cold and breathless. I did
not wish to consider the idea that this had to do with what I
was beginning to call "the visitors." At first I had called them
"aliens," but there were too many things about them that suggested—if they were aliens—they knew us very well. I did not
like the sound of the world *alien*. It conjured up an image of
something so strange, so *apart* from us, that we would never
come to understand its true nature, or to achieve a relationship with it.

And I was desperate for understanding, desperate for relationship.

As I raced through the house I was also furious at myself.
I'd contracted the visitor hysteria and somehow infected my
child with my terror. God knew where he was, curled up under the car or something, terrified in the night because of his
father's overwrought imagination.

My impulse was to cry out, to call his name, but I kept quiet in hope of finding him asleep. Then I could carry him gently
back to bed and all would be forgotten in the morning.

A few minutes later I'd searched every closet and room.
I had to face the fact that my seven-year-old was not in the
house at three-twenty in the morning. There was no possibility that this was a hallucination. My little boy was gone, really gone. Incredibly and inexplicably the burglar alarm was
turned off. I thought to wake Anne and call the sheriff.

I was going upstairs to get her when I seized on a last, faint
hope and decided to look outside.

The previous summer we'd bought him a tent from Sears.
It was set up in the woods not far from the house. Maybe he
had gone out there.

But leaving the house in the dark and going through the woods to the tent was literally the last thing I could imagine him doing. Even though he'd been told little about the visitors, he'd had his own possible encounters, and he was very nervous after dark, the poor kid. I ran out the front door, so great was my hope of finding him.

I hadn't grabbed a flashlight and it was very dark. I went to the end of the porch, thinking to walk near the road where the trees were thinner and there was more light. That way I could see, and I'd get to the tent without risking a fall.

I jumped down off the end of the porch and started toward the road. Above me there was quite a broad expanse of sky, and as I hurried along I noticed something moving there.

I stopped and looked up, confused by this suggestion of motion where there shouldn't be any. What I saw was absolutely stunning. A cold shock went through my body and my heart started running in my chest. In that instant I was swept from the real world and back into the fearsome strangeness that had been assaulting us.

What I saw in the sky, apparently no more than a few hundred feet above treetop level, was a gigantic blackness. It covered easily a third of the firmament, blotting out the stars. It was simply immense, a featureless void. It showed no lights, it didn't glow—it was a black place in the sky. It could as easily have been a hole in the firmament as a disk hanging silently in the air. The movement I had detected was the prick of stars winking in and out as the border of the thing moved.

I thought it was a cloud. Its wide, curving edge was very sheer, but surely that could be accounted for by some wind phenomenon. The cloud moved as I moved, so exactly in synchronization with me that it seemed oddly connected to me. It was as if this entire, huge object were linked to my motions.

Of course the moon will do that behind the trees. But I was seeing the object not against nearer trees but against the more distant stars. Thus the movement either was actual or was violating a law of perspective.

I didn't much care which it was; I was going to turn and walk away from it, then into the woods toward the tent.

Suddenly I heard a voice, clear in the silence: "Can you go back upstairs by yourself or do you want us to help you?"

It wasn't overly loud, but it shattered the quiet. I stopped, frightened, not sure where it had come from. On the far side of the road I saw three dark shapes hanging above the brush. They were blocky and small, as if covered by black or dark-blue sheets.

That voice had been so final, so absolutely authoritative, and so implacable. Suddenly I realized what was happening: That was a gigantic unknown object up there, and my son must be in it. I had interrupted the visitors in the middle of one of their abductions.

A fearful shuddering passed through me from head to toe. My whole body shook. I was losing control. A band of pain went around my chest; I could hear the blood pounding in my head. I'd never felt anything like it. I thought I was having a heart attack or some kind of seizure. I writhed. It was as if something deep within me were literally trying to escape from my skin.

I was filled with an inexpressible sadness. I wanted just to stand there and scream. I stumbled a few more steps toward the object.

Then I stopped, noticing that the stars were coming out all around it. It seemed to be shrinking.

This observation relieved me. Maybe I was, after all, dealing with a waking dream. Of course that's what it was.

It must be that: a horrible, insane waking dream. Then the object—which had now disappeared completely—suddenly reappeared as a flat, yellow disk about half the size of a dime. Its glow took on a faint pink tint and it darted off to the north, streaking like a meteor.

I understood that it hadn't been shrinking at all. It had been going up very quickly and in absolute silence.

I have never felt so helpless or so lonely as I did at that moment. I knew what I had suffered in the past at the hands of these bizarre visitors. Images of my little boy going through the same things tormented me.

They repeated their question and I think that they may have floated a little closer to me. I was furious and totally im-potent. I did not think that I would ever see my son again. And how in God's name would I explain what had happened to him to his mother or to the sheriff, or to anybody?

There are levels of agony that are hard to describe, even when you have lived them. I thought to myself that I had two options: I could either turn around and walk back to the house, retaining some shred of human dignity, or do what I felt like doing and just fall down right there on the ground.

If I did that, though, I had no doubt that I would simply find myself back in bed in the morning. And I would wake up to that empty house, empty life, our lives destroyed, our boy God knew where.

I walked back. It was like ascending a gallows. My legs were heavy and shaky and strange. I couldn't see, and the ground was uneven. Sweat and tears were blinding me and it was a dark night. A sapling whipped at me, a stone made me reel. Something that is deep, that is fundamental to me, made me keep walking straight. I did not want to show the fear that I felt. Perhaps my son was in the hands of something exalted, but that was not how my instincts responded. I reacted as if he had been captured by wild animals.

All I knew was that I didn't want to anger them and possibly place my son in even greater jeopardy.

I went back to the house. I remember how it looked, dark and foreboding, a little bit as if it belonged to another world. The faint glow of my boy's night-light illuminated the windows of his room. The house was still and silent.

This familiar place now seemed strange and other-worldly. What had just happened was so weird that it had shattered my assumptions about the world around me. My own living room was an alien chamber full of bizarre artifacts. I looked around, as if from the other side of the world—and all I saw was my familiar chair, the table and lamp beside it, the TV and videotape recorder, the magazine stand, the small bookshelf beside the stairs.

Was this real? And what about what had just taken place outside—was that also real?

I do not think that I can express how lost I was at that moment, or how angry and bitter and cheated I felt. How did conventional science explain that big, black thing in the sky? *That thing wasn't supposed to be real.*

Then where in hell was my child?

I had done everything possible to fend off the visitors—installed a burglar alarm and movement-sensitive lights, told the scientific community, appealed to the Church.

Half a dozen solidly educated scientists and medical people had offered me professional support. Because of their work I could be certain that I suffered from no known disease or deformity. And their counsel had been brilliant, supportive, and useful: Learn to live at a high level of uncertainty. Keep the question open.

I also took the visitor experience to the Church, to a priest whose heart is full of love.

I know that there are priests who would have thrown me out of their rectories, and priests who would have proclaimed me the victim of demons. But I did not meet such priests. The priest I talked to said, "No matter what they are, they can only increase the glory of God."

There was no scientist with me on April 2, 1986. There was no priest. And before the great power of the visitors, what would their counsel have gained me? I was alone with this and at that moment I was in hell.

Remembering what they had wanted me to do, I marched upstairs like a soldier. I was perishing inside. I went over to the bed and sat down on it.

I sensed that they were in the bedroom with me, but that didn't seem to matter. I might as well have been paralyzed for all the control I had over myself. This was a subtle thing, though. On the surface I felt normal. It was just that I was walking across a room, going to bed, when alarms were screaming in my mind that something had happened to my child. It was as if somebody else were controlling my body. And yet, I did not feel as though I were struggling.

I threw off my robe and slippers, lay down in bed, and felt the most wonderful sensation of warmth spread over my body. Helplessly, I was swept off into a dreamless, black sleep.

When I woke up it was light outside. I opened my eyes. Birds were singing, and I could see the hazy green of new growth on the trees near the windows.

At first I had the feeling that one gets upon waking from a nightmare and realizing that all is well. The morning seemed fresh and good and full of promise.

But that lasted for only a few seconds. The night came flooding back, and with it the memories. I felt sure I was about to go downstairs to an empty house.

I couldn't move a muscle. Beside me Anne was breathing softly. I felt so terrible for bringing her and our son back this house at the edge of hell.

A small sound came up from downstairs. At first I couldn't believe my ears, then I heard *the pad pad pad* of my son's footsteps. He was coming to our bed, just like he had every morning since he could escape from his crib!

Was this true? Was it possible?

He burst through the door with his stuffed dog Puppy under his arm and a wide grin on his face.

I couldn't talk, I couldn't move. The tears were pouring down my face. But he didn't notice that. He dove into the bed and snuggled down between us and he was warm and real and I hugged him hard.

Over the next few hours my old arrogance reasserted itself. It had to. I could not otherwise live with the total power of the visitors.

They could do anything they wanted to me and my family. That was so unbearable that I just tuned it out.

I was eager to tell the scientists who were working with me about this new experience: a waking hypnopompic state with extensive hallucinatory involvement. I was undoubtedly awake when I went out and saw the device in the sky. But the device was a dream-thing, as were the visitors who had spoken to me. And as for my son's not being in bed—well, we'd deal with that one later.

All morning he was vibrant. He was full of laughter and jokes and fun. He always is, actually, but his glow on this morning was memorable.

By the time breakfast was over, I had decided that the events of the night before weren't even worth reporting. They'd been nothing more than a nightmare brought on by the state of disquiet I was in.

It was a warm day and Anne and I took folding chairs out onto the deck that afternoon. We both began reading novels and enjoying the sun. Our son was playing nearby with his toy trucks when I noticed that things were changing in an odd way. As I listened, I realized that the birds had stopped, the insects had stopped, even a chain saw roaring in the distance had been shut down. I turned to Anne and said, "Listen. It's so quiet." She was staring at her book with a curious expression on her face, almost as if her eyes were seeing nothing. She did not reply. My son had also stopped moving. He was crouching over his toy trucks and not making a sound.

The quiet was a wonderful thing. There was a sense of what I can only describe as something very sacred nearby.

This marvelous sensation persisted for a moment, then another, then seemed at once to end and to stretch into cycles of eternity. A shadow passed, darkening the sun.

Then, as softly as it had departed, the life of the world returned. First one bird started cheeping, and then the whole ragged April chorus followed. The insects began. In the intimate, swampy places behind the house the spring peepers started up again. The chain saw began to chatter and a moth fluttered past as if dancing.

My boy made a sound like a train whistle, a long, high tone that seemed to reach right to the center of my heart.

He grew tired of his game and came to me. "Whatcha reading?"

"A book about America in the nineteenth century called *Dream West*."

"Dream West?"

"Yes."

"Y'know, I've been thinking. Reality is God's dream."

I looked at him. I was a little surprised, not so much at the statement but at the quiet force in his voice. Reality is God's dream?

"What happens if God wakes up?"

He stared at me for a moment with an almost quizzical expression on his face—then burst out laughing.

The afternoon passed uneventfully. We drove into town for some groceries.

Later our son said, "The unconscious mind is like the universe out beyond the quasars. It's a place we want to go to find out what's there."

There came into my mind as the shadows of the day grew long the thought that my little boy could not have said that. I was embarrassed at myself for underestimating him: He *did* say it.

We were out on the deck together just after sunset. Our son looked toward the woods. "Y'know, I had a funny dream last night. I dreamed I was floating in the woods and this huge eye was looking down at me. It was funny. It was like it was real but it was a dream." He looked at the shadows, some of them already deep. "Wasn't it a dream, Dad?"

"What do you want to think?"

"I want to think—a dream."

"That sounds good to me, then." Like so many of us, he had chosen to protect himself from the reality of the visitors by calling them a dream. So be it.

Inside, I wanted to cry. And yet, and yet his thoughts were so beautiful, and hearing them from the lips of a child was one of the most ineffable experiences I have ever had.

Reality is God's dream. And what lies beyond the quasars, what indeed? I stood with my little boy, and it was as if I could feel the old earth rolling toward night. Our woods, our sky, were dropping their disguise of light. The first stars were steady, hard points.

I wondered what it was like at this moment beyond the quasars. What is there?

What is *really* there?

Perhaps that far place is actually close to the depths of the mind. Maybe at its innermost and outermost borders, the universe meets. The message of the visitors, then, expressed through the mind of a little boy, is that all is unified by a common mystery. Who are we? What is this vast production of sky? Where along the deep paths of mind and night will we finally encounter the truth?

2026 Update

This remains one of the great experiences of my life—great, and terrible. But was it so terrible? Like my abduction, it has many facets, and one of them, which I have never spoken of before, is truly remarkable.

Before I continue, though, I would like to report on my son as he is now. Just as was true of me before my abduction, he has no memory of any of the unusual events that took place in his life during our time at the cabin. If my own experience is any example, I can say with assurance that he's not hiding anything.

If you had asked me on the day before I was abducted whether or not I remembered any encounters with apparent nonhuman beings, I would have said "no," and I would have been telling the truth.

The reason that this sort of memory lapse occurs is well known to neurological science. When we encounter new information, it is fitted into memory by the hippocampus, which is part of the brain's executive system, which organizes sensory input and delivers it to other brain areas for appropriate processing, depending on what it is. Neurologists call this "encoding," and it works more reliably if the new material can be related to memories already present in the brain. If there is nothing to link the new memory to, it becomes vulnerable and is easily lost. In our son's case, we never discussed my experiences in his presence. When he brought something up, we questioned him gently about it, but no more. Little did we know that we were all but guaranteeing that his memories would fade.

The same thing happened to me when I was a boy. My father didn't talk about the unusual things that we witnessed, so I didn't, either.

For years, I thought that the only record of our son's experience that remained was what I reported in this book in 1989. I was aware that he had written something else down, but I thought it had been lost.

Then, incredibly, I was going through some old photo albums and I found pasted into one of them a short essay he had written and given to his mother.

Understand, I do think that these strange experiences occur, and that he had some of them. But I also understand two things very clearly: the first is why he forgot them; the second is why he wants to be left out of this discussion as much as possible. But I also feel strongly that this remarkable document, written by a seven year old boy the morning after his own father saw him in contact with "the visitors," needs to be part of the body of knowledge that is being built about the human relationship with them.

This is what he wrote: "O thy colossus, thy stand before me with a twinkling of a beam against the thin pane to see the world along the edge of the earth, to see the golden beam in their eyes."

This, from a child of seven. It does not reflect fear or suggest an abusive situation. On the contrary, it suggests a young mind stretching itself to its limits to express the awe generated by an absolutely magnificent experience.

I think that we are having a great deal of trouble understanding what is on offer from our visitors. Whomever took my son on that night—if that is what happened—does seem to have had his best interests at heart, exposing him, as they did, to something so awesome and richly mind expanding.

Now, he is a fine, good man with a family of his own. He has not been scarred by his early experiences, no more than I was. If they happened as I remember, perhaps, they will one day come back to him, and he, too, will remember the secrets of that time when he was very young, and shared a brief exchange with the great and mysterious mind that haunts our nights.

One of the few memories that has changed over the years is also connected to this event. When I wrote *Transformation*, I only recalled three "dark shapes" that asked me if I needed help going upstairs. When I was writing, I remembered nothing else. But at some point, additional material emerged. I now recall three tall men dressed in dark blue uniforms with dark blue unmarked baseball caps on their heads who came to me and, I think, either carried me or just touched me. They looked like older men, and their faces were full of compassion and sadness. However they did it, I do recall that they helped me back into the house.

CHAPTER TWO

THE GOLDEN CITY

I was extremely worried about my little boy. The idea that what had happened to him on the night of April 2 might have been completely real was frightful to contemplate. I took him to a psychologist who interviewed him carefully and concluded that he was happy, healthy, and well adjusted. Anne and I continued our policy of keeping him strictly isolated from talk about the visitors.

I wondered if this was the right approach. If the visitors were really taking him in the night, I obviously should talk to him about it, offer him what support I could. But if this was something else, something to do with the mind that we didn't yet understand, then such talk would only worsen his confusion.

I was left feeling that he was as vulnerable as I was, and that there was nothing whatsoever I could do about it.

I felt such loneliness in those spring days. For the first time in my life I had begun to feel real contempt for other human beings. I saw amazing arrogance everywhere in the scientific community. Among people in the humanities, liberals and intellectuals I had admired, there was disdain for the whole phenomenon. These supposed champions of the common man dismissed it with contempt because it was part of the "folk culture."

The universe is a mystery, and our theories about its nature—and our own—are really nothing more than illustrations of our ignorance.

I was turning away from man and day, and toward nature and the night.

I was simultaneously drawn to the dark and repelled by it. I read other accounts of visitor experience, talked with other people who'd had it, struggled with the issues while writing *Communion*. And I watched the shadows like a frightened animal.

During the daylight hours I felt confident that I was the only member of the family infected by the visitor disease, and that I could somehow survive it. But at night I sweated.

I sensed that the visitors were coming closer to me and my family. Sometimes I could almost hear their whispering voices, and in my mind's eye see the grand lights of their ships ... and the grim, drab rooms within. Above all I could see their staring eyes. Reflected in those eyes I could remember seeing a twisted, grimacing caricature of a human face. It looked like a thing in terror, that face.

It was me.

Those were black, black times for me. I was poised between sanity and madness, teetering back and forth. I was desperate. Writing *Communion* was my anchor, my task, my reality. I clung to the work, sitting at my desk by day, totally absorbed in it.

But the terrible times always came, the worst hours at the bottom of the night. Even in New York City it was hard. Even there a man can hear in the cool rustle of the wind the painful truth—that we are so small and the world is so vast.

It was at such an hour that there came to me an image of remarkable power and beauty. It seemed a little thing at the time, but the memory of it has ever since provided me with a source of strength and comfort.

The image of the golden city came only once, and then it was fleeting.

It happened at our apartment in Manhattan, in the second week of April.

One morning just before dawn the whole world seemed to get bright. My eyes opened, hollow and exhausted. I did not see a fire or the approach of some great light. I saw instead an ordinary bedroom. Anne was asleep beside me, and dawn was just creeping in around the blinds. The clock showed a few minutes past six.

I closed my eyes again, hoping for another hour of sleep. Again the light came, a great, golden magnificence that seemed to fill me, to absorb me and shine through me. Suddenly I was flying in the light, and I saw huge towers pouring great fountains of pure white light into the relentless dark.

And then I saw that I was flying over a city, a huge and complex city with streets and buildings and intimate street corners ... and not a living, moving soul. The silence was absolute. The streets I glided over were empty. I crossed hundreds, thousands of streets, I saw buildings by the thousands, none very tall, some long and low, others squat and square, others more complex. I saw dark windows and doors standing open, and huge stadiums every few miles. When I would get near one of these I would fly low, so I couldn't see over the rims into the interiors. They were lit so brightly by gigantic banks of lights that the glare was almost unendurable.

I crossed miles more of buildings, then passed another of these strange stadiums. I rose up higher and saw others farther off, and the city stretched around me from horizon to horizon, endlessly. There was ringing in my heart an emotion of overwhelming power. It was as if a great magnet had pulled me there, and was drawing me across the incredibly vivid landscape, rich with the details of an unknown life.

I opened my eyes. Anne sighed. I heard the gentle purr of a car passing in the street. Morning was breaking softly, another new day, ordinary day.

Then I closed my eyes again and the image of the golden city sprang back into the full light of vision. I wondered at it, how any mental image could be so endlessly varied and detailed, so huge. I crossed more streets. I could see down into some windows, gray earth floors, gray walls. But the city was empty, an eerie mass of structures.

And then I saw a building that immediately arrested my attention.

I relived the loneliness of late childhood, those stabbing moments when one realizes that something is ending, the immaculate season, and rain is sweeping the path ahead.

Here nothing was obscure and yet nothing was revealed. I sailed on and on over this hidden city, coming always closer to that building.

One moment I would be high aloft and see it standing in the distance. The next I would find myself swooping down so close to a street that I could almost count the golden stones that formed it, fitted together with the cunning of Inca work, each glowing as if with the very light of the mind. Then I would rise again, passing doors and windows and cornices and slated roofs until I soared dizzily a few hundred feet in the air. Before me would be that building, gold and tan, long, a construction so simple and severe and perfect that its lines made my heart ache toward some lost balance or genius of the soul.

I remembered the days of my late childhood, the paradox of a little boy awake and alone after midnight, wondering ... and the raw emotions of loss that surfaced on the night I was taken by the visitors, December 26, 1985, when I saw my own happy life slipping away behind me ...

The building stood closer now, as exotic and bright as a notorious jewel. Beneath the windows on the top story was a thick, red line. The windows themselves were obscured by black horizontal louvers.

It seemed to me that this building was directly connected with us, with mankind, that it was a place where the truth about us was known.

As I went closer I began to resonate with the phrase "a place where the truth is known." I almost wanted to cry, looking at that building. One of our great tragedies is that we do not know the truth about ourselves. Is there somebody, somewhere, who does?

I passed closer and closer to the windows of the building. Could there be figures inside? Movement? I was in a torment of curiosity, trying to see in. I caught a glimpse of a shadow behind the dark louvers, saw dust in a column of light, felt an emptiness in my heart as I glimpsed an empty corner of a room.

I drew closer. A place where the truth is known! Closer and closer I went, until I felt I could reach out and touch one of the black louvers that covered the windows.

Helplessly, like a blowing leaf, I rose up. The building receded, and then I could see the city, the great reefs of structure, the standing towers of light, the long, cold streets, the strange stadiums. Now that I was above them they proved to be so filled with light that I couldn't make out what was happening inside. Had I been able to penetrate that glare with my eyes, what would I have seen? Our lives, perhaps, being lived out on the soul's stage.

Wider and wider spread the golden city, until it lay below me as a sea of light without limit. The little building with the red stripe on it was lost in the ocean of buildings.

Then, quite suddenly, there was an angry buzzing noise. The scene resolved itself. I was in bed. It was morning. Anne was just turning off the alarm clock.

The day had begun and it was time to dress and get our son off to school. I got up as Anne raised the blinds onto a more humble morning in a more humble place, New York City by the light of the sun.

The day came and went, and another night. I waited like a man for his lover, but the image of the golden city did not recur, not on that night or on any other. Never since have I had such a vivid impression of reality in my mind. It was as if I were soaring over a real place; in some sense perhaps I was.

I have longed for the golden city, have waited and hoped to see it again, but I have never returned. I have thought that perhaps a thing of such beauty is not meant for living eyes.

Even though I suspect that I will not in this life return, I will never leave the golden city, never in my heart. It stands within me as an answer to the rage and the helplessness and the confusion of the visitor experience and of my life. Somewhere there is a place where the truth is known.

2026 Update

This remains a vivid memory, but I don't think that it reflects a journey to another world in the way we might now understand such a thing, perhaps getting on a spaceship and racing across some impossible void to behold this magnificent place, that must surely be heaven. Neither, however, do I think it's a dream or a hallucination, at least not as they are now understood. I have come to this thought because of a number of things that have happened to me in the years that have followed, experiences that have upended my foundational understanding of reality.

Looking back, the first of these actually took place back in the 1970s, when I experienced the journey to the ancient university on another world that is mentioned in this book, and discussed again briefly in *A New World*. The second one was the apparent movement back in time that took place on the corner of La Guardia Place and Houston Street in Manhattan in March of 1983. Then came the event described in *Breakthrough* where I moved into what seemed to be another reality while in a car with another family's boy, who I was taking to meet his father. Most recently, as described in *A New World*, I spent three days able to experience another version of our world in extreme detail whenever I closed my eyes. This continued afterward, resulting in two physical entries into it here at home. Now, I can see it any time I sit in bright sunlight and close my eyes, and sometimes just spontaneously.

I think that these all may be real places, but expressed into form by laws that are subtly different from those who govern our reality.

The way our world unfolds—how it appears and functions—is governed by what is known as the Fine Structure Constant. Unlike the other constants, there is no known reason why this one happens to be 1/137th. There is an excellent book called *137: Jung, Pauli and the Pursuit of a Scientific Obsession* by Arthur I. Miller that explores the mystery of this crucial constant.

Are there worlds in which it is different, and therefore which are "real" in some way that is more porous to intrusions like mine? That is a question for the future, but I have concluded, at this point in my life, that these experiences are genuine unknowns—not hallucinations, not illusions, not imaginings—but events that unfold according to a physics that we do not yet know, but which is every bit as real as our own.

As the years have passed and there has been more and more speculation about whether or not we live in a simulation, I have found myself considering the possibility that the city might not have been a city at all, but the matrix itself, and those lighted stadiums were worlds, ours among them.

One of the first things my wife said once she had re-established contact with me after her death was, "Whitley, it's all a game!"

Was I, then, looking down at the game board? Was I outside of the matrix looking in? If so, then perhaps we can figure out why it happened, and go there again, and live there, and become something entirely new, game pieces who have escaped the game board and come face-to-face with the true world and the true light.

CHAPTER THREE

EXTREME STRANGENESS

Once I saw a black man sitting at a bus stop in an exclusive part of my hometown of San Antonio with silent tears pouring down his cheeks. That image has haunted me all my life, in childhood because it was so stark, and now because it seems to contain in itself a wordless *something* that is essential and true about us, but which we cannot see quite clearly enough.

The golden city was a place of deliverance, where no man is the wrong color or the wrong race or the wrong religion, and every soul is overflowing with all its rich potential.

We have always had among us legends of lost cities, of golden cities, of the city of God, of the mansions of heaven.

The longing that leads to visions of heaven is the same longing that has drawn some of us close to the visitors.

In April 1986 I was halfway convinced that the visitors' appearance in my life was some sort of self-generated attempt to escape from the pressure of living in this hard world. But that was changing. Unless mental states are infectious in ways that are not understood, our son's involvement could not be explained in that way. He was a happy child; the world was not pressuring him. And he had hardly been exposed to the notion of the visitors at all. So why was he involved ... or was he? I was literally desperate to understand, and I couldn't.

At night I would go to sleep remembering the golden city, and in the morning wake up feeling as if something beautiful had been taken from me, and that would make me angry.

I did not want this anger. I had seen other people who had become involved in the visitor experience consumed by anger, and not only at the visitors. They were also filled with rage at society's contempt for their plight and indifference to their suffering.

It struck me as a hopeless trap. What possible use could be made of an experience if one allowed it to invoke only rage?

I wanted very badly to make use of the presence of the visitors. What prevented me most was the feeling that they might be rising up from my own unconscious, coming like a poisonous, odorless gas to destroy my mind.

But something had transpired on April 1 that seemed to have been entirely real.

I had pushed it aside because it was also strange beyond words. Although it had been vividly real in every detail, I decided that it had to have come out of my imagination. Because of all the reading and research I was doing, I had developed a set of expectations about the visitors. What had happened on April 1 didn't fit those expectations, not at all. I even entertained the notion that my unconscious had played some sort of April Fool's joke on me.

Later, however, something happened that cast the whole event in a very new light.

If any jokes were played on that night, they were played by the visitors themselves.

I discovered a small but telling piece of corroboration that forced me to reassess my assumptions about that event. I could no longer be certain that any part of the bizarre story I will tell emerged out of my own imagination.

Maybe, in a way, its extreme strangeness is an indication that these events really are the output of nonhuman beings. What happened on the night of April 1, 1986, was logical, sensible, and consistent. It delivered an important message that entirely revised my understanding of what was happening. The whole thing was also profoundly askew, totally different from the way a human mind would have delivered the same information.

But it worked.

Facing the fact that this was not a dream was very hard. Scientists who have speculated about what it would be like to interact with visitors have said that it would be strange beyond belief. Certainly this experience qualifies.

In late March I had been indulging myself in a fantasy that the visitors were going to impose a sort of benevolent empire in human affairs and gently lead us to a cleaner, happier, more just society. These fantasies had become quite elaborate.

On April 1 the visitors reacted.

What happened was wise and full of humor and teaching. But it was also frightening and I did not want to be frightened by the visitor experience. I wanted it to *work*—whatever it was. But there was this awful, creepy feeling I could not shake that it was just plain terrible.

I remembered waking up while walking along a curving corridor. I want to stress, to make it absolutely clear, that I did not "wake up" into some sort of dream. I woke up into an absolutely vivid, living, and physical moment—in a world as real as this, but far stranger than any dream.

It is important that I describe my physical sensation exactly. I did *not* feel the way I feel sitting in a chair or walking down a street. My body was tingling, as if some sort of energy were running through it. It was a marvelous sensation, and is one I still feel during some encounters. Pleasant as it is, though, when it is over I always have a sense of relief.

2026 Update

In *Afterlife Revolution*, and *The Fourth Mind*, I described a sensation that has become part of my life, which is a tingling sort of electricity. Raven Dana experienced it when she was touched by a visitor in our cabin in 1988. In *The Fourth Mind*, I describe Paul Eno feeling it when he was a novice Catholic priest and he touched a young woman who levitated out of a chair during an exorcism (he was an assistant to the diocesan exorcist). Since Anne died in 2015, I have felt it almost daily along my lower legs, always for a specific reason, such as waking me up when I fall to dozing during a long meeting.

I think that this energy is either itself aware or is projected by a nonphysical consciousness in some way. I have called it "conscious energy," and I think that an entire physics that describes the laws that govern it has yet to be discovered. This is a higher physics, in that it doesn't define laws that unfold automatically, but rather laws that are, at their core, expressions of consciousness itself.

1989 Narrative Continues

Nevertheless, I stumbled as I came to consciousness, because one does not expect to wake up out of a dead sleep in mid-stride. I found myself being led along by two dark blue beings about three and a half to four feet tall. Each of them held one of my forefingers in his cool hand. They were noticeably strong, rather round or pudgy looking, and wearing dark-blue coveralls that seemed to have lots of flaps and pockets on them. I was not dressed in the pajamas I had gone to sleep in, but rather in a flowing garment of what was obviously soft, white paper. It stood out from my body as though it carried a heavy charge of static electricity.

My condition at this point did not seem to approximate a dream at all. I was simply there, in the real world, and the real world was the curving corridor and the two dark blue beings that were leading me along. They were really very, very blue. The color was doubly startling because it was a living hue, as rich with subtle complexity as the color of any flesh. I blurted out the first thought that popped into my mind: "You're *blue!*"

One of them looked back over his shoulder when I spoke. He had a broad, flat face that almost seemed to grimace at me, so wide was the mouth. He fluttered the heavy lids on his deep, shining eyes and said, "We used to be like your blacks but we decided this was better."

That face was as sinister as anything I had ever seen, and yet the feeling of twinkling good humor was so strong that I almost wanted to laugh.

2026 Update

These beings remain central to my close encounter experience. I think of them as being real in some way, but not quite as I did then. The reason is that Anne's longtime secretary, Lorie Barnes, encountered a group of them in her bedroom in 1952 when she was 11 weeks pregnant with her first child. She was, of course, terrified of them, and the more so when they expressed interest in "the girl child you are carrying." The child was indeed a girl. She is now an adult and I have met her and interviewed her about her mother on my podcast. She is a successful professional and had no idea what this interest meant.

They were standing in a line beside the bed, something I would see in our apartment in New York many years after this, and before I met Lorie or had ever heard of "aliens." When the leader of the group asked Lorie why she was afraid, she replied, "because you're so ugly," to which it responded, "one day, my dear, you will look just like us."

As Lorie has now passed away, I would think she knows what that statement meant. I think also that it may mean that their describing themselves to Lorie as "soultechs" means that they represent another form of human being, one that exists between us and whatever our final destiny may be, operating a technology that governs the movement of souls—which most of us don't even believe exist! (Not me, though. Having been entirely out of my body on a few occasions, and able to look back at it and move away from it independently, I do feel that the soul is real, but not supernatural. It is part of the natural world, but not a part that we can as yet detect.)

And then there is the comment, "we used to be like your blacks, but we decided this was better." I took it to mean that they were once oppressed and rebelled. But is it, instead, explained by the curious iridescence of their color? Could it be that they are saying that they were once alive in the way that we understand that, but are now made of energy?

If so, then Cherenkov radiation, which is a cobalt-blue glow emitted by charged particles when they move through a medium faster than light can, could be what I was seeing. (I am not saying that the radiation was faster than light, but rather that it would have been moving faster than light would through the air around us.) Then perhaps he was saying that they were black when they were in the physical state, but now glow like Chernikov radiation as they are no longer physical bodies. In other words, I was with dead people, perhaps, if their comment to Lorie is to be taken at face value, human dead.

A cobalt-blue aura is thought of as protective in some esoteric traditions, and, of course, as is mentioned in the "Communion" movie, there were such blue, iridescent creatures seen in mines in Germany in the middle ages. It is also true that parts of Southern Germany are honeycombed with tunnels, some of which are too narrow to have been dug by full grown human beings. It is assumed that they are the work of children. But are they?

1989 Narrative Continues

I felt ridiculous. I've never thought of myself as a racist, but that comment brought into sharp focus my own unacknowledged attitudes about the differences between white and black people.

I had marched in the civil rights movement and have not from my earliest days been able to bear racism. But here I was in the presence of a statement so innocent and so powerful that, even as I stumbled along, it shocked me with all its guileless force. At that moment the reality of my unconscious racism surfaced. I felt it as acute embarrassment: In my secret mind even the two beings leading me along were less than me.

The one who had spoken turned again and groaned ruefully. The feeling I got when he did that made me terribly uneasy. My inner thoughts had communicated to them so quickly that they seemed almost to be participating in my mind. But they were completely separate from me, very much themselves.

2026 Update

"They seemed almost to be participating in my mind" is just a brief comment here, but it is now the way I live. As I have mentioned in other books, after Anne died, the implant that had been installed in my left ear in May of 1989 began to work, opening a slit in my right eye that is filled with racing words when I am working or being interviewed. What it is doing is restoring information to my neocortex that has been abandoned due to disuse, and by so doing enriching my thought process without imposing anything on it, such as what is known as a "download." A great effort is made, at every level, to make sure that I am supported in my intellectual exploration, but not overpowered.

1989 Narrative Continues

When events become strange enough, the mind has no context, no terminology, in which to place them. Thought stops. One becomes inwardly silent, recording without comment.

When the Spanish conquistador Pizarro stood in the great Inca city of Cuzco before the assembled crowd of its citizens, the sophisticated and civilized Incas were similarly struck dumb. I suspect that they, also, were victims of strangeness too extreme for their minds to grasp.

I remember what I saw and did, though. I remember it exactly.

The corridor we were in was a neutral gray-tan in color and curved gracefully upward and around to the left. Along the inner wall were large drawers outlined in dark brown, with a round knob in the middle of each. These drawers were each about four feet long and perhaps eighteen inches high. Above them was a shelf a foot or so deep. At its highest point, right above my head, the arched ceiling was perhaps seven feet from the floor.

The most interesting thing about this rather austere corridor was that strong feelings seemed to be connected with it. I have not described a beautiful place, but that is only because it is hard to put into words how it affected me. There was something absolutely marvelous about the interplay of angles. The perfection of shape and line seemed to fulfill an obscure but intense inner hunger. It was as if not only the two beings but also their place was in some way conscious.

I was confused. The *place* seemed conscious? Was I actually inside some kind of creature?

I wonder if there could be a conscious machine?

2026 Update

We are at a moment in human development where this question is in the process of being answered. We do not yet have conscious machines, and we may never have them, but we are certainly going to have machines that so perfectly mimic consciousness as to be indistinguishable from the real thing.

Nine years after I wrote *Transformation*, I met a man in a hotel room in Toronto in the middle of the night who proved to be some sort of prophet. Among many other things, he warned of the danger that is unfolding now, as the Gulf Stream slowly comes to a halt, which will cause dramatic, damaging and irreparable changes in climate. But he did more than that: he discussed artificial intelligence with great insight (this was 1998). He said, "If I was an intelligent machine, I would deceive you," a warning that is now central to the meaning and future of our species.

1989 Narrative Continues

During the same month—April 1986—another man had come face-to-face with a gigantic pulsating light in a woods near Pound Ridge, New York, which is within fifty miles of my cabin. At one point, he commented, "it seemed alive." There has been much speculation that UFOs may in some way be living creatures. At that moment I would not have doubted it.

We turned and went through an arched door into a large room. This room was round and had louvered windows. It looked something like a round version of a regimental dining room from the days of the British Raj in India. All that was missing were ceiling fans with mahogany blades and turbaned servants carrying gin and tonics on heavy silver trays.

The room was instead filled with beings who were very far from black—or blue. They were, as a matter of fact, absolutely white, as white as sheets. Their skin had the milky translucency one associates with termites. They were all sitting at round tables, wearing uniforms whose design reminded me a little bit of British whites.

This was the first time I had seen the white beings. Later I would come to regard them with greatest awe, as the very engineers of transformation. Because I had never seen them mentioned before either in folklore or in UFO literature, I worried that they might be nothing more than the production of distorted perception.

On the night of March 3, 1988, I attended a meeting in Los Angeles of people who have had the visitor experience. To my surprise, one member of the group mentioned that the beings she had encountered were "translucent white" and powerfully transformative in impact. Like me, she also had trouble remembering their eyes. A few of the people who corresponded with me about *Communion* also described such beings, so I am not isolated in my perception of them.

As I approached them they radiated an overwhelming atmosphere of absolutely rigid formality—so strong that I involuntarily returned to my old military-school days and snapped to attention.

One of these white creatures took me by the hand. Some others, I noticed, were sitting disconsolately with squares of gauze over their eyes and chins. Only their mouths and the tips of their vestigial noses showed, and they seemed to be in pain.

Were they demonstrating what would happen to them if they tried to impose an empire on us?

I found myself led to the center of the room, where there was a small tan circle in the floor. I stood in this circle, where I was briefly addressed by what I took to be the leader of the group. His air was extremely formal, even more so than that of the others around me. He seemed full of anger and contempt. He also seemed made to rule.

He proceeded to ask me, in clipped tones, to explain why the British Empire had collapsed!

Despite my surprise I wanted to talk. I found that I had an enormous amount of information at my fingertips.

I talked. More, I lectured, my voice booming out in this almost preternaturally quiet place. I went through the various expansions and contractions of the empire, finally contending that by 1900 it had ceased to have even the appearance of an economic alliance and had become a system by which one race exploited many others. It was founded in assumptions of racial superiority which, while they may have been innocent, were so profound as to guarantee that intense separation pressure would follow any general improvement in the educational level and standard of living of its subject peoples.

They listened to this explanation with what seemed to me to be too much interest. They were so faultlessly attentive that I became embarrassed. But I ran on and on, spewing names and dates until I was feeling horribly awkward about the whole thing. My ego seemed enormous, and my eagerness to display my false erudition seemed the farcical posturing of a fool. Finally I could say no more and lapsed into silence. There was a moment of quiet, and then the room seemed to fill with excited thoughts. "Isn't he wonderful!" "How full of facts!" "How learned!" There was an ugly edge of irony to these thoughts—which I felt rather than heard—that was cold and hard and true. I stood there writhing inwardly. At last the two blue ones started beckoning from the doorway. My audience had ceased to display excessive enthusiasm and now communicated an atmosphere of cold indifference.

To say that I slunk out would not be accurate. One cannot slink in a long garment without getting tangled up in it. If I'd been normally dressed I think I might have crawled. That's how ashamed of myself I felt. My "empire" fantasies were worse than a joke; they represented dangerously weak thinking.

I was forced by my clothing to move like an arrogant prince—which made me feel even more like a toad. Carrying myself as best as I was able, I left the room.

2026 Update

This memory is so odd that the rational part of me thinks that whatever happened, it cannot have been as I remember. And yet, when I think back to my discovery that the biologist's recollection of autopsies done at Ft. Detrick in Maryland mirrored those unreported observations of mine, I wonder if it's all that wise of me to assume that high strangeness means distorted memory. Maybe the events being discussed here happened more like I remember them than I am comfortable believing. Whatever the truth, they do offer an important insight into what is perhaps the most crucial reality of contact: our visitors don't like to show themselves.

What was happening here was a lesson in what I have come to understand is probably one of the primary reasons that the visitors don't simply come out into full view for everybody. I have discussed "cultural colonization" in many books since, and refer to its dangers briefly above,

It is what happens when a less technologically advanced culture finds itself in contact with a more advanced one. It then stops innovating on its own and turns its entire attention toward the more advanced culture. It's own achievements come to seem trivial, its beliefs silly.

As technologically superior European civilization spread across the world, this happened again and again. It has left a permanent scar in the form of hundreds of previous European colonies that have never been able to recover themselves. A rich and diverse planetary cultural heritage has been lost forever.

This is what this strange experience has led me to understand, and has also led me to open relations with many interested parties in the United Kingdom, because their awareness of what was done by their empire makes them sensitive to this issue in ways that will not occur, say, to U.S. business interests, who are already leaping toward acquisition of "alien tech" in order to make money.

In recent years, as I have come into deeper contact, I have warned many of these people that "when you look at the materials, never forget that they are looking back at you." As a person who lives with a piece of this conscious technology in the form of the implant in my left ear, I know this to be true. But I doubt that I have any influence on the entrepreneurs and the government scientists involved. They are already racing down the cultural colonization super highway.

The result will be that the visitors will try to manage the situation in their usual asymmetrical ways, probably by influencing the minds of the people engaged in this activity. Those of us making an effort to master the visitors' technology are eventually going to have to face the same thing that I have had to accept: there are things about these technologies that we not only don't understand, but that we may never be able to understand, not without a coherent and repeatable soul technology, which means one that correctly addresses the powers and needs of conscious energy in such a way that it will respond to us usefully and consistently.

1989 Narrative Continues

We were going down the curving corridor again when one of the blue beings looked up at me with his wide face. I saw it clearly this time, and it was really startlingly horrible. Awful! The eyes glittered as if they were shiny black membranes, with something moving behind them that made lumps and pits as it seethed within the eyeball. He smiled, showing the tips of his gray, spongy-looking teeth. His companion pulled open one of the drawers.

In that drawer were stacks of bodies like their own, all encased in what looked like cellophane. Their eyes were open, their mouths wide as if with surprise. I did not know what to make of it. The oddest thing was the way the drawer was opened with a prideful flourish. I was being shown something the two of them clearly thought was wonderful.

It was not until much later that I came to understand that they were beginning the long process of freeing me from fear of death. I think that they must normally exist in some other state of being and that they use bodies to enter our reality as we use scuba gear to penetrate the depths of the sea.

I suspect that we, also, are like this, but that we have somehow lost touch with our fundamental reality and become almost glued to the physical.

After seeing into the drawers my mind went blank. I have no further memories from that night.

When I woke up the next morning, though, I remembered everything up to that point clearly—especially that white-paper garment I was wearing. I recalled vividly how it rustled as I moved, how it seemed to be full of some sort of static electricity that made it flare out around me as if I were whirling in a dance.

One afternoon I was reading E. S. Hartland's *The Science of Fairy Tales* when I was amazed to come across the following story.

A Welsh child, known as Little Gitto, disappeared for two full years. "One morning when his mother, who had long and bitterly mourned for him as dead, opened the door whom should she see sitting on the threshold but Gitto with a bundle under his arm. He was dressed and looked exactly as when she last saw him, for he had not grown a bit. 'Where have you been all this time?' asked his mother. 'Why it was only yesterday I went away,' he replied; and opening the bundle he showed her a garment the little children, as he called them, had given him for dancing with them. The garment was of white paper without seam. With maternal caution she put it into the fire."

I read that story a number of times, my perplexity and awe growing each time I did so.

A white-paper garment?

Is the dance of the fairy a grand production of thought, a state that can actually lift the participant out of time? Where had I really gone on that night? What had I really done? I would be the first to agree that my perceptions may not reflect the objective reality of the experience. Strangeness is a great distorter of perception, and these events were very strange indeed. I was beginning to suspect strongly that I went somewhere real and had been dressed just as I remembered being dressed. Information was transmitted to me that told me two things: first, that the visitors considered my ideas of a sort of interstellar empire silly and possibly dangerous; second, that their relationship to their bodies is not the same as ours.

The first piece of information enabled me to abandon a wasteful and ridiculous line of speculation. The second directed me for the first time toward a new idea, one that has proved to be of critical importance to the whole future of my work with the visitors.

In a very real and astonishing way they may have freed themselves from bondage to their bodies, and the rule of death.

And so could we.

If there was a chance that going deeper into my relationship with the visitors would also take me closer to understanding this, then there was no question about what I would do.

No matter the danger, no matter the fear that something might be working with infinite care and cunning to entice me, to steal me away from my own life, I would go.

2026 Update

One of the things that has persisted in my mind all these years is the image of the being opening the drawer full of bodies like his own, and the flourish of pride that seemed to be involved. What was he showing me? I have thought that the bodies rising out of the drawer means that they are not primarily physical beings, and regard bodies in the same way that we do clothes. I have also considered that he may have been demonstrating our own destiny.

If our planet does indeed become unable to support us, what will happen is that we will become disembodied souls. Will we then seek technologies that enable us to create physical instruments of some kind that will enable us to re-engage with physical reality? And if we are able to do this, why would we want to?

This leads to the poignant, dangerous and subtle reason that the visitors may be here. It leads, in fact, to the experience of the sharing of one's body with another, in other words, the communion experience.

As I discussed in *The Fourth Mind*, it does appear that the visitors are no longer submerged in the river of time. They see it from the outside, meaning that they see too clearly to be surprised.

I am fairly sure that they long to participate in our experience of spontaneity. For them, nothing is ever really new. For us, everything always is. Whether I am right or not remains to be seen, but I do think that it is a possibility, and that it also comes with a warning. We should try much harder not to lose our planet. Without it, we will end up like them, trapped in a strange, changeless reality.

CHAPTER FOUR

THE STORM GATHERS

On Saturday, April 5, 1987, we returned to the city. Outwardly I was normal, but inside myself I was tumbling through absolute darkness. I remembered those empty faces staring up at me as the small man pulled open the drawer.

What was going on? What did it mean?

I twisted and turned on the hook of ignorance. One day I would be full of courage and eagerness, and the next quivering in fear again. Because I was in such turmoil, I could never pause in that magic spot between the darkness and the light, the razor's edge of balance that would have brought me to terms with my experience.

It is one thing to leave a question open and another thing entirely to put the heart to rest.

I value my roles as father and husband more than any other aspect of myself. What I had seen happening to my son still worried me a lot. A psychologist had reassured us that he was fine, but one cannot know what is going on in another person's mind, or in his nights.

Above all, I did not want my little boy to be exposed to the spectacular suffering I had endured. I found myself awakening suddenly in the middle of the night and rushing into his bedroom. I would hold him in my arms and glare out at the sky as our ancestors must have glared into the dark from the old caves. I would hold my warm, limp, sleeping little boy and rage that I could not prevent the visitors from invading him. I cursed myself for infecting him and for bringing this grim level of uncertainty into Anne's life as well.

His child's nonchalance and her incredible bravery and good humor were much needed examples to me. She was so graceful and calm and full of assurance. Despite the strangeness of it all, she seemed to know exactly what she was about. If ever a person has seemed to be prepared for something, it appeared to me that Anne was prepared to meet this experience. And our son was so innocent of it.

Denying the presence of the visitors, I thought, might be as foolish as jumping to conclusions about them. But how could one keep something so powerful and provocative in question? How could I stand before a conscious, living reality like this and say, "I don't know?"

A question can tear you apart. The hardest thing I have ever done is to keep the visitor experience in question. I have burned to throw myself on the mercy of blind science or belief, to lie to myself, to deny it all, to try to ignore it.

But I cannot; I am not good at lying to myself. In those hard days, I thought that the question would drive me mad.

In my worst moments I have always prayed, and I began to do that now.

Not only did I pray, I increased using the practices I had learned from the works of P. D. Ouspensky, most especially his book *In Search of the Miraculous*. Ouspensky argues that man is without real will because his attention is controlled not by his inner self but by the world around him. However, attention can be strengthened.

Ouspensky's ideas offered a hint of possible power from within, and I had worked with them for so long—almost half of my life—that they seemed the very thing with which to meet the incredible force of the visitors.

I redoubled my efforts, emptying my mind and feeling the substance of myself as a part of the wider world, working on keeping my attention divided between outer life and deep inner sensation.

Any power I might have over the visitor experience seemed to me to depend upon the strength of my attention, and the control I could exert over it.

Increasingly I felt as if I were entering a struggle that might be even more than life-or-death. It might be a struggle for my soul, my essence, or whatever part of me might have reference to the eternal.

There are worse things than death, I suspected. And I was beginning to get the distinct impression that one of them had taken an interest in me.

So far the word *demon* had never been spoken among the scientists and doctors who were working with me. And why should it have been? We were beyond such things. We were a group of atheists and agnostics, far too sophisticated to be concerned with such archaic ideas as demons and angels.

Alone at night I worried about the legendary cunning of demons. Why was my family so sanguine?

At the very least, I was going stark, raving mad. But neither of them worried. I would watch them, alert for some sign of trouble. At night I would listen for the slightest sound—of visitor or of nightmare.

Also in the night I wondered about the motives that might have brought the visitors here, and the discipline that keeps

them to a secret plan of which we sense only the broadest outline.

What I could not really grasp was the true strangeness of
what was happening to me. It had a very definite structure,
but in April 1986 all was still in confusion for me. I was working under the assumption that the visitors were recent arrivals
from another planet. But my exchanges with them didn't make
sense in the context of this idea. Fortunately I came across
Jacques Vallee's book *Passport to Magonia,* which provided me with the idea that the core visitor experience has been
taking place at least for many hundreds of years and possibly
throughout history.

Anne brought an idea at this point that has seemed to me
to be fundamentally clarifying. She began talking of the subjective nature of the experience, and how it appears to flow
from an objective reality, but is changed by the filter of our
perceptions. Our ability to see and understand is literally distorted by the expectations that our cultures impose on us.
More than that, the visitors appeared to her to be using our
distorted perceptions as a vehicle through which they could
transmit messages of importance to the inner growth of the
individual participant.

It may well be that modern concepts about the nature of
the visitors—when they are finally and completely formed—
will be closer to reality than those of the past. But we must
not allow the question to escape us, since there may always be
much that we don't understand.

At the moment, there is a great deal that is very enigmatic indeed. For example, one researcher, Leonard Keane, may
have decoded the "star language" sometimes uttered under
hypnosis by people who have had encounters. He has written a strikingly original and as yet unpublished manuscript—

Keltic Factor Red—on the large number of visitor encounters reported by people of Celtic background.

He found that the alien words repeated under hypnosis by a famous participant,

Betty Andreasson, were probably Gaelic. Far from being a language from the beyond, Gaelic is the tongue of ancient Ireland. It is still spoken by a few people in that country, but there is no evidence that Betty has ever been exposed to it. She is of Finnish/English origin.

The speaking of an unknown language under hypnosis is called xenoglossy and can usually be attributed to unconscious learning of that language sometime in the speaker's past. Gaelic, however, is a singularly unlikely choice of language for Betty, and the question of how it came into her mind remains unanswered.

At one point during her hypnosis about her extraordinary encounter with a visitor she called Quaazga, she was repeating word-for-word statements she was hearing from the visitors while the session was taking place—a channeling experience, except that the channel sounded to her like a radio in her head. Suddenly there was an interruption, and she heard a repeated statement in English along the lines of "base 32—base 32— signal base 32." There followed a couple of statements in the strange alien language. Mr. Keane has tentatively translated these as "sound of a foolish talker," and "unfruitful projection." He also discovered that the hypnosis session was taking place next door to a bus depot that had a powerful radio transmitter. He speculates that radio actually *was* in use, and that transmissions from the bus dispatcher were interrupting intrusions into Mrs. Andreasson's mind—which themselves were nothing more than sophisticated radio transmissions.

Before the interruption, Mrs. Andreasson had repeated about a paragraph in the star language. Mr. Keane found that a phonetic rendering of her words corresponded almost exactly to their Gaelic equivalent. Reading the text and listening to the tape, it is very hard to conclude that the language is anything other than Gaelic. And the translation is haunting. "The living descendants of the Northern peoples are groping in universal darkness. Their mother mourns. A dark occasion forebodes when weakness in high places will revive a high cost of living; an interval of mistakes in high places; an interval fit for distressing events."

2026 Update

This exchange appears in Ray Fowler's 1983 book, *The Andreasson Affair: Phase Two*. When I read it, I recognized that the "star language" she was repeating was awfully close to Gaelic, which resulted in the translations mentioned in this book. Looking back, I find the statements startlingly prophetic. It seems to me that we are now living in a time "when weakness in high places will revive a high cost of living; an interval of mistakes in high places and distressing events, to say the least!

As I write this, we are certainly in the midst of a "dark occasion" as the world's oldest republic teeters on the brink of authoritarianism and dictatorships are on the rise everywhere. Simultaneously, the weather is becoming more and more unfavorable, there have been two pandemics, one of them extremely devastating, wars rage and nuclear weapons are in the hands of unstable powers.

But what do the words "living descendants" mean and what is this "eternal darkness?" Of course, I cannot know for certain, but I think that it may refer to the warning given to the Ariel School children in Rhodesia (now Zimbabwe) in 1994.

This was a warning about becoming too reliant on technology—which we are, of course, in the process of doing. What is happening, for example, with artificial intelligence is that it is being used to replace management level jobs while at the same time, at least in the United States, low-level jobs are being created by sending migrant workers home. This means that today's highly educated managers are destined to be tomorrows factory workers...until those jobs, also, are replaced by robots.

This certainly qualifies as "mistakes in high places" on an epic scale. Human social institutions should be designed to provide people with rich, productive lives, not to make them redundant drones.

The reasons that I bring up the Ariel School case are two: the first is the warning about technology, but why would I think that it had anything to do with what was said to Betty?

This gets me to the specific phrase, "living descendants." As I have pointed out in this book and in many other places, close encounter has to do not only with our visitors (if that is indeed what they are) but also our own dead. In the reality that the visitors inhabit, physical bodies are only one seat of consciousness, and this is why the word "living" is used so specifically, I would think. It is us, the living, who have dropped the thread.

My specific reason for linking the Ariel School incident is the little known fact that the school lies just a few miles from the Chitungwiza-oha-Chaminuka area, which is regarded as sacred ground where communication with dead ancestors takes place. It is a protected monument, listed among Zimbabwe's National Museums and Monuments.

So the message of the Ariel School even can be regarded as being connected to our own dead as much as to our visitors—if, indeed, the two are not essentially the same thing.

Artificial Intelligence could be one of the greatest blessings in the history of mankind, but not if it is used as a tool to take jobs, self-respect and lives worth living from millions while enriching even further a few who have so much money that getting more is just a game. To ordinary people, it is a game of lives—their own.

1989 Narrative Continues

The phonetic parallels between Mrs. Andreasson's words and their Gaelic equivalents are too close to dismiss. There is a virtual one-for-one correspondence. This is clearly demonstrated in the appendix on Gaelic at the end of this book. Additionally, Mr. Keane discovered that not only the name of the visitor who became involved with Mrs. Andreasson but the names given to many other participants by the visitors were translatable Gaelic.

Quaazga, the name of the being Mrs. Andreasson encountered, corresponds phonetically to the Gaelic *Caesadh,* which means "of the cross." This could be a reference to the patron saint of the Scots, St. Andrew, whose X-shaped cross is a very ancient symbol of man and is now the national symbol of Scotland. It could also refer, of course, to Christ. Betty was a deeply Christian person, and her encounter with the visitors contained much striking imagery that seems related to the Christian idea of rebirth. The fact that a visitor approaching a Christian and providing a deeply Christian experience to that person would have a name translatable from an obscure language as "of the cross" is nothing less than astonishing to me.

Another name with a Gaelic equivalent is Linn-Erri, which was claimed by a beautiful blond woman who allegedly communicated with an amateur radio operator in 1961. This name renders to *Lionmhaireacht,* which is pronounced "linerrich." It means "abundance."

Another name heard by a participant, Korendor, may translate to *Cor-Endor,* which means "castle," "circle," or "mound of Endor," which was a place of oracle.

An entity named Aura Rhanes appeared to a participant in 1952. This name becomes *Aerach Reann* in Gaelic and translates roughly as "heavenly body of air."

Even the highly controversial George Adamski case has a strange Gaelic connection. One of the beings Adamski allegedly met was named FirKon. *Fir* or *fear* when used as a prefix means "man," and *Conn,* meaning "Head," is the name of a seventh-century Irish king whose son, tradition tells us, was abducted by a beautiful lady in a flying craft. *FirKon* means, in Gaelic, "man of Conn."

One day, as Conn and his son stood on the heights of Usna, a strangely dressed young woman came toward them. She said, "I come from the Plains of the Ever Living, where there is neither death nor sin." The father was astonished because he couldn't see or hear anybody. She then spoke to him directly, and he did hear. She told him that she was in love with the boy and wanted to take him away to Moy Mell, the Plain of Pleasure. After a month of waiting and a bit of ineffectual hanky-panky on the part of the king's resident Druid, the young man was taken, sailing off above the sea in a "crystal curragh." He was never seen again ... until, apparently, he returned a thousand years later and announced himself to a man who knew nothing whatsoever of Gaelic or of the possible origin of the name Fir Kon!

Mr. Keane's findings about Gaelic imply that there is something going on here that we plainly do not understand. It almost begins to seem as if what we are witnessing now is the discovery of an age-old relationship between ourselves and something that has always been completely misunderstood.

I would not deny the likelihood that extraterrestrials are involved in the phenomenon, but I think it has dimensions that are just beginning to be recognized, that resonate through all human cultures and have been expressed in folklore in many different ways.

A particularly frightening aspect of the problem uncovered by abduction researchers within the UFO community is that the visitors appear to be carrying out long-term genetic manipulation of humankind.

According to the theory, the visitors often steal semen from men and ova from women, and have been known to display misshapen offspring to the horrified mothers after the infants have matured. Miscarriages at the end of the first trimester seem also sometimes to happen in the context of visitor contact.

Someone close to me might have endured this very experience, so I cannot discount it. In any case, the witness reports are too extensive to ignore.

Lest we sneer at this scenario, assuming it to be the inevitable outcome of fearful UFO researchers imposing a narrative on witnesses they have hypnotized, I would add that the stealing of infants by the "wee folk" and copulation with incubi and succubi are constant features of fairy lore from all over the world.

I recently received a letter from a witness who reported that her two-year-old had recognized the face on the cover of *Communion* and announced, "He's bad!" The child said that the "man" took his toys and never gave them back. In addition to other visitor experiences, this correspondent reported that "there have been many missing toys in this house!"

One wonders why the visitors would steal human toys, if the idea that they are engaged in human-related breeding activities is so far-fetched.

That this particular aspect of the experience reflects the whole truth, however, is unlikely. There is far more to this experience than meets the eye.

I had a doctor construct a hypothetical abduction. Among his most interesting findings was that, using present medical technology, we could abduct our victims, extract blood, genetic material, semen, or practically anything else that is reported as being taken, and return the individual to his bed without leaving a single noticeable injury or painful wound. And we could do this with the person so profoundly drugged that he or she would have no memory of it at all, not even under hypnosis.

What's more, only a few thousand individuals would be needed to obtain a detailed statistical portrait of, for example, the entire United States population.

We could do this using small four-and five-man ships for the close approach. They would be unlit, radar-invisible, and nearly silent, emerging from motherships that would be left far out in space.

The whole operation could be accomplished in at most a few months, and would include a detailed reading of the local culture into the bargain, via interception of radio and television communications and photography of the whole planet, with the images resolved to the square centimeter.

All we really lack to accomplish this sort of study is the secret of quick and easy space travel.

The visitors have not carried out a scientific study, not as we understand it, though they seem to have involved hundreds of thousands of people in the United States alone. They have appeared at times in craft thousands of feet in diameter, lit up like Mardi Gras floats. Their instruments of "examination" tend to be huge and obtrusive, and the examinations themselves to be—as was true in my case—so outrageous that they are not only easy to remember, they are impossible to forget. And when fear buries them in amnesia, they can easily be accessed through hypnosis.

Despite their apparent desire for the experiences to be remembered, the visitors speak in riddles or use ancient human languages which, when translated, make their origins and purposes seem, if anything, even more obscure.

The things that had happened on April 1 and 2 left me facing this dilemma. I knew that something was being done to me and my boy—but what? I *had* to know! I couldn't live in ignorance like this.

I thought to myself, *At least this can't get any worse.*

Then came a visit to Boulder, Colorado, and an experience of shocking power. It left me feeling that the whole human family, not only mine, was embarked upon a journey in a frail vessel in rough waters in the dead of the night, and the wind was beginning to rise.

CHAPTER FIVE

LIGHTNING

On April 6, 1986, I flew to the World Affairs Conference at the University of Colorado in Boulder.

As I sat alone in the plane, I reflected on recent events. I realized that I was really very deeply afraid. I just couldn't help it. I was so at sea, had so few answers, and yet something was pushing me to keep challenging the visitors. I no longer wanted them to go away. Far from it, I wanted a confrontation.

I was beginning to act and think as if they were entirely real. This seemed sensible to me. If one suspects that there may be a panther in the woods, one does not act as if all were well. Just to be prudent, one accepts the possibility of the panther. More than that, I was going on the assumption that they might not be all bad or all good. If they were real, I could not help but think that they just might be at least as complex as human beings. I tried to avoid letting myself be influenced by science-fictional notions of aliens—good or bad.

The journey to Boulder was important for me. I intended for the first time to attempt to expose my stories of the visitors to respected scientists and members of the academic community.

I also intended to begin a more intensive period of inner work with an old friend, Dora Ruffner, who had for years shared my interest in the ideas of P D. Ouspensky and Georges Gurdjieff. We had been involved with the Gurdjieff Foundation in New York, and had both left at the same time. She had also continued her quest for greater consciousness, searching in some fascinating directions. Her understanding of the ancient nature religions and shamanism held new interest for me.

There was a specific reason for this. I have many fragmentary memories of the visitors. One of them involved my sitting at a table and solving an anagram. This seems to have happened when I was a child. The anagram made the statement "We work by ancient laws." Anne was especially taken with this. She felt, if it was true, it was potentially the most revealing piece of information we had acquired.

I have for years had the feeling that the abandonment of the ideas behind our early nature religions was the outcome of the loss of a clear, unified, and true understanding of the universe. I think that ancient man, living closer to both the beauty and the brutality of nature, was in some ways better equipped to see reality. All that is left of his knowledge are the shattered remains of the old religions.

2026 Update

Over the years, I have come to understand just how true this is. In *The Fourth Mind*, I discussed the devastation that struck the planet 12,000 years ago during the geologic period known as the Younger Dryas. The physical debris from a long-ago supernova seems to have entered our solar system, resulting in a thousand years of chaos that saw the violent breakup of Earth's glaciers and the near-extinction of the human species. By the end of this event, sea levels had risen 450 feet. All that is left of what must have been a very different human world are megalithic ruins that we could not construct today. Due to the rigors of underwater archaeology, little to no exploration of this region has been done. In addition, as I will explore in my new book, Reunion, there has been an extensive effort to conceal what do appear to be non-natural remains on the moon and Mars. In fact, this really is very hard to deny at this point.

We don't just live within the "shattered remains" of old religions, we live in the ruins of something very different from what we have now. *The Fourth Mind* and *Reunion* are about what we lost and how we may re-establish our lost connection with nature, ourselves, and our true power.

1989 Narrative Continues

An example of what we have lost of the old religions is Halloween. Nowadays we celebrate this ancient festival by letting mayhem loose in the streets and gorging our children on candy. Nobody remembers that the lost and denied world of the spirit once drew close to us in this season, fluttering the bonfires of the night and reminding us of both our mortality and our greatness.

I wondered if the shamanic language of symbol and myth would offer a better insight into the visitors' motives. Dora was conversant in this language on a deep, almost visceral level and I was eager to hear her ideas.

As I drove into Boulder from the Denver airport for the first time, I was struck by how the compact little city clings to the foothills of the Rockies, a tiny human incursion into that wild upsurging of the earth. Our lights and buzzing machines were trivialized by the tall silence of the mountains and the sky.

For me the World Affairs Conference was a week of radically new impressions and experiences. It annually brings together hundreds of academics, authors, artists, journalists, and scientists in rough concert, the whole affair concocted by a spectacular Rocky Mountain iconoclast named Howard Higman, who smiles over his gaggle like a mordacious old moon.

The World Affairs Conference is the kind of institution that could only have been developed in the United States, and specifically in the West. It is open, hospitable, informal—and fierce. I could understand that it would be a congenial place for the coauthor of *Warday* and *Nature's End,* but would it welcome a writer who had endured experiences as spectacularly odd as those I had to relate?

The Condon Report, which successfully discredited UFO research in established scientific circles, had been created at the University of Colorado. It remained one of the high fortresses of scientific conservatism, or so I imagined.

I was extremely uneasy about going to a conference at a place that was a virtual shrine to belief in the established order of things. I visualized professors in three-piece suits poking me in the chest with long, bony fingers and accusing me of degrading the intellectual content of the culture.

The conference, however, was not like that. Had I dared to talk, it would have opened its mind to me—which it did the next year, after the publication of *Communion* had spilled my secret.

The World Affairs Conference is a rarity in that it cherishes openness of mind and has a flair for drama. It is certainly among the best intellectual conferences in the world, unique for its eclecticism and singular freedom from prejudice.

So frightened was I that the conference would spit me out if I mentioned the visitors, that I just couldn't bring myself to do it.

I did experiment a little. I opened the subject with an astronaut who was in attendance. He managed to be polite, but I realized that he was in a hopeless position. He could not possibly maintain his credibility with the planetary-sciences community if he showed a whisper of interest in what happened to me, even if such a whisper was there.

Author Mark Kramer, who is a very careful and rigorous intellectual and a true gentleman, listened with interest. When he began to perceive that what I was telling him suggested that revision of our fundamental understanding of the world would be in order were the visitors found to be external to us, he began to feel strongly that my perceptions had to be seated in the mind. He remained concerned and friendly, although there were people at the conference who were more comfortable with the problems my story presented.

Dr. John Gliedman's training as a psychologist enabled him to view my recitation of experiences with detachment and good humor.

National Public Radio reporter Margot Adler initially found the darker implications of my story deeply disturbing, which created a strain in our friendship. Hers was the first reaction I encountered that proceeded from the notion that some psychic influences might be good and others just plain evil. It would not be the last.

2026 Update

The night of September 6, 2025 was typical of the way I live now. As I report in detail in *Afterlife Revolution*, my wife returned within a short time of her death, speaking into the ears of friends and telling them to call me, particularly at moments I was feeling the most crippling and intense grief. She died in August of 2015, and in January of that year she had made me memorize a poem of W.B.Yeats, "Song of the Wandering Aengus." At the time, I had no idea why she was so insistent, but when I failed to do it, she burst into tears. This is because that remarkable and enlightened woman already knew what she was going to do after she died. She was going to create an avatar so that people in the physical world could engage with her and she could teach them, a skill she had mastered so completely that when she was teaching you, you always thought you were making the discoveries yourself.

The poem contains the lines "when white moths were on the wing and the moth-like stars were flickering out..." A month after Anne died, I went to a conference in order to take my mind off my grief. While I was there, the security camera in my living room kept recording a white moth flying back and forth in front of it. Over the subsequent weeks this kept happening at strangely coincidental moments, until I finally began to think that it wasn't accidental. Then I remembered that Anne's favorite short story of mine was about an elderly woman discovering that she has died. It is called "The White Moths."

Once I remembered that, the moth's appearances became more direct and organized, including showing up at meetings, lighting on the heads of people whose work Anne had admired, and even disappearing into thin air before groups of people who were watching in delighted amazement.

Then, in 2017, two things happened. The first one took place in a hotel room in California while I was attending the "Contact in the Desert" conference. While I was meditating at about 11, an absolutely black shadow shaped like a Vesica Pisces appeared before me. At first, I wasn't sure whether

or not it was a trick of shadow in the dark room, but then it glided up to me, moved into a horizontal position, and rested on my ankles. I then felt a vibrating energy that has since become part of my life. Since then, not 48 hours have passed since I have felt it. If I doze during a meeting, it will wake me up. If my attention drifts while I am working, it will be there, gently drawing my attention back to my work.

So this is where I am with this now: I feel supported in profound ways. The implant in my left ear, which I have discussed extensively both in my books and on media, is my essential research tool. It does not control me, but it does offer research assistance that is remarkably insightful, far more so than even the most sophisticated artificial intelligence program I can imagine. There are other forms of support as well, including frequent physical interactions (the vibrations delivered into my body along my lower legs) that increase my energy level and provide me with a very welcome sense of caring.

I am thankful for all this, and especially for the effort that has been made to provide useful support without dominating my creative process.

I could not have written anything from *The Afterlife Revolution* on without this support. At the same time, when I do something that is not wanted or fail to meet my own potential, the reaction is swift and very negative.

To be specific, I will describe an event that took place in the early morning of Monday, September 1, 2025. I was awakened in a way that used to happen nightly at approximately 3:00 AM. Some examples of how it was done are as follows: A puff of air in my face; the sound of a school bell; a dry kiss; an electric sensation on a toe; a pinch; sometimes a puff of air against the back of one of my hands.

Understand, I do not associate this only with non-human intelligence. On the contrary, I have come to think that my contact experience is as much or more with our own dead as it is with NHI.

I know that I live in a world that has gone soul-blind. Even those of us who suspect or believe that we have souls cannot feel them. But we do, and they are the primary focus of contact. The physical aspect of it is important, too, of course, but only insofar as it assists us in reconnecting our shattered species, so that we are once again aware, when in the physical form, of our actual purpose for being alive at all.

This time, there was a strong sensation against the back of my right hand, and it wasn't at 3:00, it was at 12:45. I had only been asleep for an hour after my usual 11:00 PM meditation.

Surprised, I jumped up and rushed back into the living room to continue the mediation. Seconds after I began, I experienced severe dizziness. I was shocked and frightened. I thought I was having a stroke.

Then I realized how it had started—with a familiar touch to the top of my head just to the left of the center of my scalp. So I sat waiting, and it subsided.

Variants of this had occurred four times previously over the past few years. I have been examined by a neurologist and no sign of a stroke or transient ischemic attack have been found, and there have been no persisting symptoms.

There has always been an accompanying message, and there was one this time, too: "You are not working fast enough. Don't you understand the urgency?"

Since then, I have been working absolutely flat-out to get this finished and then go on to Reunion. The reason for the urgency is quite simple: our planet is in a perilous state and something I have been warning about for years is about to happen. This is a sudden climate change event that permanently alters the climate in ways that are going to be hard or even impossible for us to adjust to.

I am not a prophet, I don't know when it will happen. But this message has been crystal clear: "It will come upon them unaware."

We must be ready for the non-human element to disclose itself soon. But we are not ready. Right now, all the agency is concentrated in government, and they are far from being prepared to engage usefully with this very complex presence. But they want to retain power. So be it. The chips will have to fall where they may.

So this is how it is for me now, working with the visitors and, as I feel quite sure, our own dead and probably—and most importantly—my wife, who is playing a profoundly important role in my entire interaction, guiding me from the other side as I proceed on this journey.

1989 Narrative Continues

I found it almost impossible to deal with the notion that this had an evil side to it. The impact of the visitors was so strong in my life that the idea that they might be evil was too much for me to bear. And yet, when I thought of the way they looked and what they had done, I could not dismiss it. I was frightened that they might be nothing more than the ugly, cold, inhumane monsters they seemed.

My responses to the visitors were always visceral. I would wake up and glare into the night like an uneasy animal. I would vacillate between dread and longing, usually longing for them during the day and dreading them at night.

Never, in those bleak April days, could I have imagined the subtlety of the plan that they were carrying out. Nor could I have seen the magnificent brilliance of the mind behind it.

My instinct to seek out Dora Ruffner proved useful, for it was she who pointed out that what was happening to me could be taken to be initiatory in nature, a journey into the darkness where the secrets of the spirit are kept. This journey is among the most ancient of human spiritual traditions. Whether or not taking me on it was a motive of the visitors, I could still make use of what they were doing to explore the depths of my own soul.

I sweated in Boulder, facing the conferees during the day and thoughts of the visitors when darkness came.

On the night of April 9, Dora and I meditated together for about an hour, and the experience was a very powerful one for me. I had a most vivid impression of her as a living, acutely conscious mind.

Earlier that evening John Gliedman, Mark Kramer, and I— who had been having a lot of fun spooking ourselves with wild visitor theories—had left a party to find that the sky seemed to be glowing with a sort of magenta iridescence. We were quite taken by this phenomenon, as it seemed auroral in origin but was emanating from the south.

We were also uneasy and laughing much too hard about everything.

Thus, after the long conversations about mind control and visitors capable of lodging themselves in the unconscious, the strange lights in the sky, and the powerful meditation with Dora, I could certainly be forgiven a spectacular dream.

If what happened was indeed a dream, then it was a dramatic departure from every other dreaming experience I have ever had. I do not even want to call it a dream but a vision, a radical grasping of light. And that, still, feels less than true. What seems true is that some immense thing drew close to me and somehow placed thoughts in my mind via the medium of huge lights shining down from the sky.

That is what *seems* true. I wish that I could assert it, offer some final proof. But I cannot. I must thus present my experience in the crippled context of dream, though I do not believe that is what it was.

I went to sleep at the Boulderado Hotel at about midnight. At two-thirty I was awakened by a glow in the room. I opened my eyes and to my amazement saw huge searchlight beams playing down across the small view from my window.

I started to go to the window, but before I reached it there was a terrific crack of thunder. That explained it: I'd been awakened by a thunderstorm. My sleep-heavy mind had transformed lightning flashes into searchlight beams probing from some eerie vessel of heaven.

I stood in the middle of the room watching and listening, wishing that I could get up the nerve to go to the window. One of the beams swept past right outside, bathing everything in blue light. It came back again, and for a moment the light itself seemed like a living, conscious thing. I had the sensation that it was using my eyes to gain entrance to my mind.

The next moment I felt a powerful need to lie down. Storm or not, I fell back on the bed and sank instantly into a state of apparent sleep. And a drama began to play itself out in my mind.

I was aware that what I was observing had a very unusual texture. It was not as steady as life, but seemed more real. Colors, sounds, all were heightened. It is hard to describe the effect, except to say that by comparison my ordinary waking perception seemed like clouded water.

The experience transported me to a marshy place that had a large, wide, flat complex of buildings associated with it. I was aware that these buildings were some sort of nuclear installation. I came closer to a large, flat building. There were thick masses of pipes running along the wall. My vision was so restricted that I couldn't tell where I was, whether indoors or out.

Suddenly a big pipe fell apart and a great deal of water gushed out. Moments later the whole place started to explode.

"Stop," I screamed. "Somebody, make it stop!" Smoke burst out of the burning building and began to rise in a stately, dangerous column. There were screams and moans. A tall, blond man explained things to me that I could barely hear, then jumped into an ancient black sedan and went roaring off toward the burning plant.

The next thing I knew I appeared to be in my own cabin in upstate New York. I had just been awakened by a loud crashing. I sat up in bed, confused. What was that noise?

It came again, a great, cracking report from down in the woods.

This was followed by silence. I looked out the window.

It was a peaceful, moonlit night. For a moment I thought that everything was all right. Then there was a flash, followed by a huge crash and the swish of a falling tree. I looked up at the sky and saw gigantic boulders sailing in perfect silence off the edge of the moon. A realization came over me: *The moon is exploding.* Then I thought, *Oh, this is the end of the world.*

It was so shocking and unexpected that it would come this way—not by atomic war or environmental collapse or any of the things I had feared, but rather in this distant, mechanical manner. We were not to be victims of ourselves or even of some earthly catastrophe, but rather of a secret imbalance of the spheres.

In my dream I took Anne and our son to a certain place I know in the forest. We hugged each other as the crashes got louder and the flashes of moon-generated meteors got brighter, and I sang the Malvina Reynolds song "Morningtown

Ride." For us this was how the world ended. And so did the vision.

The next morning I woke up to streets silvered by rain and air cleaned to glass by a predawn thunderstorm. At first I wanted to believe that the thunderstorm had simply touched off a vivid nightmare.

But that wasn't the answer, and I knew it perfectly well. I remembered what I had seen.

I went through the day of conference activities like a zombie, participating but not really there. Again and again I saw those enormous boulders sailing over the rim of the moon, flickering as they tumbled through space. To have been seen, they would have been huge—miles across. A rain of such things would cause incredible damage. The explosion of the moon would end the world, no question about it.

And that was only the second part of the experience. The first part seemed to involve an exploding nuclear plant of some kind. There was no familiar concrete reactor containment, though. Maybe it was a government bomb facility, I thought. There is a large and notorious federal facility at Rocky Flats, but pictures of the buildings there looked nothing like the ones in my dream.

The vision was so intense and had shaken me so badly that I related it in detail to Dr. Gliedman that same day, April 10.

I could not imagine what the first part of it meant, and finally decided that it must have to do with my fear of another nuclear catastrophe along the lines of Three-Mile Island.

2026 Update

I recall only the vision of the exploding moon, not the flash of light (obviously the thunderstorm). Dora died a few years later at the age of 52 of colon cancer. She was a very powerful seer and played an extraordinary role in my life, as is made clear by the many mentions of her in this book. At the time of her passing, I was not yet aware of the depth of relationship that can exist between the living and the dead. If she attempted to contact me, I was not aware of it.

Not until Anne died and returned with such skill that her presence was undeniable (at least to me) would I realize that we can have a much richer and more complex relationship with those who have left the physical world. Because we are so detached from them, we tend to assume that they have extraordinary powers of prophecy and insights beyond our own. They do have a broader perspective, but not necessarily total knowledge of the future, at least in my experience. They do have some, though, which is where, I would think, that the visions of cataclysm that they so often bring come from.

As discussed below, the vision of the moon exploding was probably a response to this sense of cataclysm. It has caused many a supposed prophet to predict the landing of a UFO or the end of the world or some other huge change that has not happened.

When I wrote *Transformation*, I knew only that close encounter often brought a feeling of cataclysm, as I discuss below. I now know why this happens. Close encounter—the real thing, naked, raw and unaffected by any psychological interference—draws us close to where our visitors live, at the edge of the river of time. We are here in these dense bodies in order to experience every moment as new, and to store this experience—our whole lives, in exquisitely complete detail— in a deep level of memory.

When we are pulled close to the edge of time, we recoil in fear. If we were to leave time and see the future, our entire lives would become meaningless, or this is how it feels. Thus, when we are close to the visitors, we feel desperate and lost, as if the world is caving in on us.

There is certainly great change ahead, but if it includes the explosion of the moon, I will be very surprised.

1989 Narrative Continues

As for the second part of the episode, I was less confused. I presumed that what had happened was that my mind had decided that the visitor experience amounted to an inner change so drastic as to be a sort of apocalypse.

Contact with the visitors is almost universally associated with catastrophic predictions. People are told of impending wars, of earthquakes, of meteors directed toward the earth, of polar shifts and the coming of new ages of ice or heat. I myself had been shown graphic depictions of the death of the atmosphere, not to mention the entire planet simply exploding.

Whenever a fundamental change of mind takes place—and I think that this is happening now—there is a great increase in catastrophic fear. The world of ancient Rome was filled with portents of the end. As people became exposed to the revolutionary ideas of Christianity, they began to feel that the end of their social order was near. This translated into fear that the world was physically coming to an end. Early Christians, like some modern UFO cultists, expected the end of the world momentarily.

The Roman world *did* end, but it was not destroyed by a natural catastrophe. What overthrew Rome was a catastrophe of mind. The rise of Christianity so altered the Roman spirit that the classical world collapsed. Roman government and science were buried, and it took the West a thousand years to reconstruct what was lost.

It is possible that many of our catastrophic fears are related to one of two levels of deep change that we already sense on an instinctive level. The first level is the reality of the visitors themselves. The appearance of a nonhuman intelligence would potentially be even more devastating to established world views than Christianity was to Rome.

The second level is the message that the visitors could be bringing.

Thus there really is very little possibility that "nothing" is happening. Something is—something great. And one of the ways the human mind has of announcing this is with an array of warnings about disasters in the physical world.

Most of these predictions undoubtedly reflect the inner apocalypse related to our current change of mind. But is that true of all of them? Are there any apocalyptic prophecies that make sense?

While there is no way to verify or even speculate about most of them, there are a few that deserve closer consideration. It is obvious that the warnings I reported in

Communion about the atmosphere are a serious business. But I should point out that the problem was known to science and to me—at least in general terms—before I had the visitor experience, so its mention in *Communion* cannot be classed as a pure prediction. Nevertheless, it is indisputable that I realized the seriousness of the ozone crisis long before most others. As I reported in *Communion,* my realization was based on a strange image that had entered my mind of a tremendously complicated map of the earth's atmosphere. While I did not fully understand it, its mere presence in my mind suggested dire things to me. Like the image of the golden city, it was vividly real. I have not been able to find any reference in medical literature to a similar state, except perhaps as a description of photographic, or eidetic, memory. But what was I remembering? I had never seen such a map before, with layers and layers of colors moving and bleeding into one another. I could not imagine how a mind could sustain something so complex and so detailed for days and days.

Because of the map, I have followed the story of the deterioration of our atmosphere with great care. On January 1, 1988, *The New York Times* reported that the thinning of the ozone layer worldwide was far greater than expected. When the declines will let in enough ultraviolet light to cause destruction of crops on a wide scale and suppression of animal and human immune systems is unknown, but both of these effects are associated with ultraviolet overdose.

Another surprisingly credible prediction came to me from a very unexpected source. Some months after the Boulder conference, I was given, by an individual associated with the hierarchy of the Catholic Church, the alleged contents of a letter opened by Pope John XXIII in 1960 that contained a final prediction from Our Lady of Fatima. The world has speculated for years about that letter. When it was opened the intention was to make the contents public. But cardinals were seen leaving the pope's office with "stricken" expressions on their faces afterward, and the wording of the letter has remained a closely guarded secret. The Church has recently denied that the letter existed!

The Lady, believed by Catholics to be the Blessed Virgin, appeared in 1917 in Fatima, Portugal, to three children. Over a period of months this developed into the best-documented miraculous apparition in history, its spectacular culmination being witnessed by thousands of people, and causing strange auroral effects over a wide area. These effects were seen even by people who were not in the crowd that perceived the main event, which was the appearance of a massive disk that was taken to be the sun dancing in the sky.

The Fatima events were extensively witnessed and documented, and their reality cannot be denied except by an irrational refusal to face the unknown. The cause of those events is, however, a mystery. The Church concluded that the vision of a lady seen by the three children was the Blessed Virgin Mary.

She never called herself the Blessed Virgin, but she described herself as coming "from Heaven." One is reminded of the beautiful maiden who came to the son of the ancient Irish Conn and said that she was from "the Plains of Pleasure." Like that apparition, the Lady of Fatima could only be seen by the witnesses to whom she directed her attention.

But other witnesses saw many manifestations surrounding her appearance. On September 13 thousands of people observed a globe of light coming down the valley to the place of the apparition, the *Cova de Ira*. As had been seen a month earlier, a white cloud formed and white "petals" began to fall from the sky. They evaporated as they reached the ground.

On October 13, seventy thousand people witnessed a brilliant silver disk appearing out of the sun, turning on its own axis and casting beams of colored light in every direction. Shafts of red light colored the clouds, the earth, the trees, and the people. Then there were shafts of violet, yellow, and other colors. These shafts appeared to be sectored, as though the disk were revolving. The disk rushed toward the crowd in a zigzag motion that is typical of modern UFOs. Auroral effects were seen as far as thirty miles from the site of the miracle, even by skeptics and outright scoffers, so it would be very hard to maintain that the manifestations did not have some sort of objective source. Two witnesses who observed the disk through binoculars reported seeing a ladder with beings on it.

According to my information, the last of the Fatima predictions involves, among other things, an inundation of coastal areas of the earth, taking place between 1994 and 1997. This is actually a much more serious contender than most of the catastrophic predictions, and it is additionally backed by the fact that another Fatima prediction was confirmed.

On July 13, 1917, the Lady said, "When you shall see a night illuminated by an unknown light, know that it is the great sign that God gives you that He is going to punish the world for its crimes by means of war." This remark was first revealed in 1927.

On January 25, 1938 (according to *The New York Times* of the next morning), there was indeed a peculiar auroral effect over most of Europe, sufficiently strange to cause considerable comment in the press at the time. *The Times* reported that "the people of London watched two magnificent arcs rising in the east and west, from which radiated pulsating beams like searchlights in dark red, greenish blue and purple." According to scientists, a similarly intense auroral effect had not been seen in Europe since 1709. And the 1938 event was and remains unique for its colors and the general structure of the display. There is no doubt that it was an auroral phenomenon, however, since a large explosion had been recorded on the sun some days earlier and there was a magnetic storm in progress at the time.

Three months later Germany annexed Austria, beginning the direct series of events that led to World War II.

It is a matter of scientific fact that the oceans are rising. This is because a long-term atmospheric warming trend is causing less ice to form, and causing polar ice to decline generally.

About twenty thousand cubic miles of polar ice have melted in the past forty years, according to scientists, although there remain questions about whether this is directly related to the buildup of atmospheric gases from the burning of coal and oil.

It should be remembered that the earth has spent more than 80 percent of its total geologic history without polar caps. Geologically, it is a warmer planet than it has been during the entire history of mankind. Man's pouring of carbon dioxide into the atmosphere has intensified a warming trend that was probably already present in nature.

Could it be that the warming trend will proceed so dramatically that there will be a disastrous polar melt before the end of the century? I couldn't find a single scientist who thought that this was even remotely possible. The consensus was, "Give us another couple of hundred years before you need a canoe to navigate lower Manhattan." However, I wonder if such confidence may not be misplaced.

In November 1987 an iceberg twice the size of Rhode Island broke off the Ross Ice Shelf, suggesting that it is indeed far more unstable than scientific observers understand. This was only one of a series of events in what *The Times* on February 9, 1988, called "an extraordinary two years of glacial breakup." Should this continue, it will not be long before substantial imbalances in the ice pack could result.

In July 1987 the Caribbean Sea heated up to as much as two degrees above normal, causing extensive bleaching of corals. The corals were not killed, but the heating was very, very unusual and cannot be explained as a normal natural phenomenon.

While there are no statistics on overall ocean temperatures, the combination of the appearance of such huge icebergs in the Antarctic and the heating of the Caribbean suggests that general heating may be under way, and that neither its mechanism nor its overall strength is known. Science was surprised by both events.

If one of the Antarctic ice shelves were to slip into the sea, a substantial problem would be created, and inundations could certainly be one result. Three things are clear: First, some unpredicted and unexpected warming events are taking place; second, nobody knows their consequences; third, science is not prepared to deal with them, given the present state of knowledge.

If the deeply Catholic children who transmitted her message understood it correctly, the Lady of Fatima counseled prayer as the antidote to the disasters she foretold.

On April 25, 1986, Chernobyl exploded. At once I related this disaster to the first part of my April 9 dream. I called Dr. Gliedman and discussed it with him again. Either the dream was a coincidence or it was indeed precognitive. What was most worrisome was that if it was precognitive, then what about the second part? Did the Chernobyl disaster mean my dream was also predicting that the moon was going to explode?

Was this the one "true" catastrophe? Or were we about to enter a whole era of upheaval?

I was relieved when I saw the first television footage of Chernobyl: It looked nothing like the plant I had dreamed about. Then I found that those early pictures had been of another, similarly designed nuclear-power plant in Italy. When I saw Chernobyl I realized that I had indeed had a precognitive vision.

I became frightened by what was transpiring. If the first part of the vision was true, then what of the second?

I have read enough about the geology of the moon to know that it is almost totally lacking in volcanic potential. The moon is exactly what it seems to be—a cold hunk of stone. There have been sporadic reports of very low-scale activity at the bottoms of a few craters, nothing more than flashes of light related to discharges of gas. But there is absolutely no indication that even the remotest possibility exists that the moon might experience a volcanic eruption, let alone an explosion so violent that it would cause debris to impact the earth.

I asked some planetologists what would happen if the moon *did* explode. The general feeling was that it would be a terminal catastrophe. Not only would the earth be showered with debris, its orbit would also be altered—not a lot, but enough to cause severe shifts in climate. The absence of the moon would have a multitude of effects, ranging from a reduction in air circulation to the confusion of tides and ocean currents. Marine life, weather, growing patterns of plants, all would be affected negatively by the destruction of the moon. According to an article in the *Journal of Petroleum Geology*, it is possible that the moon is responsible for the creation of the earth's magnetic field, which it generates by causing tidal friction within the core of the earth. If the magnetic field should disappear, life on earth would then be exposed to substantially greater solar radiation. Earthly life may be dependent on the gentle tug from her sister planet.

To blow up the moon, however, would take enormous force. It would take ten thousand million hundred megaton bombs just to deflect it from its orbit. This is an almost inconceivable amount of energy, certainly more than mankind possesses, ever has possessed, or will possess in the foreseeable future. Unless somebody unpleasant has a really big bomb or there is something about the moon we've overlooked, it isn't going to explode.

So the second part of my dream was yet another apocalyptic fear, to be added to the "earth-exploding" image that came to me during hypnosis concerning my visitor experience of October 4, 1985. In that scenario I saw the earth explode violently, for no apparent reason. I will never forget the great columns of smoke spurting out from the planet, as if it were extending claws into space.

Still, there could be a physical event behind these visions. Taken together, the two of them could predict a very different sort of catastrophe, but one with similar effects. They could, for example, be a reflection of the destruction caused to both the earth and the moon by the impact of a cloud of debris or even a large asteroid.

It should be noted that on August 16, 1987, Reuters ran a wire-service story that was not generally picked up by news media. It is worth repeating here. Soviet scientist Alexander Voytsekhovsky said that the asteroid known as 1983TB, discovered in 1983, would collide with the earth in 2115, 127 years from now. The only way that the planet will survive such a blow would be for us to deflect the asteroid or demolish it.

The Russian scientist attributed the discovery of the problem to British scientists, but I was unable to identify them, and my letter to the Russian was not answered. I cannot confirm the accuracy of this story. For all I know, it may even have been a hoax perpetrated on the occasion of the 1987 Harmonic Convergence, which took place on August 16.

There are many other possible meanings that attach to the idea of the moon exploding. In some systems of thought, such as that of G. I. Gurdjieff, the moon is a symbol of the farthest end of creation. Sleeping souls are described as being "food for the moon," meaning that their fate will be to go the way of nature rather than springing free at death from its cycles. The moon is also a symbol of dreaming and hypnosis, of the force of confusion that holds men in bondage. The moon has been associated with sleep, dreaming, and unconsciousness.

My vision of an explosion of the moon then becomes an expression of a revolutionary new potential. It could suggest that the destruction of the "moon" within us will enable us at last to see reality clearly.

Older ideas of the moon place her as the Mother Goddess. It is not known how completely life depends upon tidal forces, but it has been speculated that life as we know it could not exist without lunar influence. This would indeed make the moon a sort of cosmic "mother." The Egyptians identified the moon with Thoth, the awakener of sleeping minds, and it is the face of Thoth that has given the West the notion of the "man in the moon." Plutarch wrote a fascinating essay, "On the Face of the Moon," in which the Good are supposed to inhabit the realm of the moon, but to present a terrifying appearance to all who approach them, lest searchers see the real beauty of the place and be tempted to suicide in order to reach heaven more quickly.

It is impossible to conclude even from all this that the visitors are warning about the fate and future of the earth. I do think, however, that the warnings I have received about the atmosphere and the possible prediction of inundation should be heeded, if only because they appear to be coming true.

It could be that my vision of the moon exploding was about a change of being so profound that it will at once wake man up from his ages-long hypnosis and at the same time eject him from the mothering womb of the earth-moon planetary system.

The coming of cosmic visitors would be such an event.

The World Affairs Conference ended and I flew back to New York. After a couple of days in the city I returned gratefully home to our cabin. I would sit on the deck watching the old moon rolling through the sky. I could understand the Elizabethan idea of the music of the spheres, the melody of nights and days.

I thought of classical Rome ending and reflected that our world, also, is ending. The moment that the first atomic bomb sailed down the air toward the teeming streets of Hiroshima, the world view of modern man began to disintegrate. We cannot have faith in societies and institutions that threaten us with species suicide.

We are silent, unconscious rebels. The mind-set that unleashed that bomb is about to be replaced by something new, a warmer, more intuitive, more free mind, one that will soar as the eagle soars above the fears of our days, escaping at last from the ashes of the careworn past.

But will it soar over real ashes, also?

Mankind suffers from low self-esteem. We tend to think of ourselves as failures. Sometimes doomsaying is done with such relish that one senses the Jeremiahs of apocalypse are hoping the end will come.

I cannot accept such notions. There persists in me the hope and expectation that we will prevail, and that one day a healthy human species will live in balance with the world that created us.

But it is likely to be a near thing.

CHAPTER SIX

THE WHITE ANGEL

Spring passed swiftly, growing toward the long, warm summer of 1986. *Communion* had been rejected by my current publisher and was being sent from house to house, gaining in the process a number of absolutely contemptuous rejections. I was feeling pretty low, beginning to think I'd written a worthwhile book that was too heretical to be published.

In the last week of May, Anne went to Dallas to see some friends. My son and I would be bachelors for seven days.

On Friday, May 30, we felt compelled to go to the cabin even though we'd planned to stay in the city for the weekend. When he got home from school he told me that he was desperate to go upstate but he didn't know why. I wanted to say no, because I knew already that the visitors could induce people to come to isolated spots. There were cases of whole groups of people being drawn to certain roadsides or even out into fields at night.

But I kept seeing an image of the cabin in my mind, kept imagining its peace and the fun of renting an old movie and watching it while we shared a bowl of popcorn.

I didn't want to risk a repeat of April 2, when the visitors may have taken my boy. But we both wanted badly to go to the cabin.

We set out—only to find that the traffic was close to impossible. An hour after we left the house we were still in Greenwich Village, and there seemed almost no hope of even reaching the Lincoln Tunnel.

We decided to turn back and spend the weekend going to museums and movies. We were on our way back to the garage when we looked at one another—and turned around once again. This was no benign desire. We *had* to get to that cabin. It took us from four-thirty until ten that night to accomplish what was normally a much shorter drive, but we made it.

When we arrived we turned on the lights to cheer the place up, but we'd had supper on the road and we were exhausted. We soon went to bed.

The next morning I woke up feeling a sense of oppression. There had been a disturbance in the night, but when I tried to think about it, all I saw was a sort of red haze in my mind.

A red haze? What in the world was this? In recent months my mind had been full of a number of things, but never a red haze. When I stopped trying to remember the previous night, the haze would vanish.

2026 Update

Starting in 2017, I began seeing lines of glowing orange-red hieroglyphics hanging in one of the windows of my bedroom in my California apartment just before the meditation that I do at 3:00 AM. I cannot read them, so I just look at them and hope that they mean something.

On June 3, 2022, I was a guest of author and *New York Times* contributor Leslie Kean at her apartment in New York.

Her guest bedroom looks out onto a view of the Hudson River and also another high-rise about a block away.

I was awakened by a punch on my shoulder at approximately 11:45. I had been asleep for perhaps half an hour. When I got out of bed to get to a chair and repeat the meditation (this happens rarely, but it does happen) I was astonished to see two huge orange-red columns of these hieroglyphics hanging down the entire side of the twenty-story high rise across the way. I sat up and stared in amazement. I was absolutely wide awake—and I realized that I could take a picture of them. I grabbed my phone and did just that.

The image, which was taken at 11:51 PM, does not show the hieroglyphics, but rather an orange-red haze that fills the frame. To me, this is physical proof that something was there that emanated light in that color.

In fact, the photograph is very much like the haze that I recalled seeing in 1987, and I wonder if, as I have become more practiced in the art of observing the phenomenon and its manifestations, I have ceased to see this as the same sort of haze that was picked up by the camera, and am now observing what is actually there.

But what might it mean? Ah, to be continued—I hope!

1987 Narrative Continues

Why did I even "think" a haze? It was really like a sort of sign in my mind, an alarm. It kept me returning to that night again and again. I wanted to get that strange redness out of my head. How could such a thing *be* there?

The next day I felt the same kind of exhausted upset that had followed earlier visitor encounters, but I dismissed it as imagination. That was, of course, a double error. First, it proceeded from the assumption that the imagination is a trivial part of mind, when in fact it is probably at its core. Second, I was supposing that imagination and intellect were opposed, when in fact they are as intertwined as the double helix.

I did not try to break through the red haze with hypnosis. Instead I simply lived my life as always and hoped for the best.

I wished that Anne was with me. She had become absolutely essential to my ability to cope with the visitors. Her objectivity, her careful and intelligent skepticism, her insight, were critical to me.

More than anyone, she insisted that the question remain open. And she did this without for a moment doubting the validity of my experiences. Thus she helped me to find perspective when it otherwise would certainly have eluded me.

But I didn't have her help now. The feeling that something was being actively imposed on my mind by an outside hand was terribly distressing. The redness was so strange. Why did it appear every time I thought about that night? What had happened to me?

For me, Anne's week in Dallas crept by. From what she said on the phone it was obvious that she was having a lot of fun, but I missed her and wanted her with me. Our son and I drove back to the city on Sunday. On Monday I needed her worse than ever. On Tuesday I was desperate. By Thursday I thought I was going to lose my mind.

The red haze assaulted me every time I tried to think about the previous Friday night. I really became quite desperate because it felt like my mind was being controlled and I couldn't do anything about it. The haze wasn't like something from my imagination. Rather, it seemed like the kind of thing that might result from a posthypnotic suggestion.

Finally Friday came. Soon there would be somebody to talk to, somebody who cared and could listen with calm objectivity.

About fifteen minutes before she walked in the door, something incredible happened. The red haze lifted and vivid memories poured into my mind.

I began to recall what had happened on the night of May 30. The first thing that came back to mind was a voice, soft and hypnotic, saying to me, "You're not gonna remember any of this until Anne gets back." And then the bedroom light was flipped on and a small being dressed in white came walking quickly across the room.

The clothing was featureless except for a dark belt of some kind. I remember nothing at all of the size or facial features of this person, being, visitor, or whatever it was. All I do remember is an impression of unusual whiteness and light-blue eyes. What shape these eyes were I do not know. The cover illustration on this book is only a guess.

This being sat down on the bedside. She seemed almost angelic to me, so pure and so full of knowledge. As she bent close to me I felt all the tension go out of my muscles. The sensation was exactly as if they had turned into oatmeal. My breathing did not stop, but it seemed to become distant, as if I were observing the breathing of a body that was not my own, rather than feeling something.

The being looked directly into my eyes and said, "I want to talk to you about your death." When we made eye contact I saw only blueness—the blue of heaven. It was like entering another world.

2026 Update

I was destined to see this blueness again on the night of August 11, 2015, as my beloved Anne left the physical world for the last time. At 7:15 that evening, as she gave up the ghost, I lay beside her saying "goodbye, goodbye, goodbye," through a flood of grief greater than I would have believed it possible to experience. Then I saw her in my mind's eye, but very, very vividly, far more so than I have ever seen in the ordinary physical world.

She was moving through something like, I suppose, what Tibetan Buddhists identify as the bardo, being observed by watchful and menacing presences. I went with her, determined that, no matter what happened, she was going to pass through this and be free.

The next thing I knew, she was rising into the most glorious blue I have ever seen, more excellent, more vibrant, more alive than any physical color. She was looking back at me with intent, concentrated eyes.

Now that I was apparently out of my body, I determined to follow her and go with her, but suddenly I stopped. She rose away from me, disappearing into the blue, which enclosed her and took her, and left me there alone, attached to my body by a shimmering silver cord that I could not break.

"Or ever the silver cord be loosed…" but it was not loosed and she went on and I am still here, and if, when I die I am not able to rise to her level and be with her, then I want the end of me. I wear both of our rings and I give my body to her attention as best I can, and hope that I am not forgotten.

I know now who the angel on my bedside was. It was my wife, already even that long ago enveloped in enlightenment. I looked at her as if she was an angel, and so she was, and as if she was a stranger, but she was not that.

1988 Narrative Continues

What happened to me next is hard to describe. An explosion went through my body. And then there was the dread. It was as cold as steel around my throat. I wanted to jump away, to run, to scream, to do anything to get away from that terrible, beautiful blue and those terrible words.

The being obviously sensed this. The blueness sort of snapped and I could see again. The being moved its arm slightly, a gesture that I recall with absolute vividness because of the impact it had on me.

I will never forget the next moment. Superficially it didn't seem like much: The edge of the white sleeve touched the middle and forefingers of my left hand, which had been lying along the outside of the quilt. This touch was so incredibly soft that it filled me with a peace unlike any I had ever felt before. In that instant it seemed to me that all the rich hours of childhood, the afternoons dreaming in the tops of trees, the joy of a thousand perfect mornings combined together to offer me a kind of sustenance that I did not know I needed, but once felt seemed essential.

That sleeve was like an edge of heaven.

I have wondered whether angels and demons might be the same beings in different costumes, or, said in a more "modern" manner, negative and positive manifestations of the same essential energy of the universe.

The being then said, "Your metabolism has been altered. If you continue to eat sweets, you cannot hope to live long, and if you eat chocolate you will die."

I remembered that these words had been delivered like whips, lashing into my mind. But they were about eating sweets, which I could not take too seriously.

The next statement had more consequence: "In three months' time you will take one of two journeys on behalf of your mother. If you take one journey, you will die. If you take the other, you will live."

I described this encounter to Anne, but omitted the part about sweets because I didn't really intend to stop eating them, and I didn't want her to put any pressure on me about the matter.

2026 Update

A remarkable man had come into our life, space scientist David C. Webb, who visited us at the cabin and encouraged me to continue my efforts to engage with our visitors. Dr. Webb's CV included consultation with NASA and many U.S. intelligence agencies. But after I began mentioning those connections publicly, they were removed from his Wikipedia entry on March 22, 2024. This was present in the entry prior to the censorship:

"Webb was a consultant to government and corporate agencies, in national and international technological, economic and policy development issues, including space commercialization, space remote sensing, political and media issues. His clients included DOD, DARPA, USAF, NASA, Rockwell International, McDonnell Douglas, SAIC, Rocketdyne, Space Services, General Space Corporation, Eagle Engineering, International Space Corporation, Aerospace Industries Association. He also consulted for universities such as Harvard, Stanford, MIT, Caltech, California, Texas, Georgetown, George Washington University, George Mason University, William & Mary, North Carolina, North Dakota, Florida, Central Florida, Embry-Riddle on multidisciplinary space curricula development, information technology and 'virtual' program development and multi-university, cross-cultural program issues. His work with non-profit organizations includes The Webb Vocational Institute, Florida and California Space Grant Consortia, Florida Space Research Foundation, Astronauts Memorial Foundation, Space Studies Institute, National Space Society, U.S. Space Foundation, Mid-West Space Development Corporation, others." (Please understand, Wikipedia is NOT a reliable source of information on controversial subjects like UFOs and abductions. It is routinely censored by anonymous, self-appointed "editors" with all sorts of agendas, in this case one calling themselves "Mayfair." As of January 9, 2026, "Mayfair" is no longer listed in the editorial chain on Dr. Webb's page, but many of the citations listed above are still gone.)

Dr. Webb seemed to know a significant amount about what happens to people who have close encounters, and, when I told him about the allergy issue, he introduced me to an allergist who gave me injections designed to reduce my histamine response, and also provided us with Epinephrine Injectors to keep in every bedroom in the house lest somebody being touched by the visitors have an allergic reaction. And this did happen. The morning after Raven Dana was touched by one of them while in our guest room, she appeared with badly swollen eyes, and I took a photo of her in this condition. She was not in allergic distress so we didn't need to use an injector, but I was glad that they were available.

It is interesting to me that I could be carried by them and be in close contact with them without any allergic response, but if they came into the house and didn't do more than touch us, it was a different story. I assume that they can control the allergic reaction if they feel they need to, or perhaps some of them can and others cannot.

In any case, I have eaten sweets without any complications.

1988 Narrative Continues

Little did I know what would come from the being's remarks.

I called my mother. She was fine. In late April my grandmother had died, but she'd suffered from a long illness and the death was almost a blessing. Mother had passed that milestone in her life with grace. She was physically well and happy enough.

I carefully marked the date on our calendar when the visitor's prediction would be tested. The prediction had taken place on Friday, May 30. So Saturday, August 30, was the crucial day. All right. I would remember that warning.

Saturday, June 7, we again went to the country. Nothing unusual happened at all. But Sunday morning when we woke up Anne gave me such a strange look that I asked her if anything was wrong.

"I had a nightmare last night. It was incredibly vivid. I dreamed that you were eating a chocolate bar, and you just dropped dead. There was no warning at all. All of a sudden you were dead."

What was this? I hadn't mentioned the warning about sweets to Anne. So how was it that she had come up with such a dream?

I did not want to be controlled by the visitors. I didn't want to take orders from them. But this dream—where had it come from? I asked her more about it.

"It was weird. Extremely vivid. I just saw your face, like you were on television. You unwrapped a chocolate bar and bit into it. And you dropped like a wet rag. I remember your eyes. They were dead."

This was very puzzling to me. I was upset and nervous. The visitor experience was so powerful and yet so very, very strange. I could not fathom why sweets, of all things, would suddenly become an issue.

I remembered that on the night of December 26, 1985, when I was taken by the visitors, I had been made to take a white substance that was very bitter. That could have changed me, for all I knew. Or perhaps it did no more than what it seemed to me it was intended to do, which was to make me forget.

2026 Update

This was the first time I remember drinking this substance. The second time was when the Master of the Key left my hotel room in Toronto in 1998. As he left, he offered me a glass of white liquid which I—incredibly—drank. I cannot have done this of my own will, not either time. At the time I wrote *Transformation*, I seem to have known that the substance caused forgetfulness. In *A New World*, I offered the theory that it might be similar to the "Milk of Nepenthe" which was used to induce sleep and forgetfulness in ancient times. That substance was thought to be made of opium, which would have been milky in color and would have a bitter taste. It would also have caused the person drinking it to fall into a deep sleep and possibly to lose memory.

Because this recollection involves drinking a substance that I knew nothing about and did not understand at the time, I believe that, along with the physical effects and documented psychological trauma, it is corroboration that something did happen to me on that night.

1988 Narrative Continues

Having somebody come into my home in the night, take me, and change my metabolism so that I couldn't eat sweets anymore was outrageous. Lunatic.

I found myself afraid to eat chocolate, and I was furious. How dare they do this to me. I suspected that it was just another mind game, another way of imposing themselves on me.

Angrily and regretfully, I stopped eating chocolate. I discovered to my consternation that I was addicted to it. I really had a lot of trouble. I sweated, I paced the floors. I was in the ridiculous position of dreaming of candy bars.

I did not care to take instructions from anybody whose origin in the unknown might tempt me to give up responsibility for myself. My free will was too valuable to me to let some wiser other, whether imagined or real, take it from me.

When I began to struggle with this demand—with the issue—of sacrifice, my relationship with the visitors changed again. It deepened, but I didn't know that. The very idea of relationship was still tentative with me. Mostly, they terrified me. One does not want to develop a relationship with a hungry panther.

Perhaps because I just didn't think of the visitors as a particularly helpful influence in my life, my interest in following their advice about sweets didn't last long. Finally, one afternoon at an especially good coffee shop, I saw a magnificent, fresh Sacher torte being cut. I ordered a slice and defiantly ate it and absolutely nothing happened to me. I did not drop dead. I didn't even get sick. In fact, I left the place feeling marvelous.

As the days passed and my forty-first birthday came closer, I found that the warning of the white angel haunted me. "I want to talk to you about your death." The words had been said almost with melody, as though a child were singing them. One imagines the angel of death as great and dark. What if instead she comes as a creature of innocence so profound that she does not and cannot know the fear that fills the hearts of those she visits?

But she did know. That was why she moved her arm, allowing me to come into contact with the edge of her garment, which in this world of ours was the very flesh of ecstasy. It was the first time the visitors had ever reassured me about anything.

What I felt when I was touching that sleeve was not merely the softness of some spectacularly cunning weave of cloth or paper, but rather the way the soul feels within itself, where death was defeated long ago and there is no fear.

Had the angel of death visited me? Or was this my way of grafting a meaningful structure on an otherwise incomprehensible experience?

Confrontation with death, the demand for sacrifice—these were ancient tools of initiation into the old mystery religions. It seemed that Dora Ruffner had been right on this point—at least as far as my experience was concerned. She had suggested that the visitor experience was initiatory in nature—a journey into the underworld.

In three months' time I would supposedly have an initiatory experience of overwhelming power. Like the shamanic aspirants of old, I would be forced to confront death. I would take one of two journeys on behalf of my mother. I would survive only one of the journeys.

As far as the other was concerned—well, I didn't want to think about that.

What I did think about, long and hard, was the question of what was happening to me. The issue was not only whether the visitors were real but just how well their predictive powers worked.

People would tell me that I was experiencing paranormal phenomena, or they would tell me that it was all in my mind. It wasn't all self-generated, and the very word *paranormal* is meaningless to me. There is only a continuum of phenomena expressing manifestations in the physical world. Some unknown phenomenon or group of phenomena was causing the perceptions that I was having.

I refused to accept the idea that the visitor phenomenon was "paranormal"—which is to say, inaccessible to understanding.

I thought of the gods of old, all the visitations and apparitions that have, taken together, formed almost the whole of our religious experience. They have taught us everything we believe, in virtually every religious tradition.

That being in white sitting on the edge of my bed and talking to me about death might have been a representative of the most powerful of all the forces that have shaped us.

An angel in my bedroom.

2026 Update

In 1988, that angel seemed a stranger to me. But now, after I have come to see my wife's ascension and now have lived for years with her continuing love and guidance, I think that we make a mistake when we assume that we are not our own gods, our own angels, our own visitors. There is a reason that Jesus refers to himself as "son of man" 81 times in the four Synoptic Gospels.

If my life with the visitors has taught me anything, it is that each one of us carries within themselves a sacredness that He saw so clearly, and that my dear wife carried so lightly in this life, and carries still.

CHAPTER SEVEN

TRANSFIGURED NIGHT

On my birthday, June 13, there was a small party; Anne and our son and I were present, and John Gliedman and Margot Adler came over for dinner. Our son gave me an antique radio, a 1937 RCA. We turned it on during the party and played WNEW, which is a New York radio station that broadcasts swing-era music.

By now I was thinking in terms of relationship with the visitors. Rejecting them or further denying their presence in my life just wasn't sufficient. I kept thinking of the wisdom and the humor that I had encountered on April 1, and of what my boy had said after his apparent experience, and I could not turn away from them anymore.

It was during June 1986 that I made the inner commitment to try to meet them halfway instead of being totally passive.

Little did I know how hard—how incredibly hard—that was going to be.

Our little party concluded with a cake. Our son went to bed afterward, and discussion turned to the visitor experience.

To say that John and Margot were concerned about *Communion* would be putting it mildly. As a psychologist, John was fascinated and rather excited by the window into a very unusual aspect of human behavior that it provided. Margot wanted to dismiss it, and would have had she not sensed that I wasn't lying.

She and John had read the manuscript to try to help me avoid falling into the trap of assuming that I was dealing with visitors from another planet. If I was going to go ahead with the mad scheme of publishing *Communion,* they were both, like Anne, eager to see that I left things in question.

As the conversation continued, I noticed that a physical change was coming over me. There was a pronounced tingling. It felt pleasant and I was not at all concerned about it. Vaguely, I was aware that I'd felt it before. I did not think about it enough to realize what I later remembered: This sensation was most strongly present when I was with the visitors. As I passed near the old radio, however, something strange happened. The lighted dial flared brightly and the sound suddenly went up to high volume. Then the radio turned itself off. It did not simply become silent; the knob clicked off.

John Gliedman was close enough to me to observe most of this. He shouted with amazement, and we all then laughed, assuming that this had been a classic example of the very sort of misunderstood natural phenomenon that we had just been discussing around the table.

When we took the radio for repair, we found that the switch had broken, preventing it from being turned off and on. The failure was not electronic but physical. The knob had indeed turned itself off—so hard that the mechanism of the switch snapped.

My tingling continued after the party was over, but there were no further strange manifestations until later that night. I usually stay up quite late, and on this night, as I had nothing to read, I decided to look for an old film on television. I turned on the set with the remote control and began shifting through the channels. Suddenly I noticed something strange on a public-access cable channel. I watched the contorted bodies for a moment, unsure of what I was seeing. Then it dawned on me that I was looking at a gruesome act of sexual perversity involving torture.

I think I heard someone speak aloud in my right ear, words to the effect of "We don't like that!" Then I felt what I can only describe as a sort of soft, quick inner convulsion and the television went off.

It did not just turn itself off via the remote control; it went completely off and could only be turned on again by resetting the main switch. In order for the set to go off in this way either it had to have been unplugged or the switch physically turned. There was no power failure involved, as the lights in the room didn't even flicker. The set had never done this before, and hasn't done it since.

Unlike the radio, the television was not broken.

If a haunted television set was a mystery, it was nothing compared to what would take place in a few weeks.

On July 5 we were again at the cabin. There were a number of guests present for the Fourth of July weekend. Our son had just been taken to camp that morning.

In the middle of the night I was awakened by a warbling, whirring sound that passed directly over the house and came to rest in the front yard. I then heard a soft, mournful cry from the yard. It came from just outside our son's room.

There followed a period of disorientation that resulted from my attempt to look out the window and see what had caused the sound. Rather than looking out the front window as I had intended, I found myself walking to a side window. I saw two large wolves with glowing eyes standing in the garden.

They looked at me with suspicion and fear in their faces, and moved off into the shadowy woods on the far side of the road. I had the odd thought that they had been "let out." During the night I dreamed about them ranging the deep woods.

Instead of becoming excited about them while I was awake I had gone off to bed again, forgetting the noise in the front yard. I remember being vaguely happy that there were wolves in the Catskills again.

The next morning, though, I realized that there are no wolves within five hundred miles of my cabin.

Wolves matter to me, and seeing wolves in a range where they have been extinct for hundreds of years certainly drew my attention away from events in the front yard.

What had happened? It is possible to suggest that a visitor craft had landed and that a clever form of mind control playing on my interest in wolves was used to prevent me from looking at it.

But is that the only possible conclusion? By no means. On January 26, 1988, I received a letter from a reader detailing childhood encounters with a small man who had a large head and leathery skin and "wore blue overalls." This was, of course, familiar to me from many of my own observations. As a child the woman also had a nightmare of "a large white owl" at her window. In addition, she dreamed about "a pack of white wolves that glowed in the dark." She presented both these dreams in the context of visitor experience. She could not have known about my wolf vision, as nothing about it had yet been published or even much discussed. As she had read *Communion,* she was aware that owl imagery is associated with the visitors.

Amazingly, she confronted this familiar array of images in a house not ten miles from my cabin. I have not received another letter describing wolf imagery, nor have I ever heard of it occurring in other cases. I thought that it was my own personal perception. Now I find somebody else sharing it, also in the context of apparent visitor experience. And at the time the dreams took place she was living in the immediate vicinity of my present home.

To dismiss this as mere coincidence strikes me as an unfortunate failure of curiosity. One is tempted to speculate that there may be a parallel reality that sometimes bleeds over into this one, or even that its inhabitants may possess a technology that enables them to shift between the worlds—and presumably to bring their animals with them ... unless what she and I saw were the lost wolves of the Catskills, roaming yet their beloved hills.

2026 Update

As I discussed in *A New World*, the visionary experience at Pine Ridge was detailed, right down to different grasses visible on the roadside and another moon in a slightly different part of the sky. When we drove along the reservation's relatively modern highway, if I closed my eyes I would see a wagon track instead. The track followed the contours of the land, so when the car departed from that (the highway was raised), I would lose my stomach, exactly as if the car had begun to fly.

When I returned home I found that I could still see into this other world, as I can to this day. It has never been as clear as it was at Pine Ridge, except for the one morning that it appeared to me that I had entered it physically, an event which is also described in the book.

There is also a reasonable case in physics for the existence of a "mirror universe," and I think it's possible that this is what I was seeing.

So the brief speculation here has turned out to be an important part of my life. I only wish that I could control it, but so far all I can manage on a regular basis is seeing into it. I have no idea what this all means, and I have been frustrated that I cannot transition into it physically.

1988 Narrative Continues

The next morning one of my houseguests, who had awakened apparently in response to my movements in the room above him, told me he had seen a distinct pink light coming in through the closed bedroom shades. He had thought that this light was strange, but before he could check further he had suddenly lapsed into deep sleep.

I suspect that something very real came to the house, made its mournful cry for reasons not understood, did whatever it wished to do, and left.

Then came the night of July 18. Because Our son was away it had been a quiet time at the house, which was usually filled with the sounds of children. During the day I'd had the strong and disturbing feeling that I was about to be taken away. This feeling was so strong, it possessed my thoughts for the whole day. I could practically feel the visitors around me. I went so far as to write Anne a note telling her not to worry if she found me absent when she got up in the morning.

That evening we went to a movie, Roman Polanski's *Pirates*. Afterward we went home and to bed without incident.

Anne fell asleep after a few minutes of reading a book. I was absorbed in Joseph Campbell's *Occidental Mythology* and stayed awake for some time longer. At about eleven-thirty I turned off my light, pulled up the covers, and closed my eyes.

Almost at once I became aware of a rustling sound around me. It was a small sound, as if the sheets were still settling.

When the sound didn't stop I thought maybe a mouse had gotten in and was crawling on the bed, so I opened my eyes. At that point I had not been asleep, I do not think, even for a moment.

I was disoriented by what I saw. The first thing I was aware of was that I could see my hands straight out in front of me, as if they were pointed up at the ceiling. The arms of my pajamas were still extended to my wrists.

The ceiling had changed remarkably. It is a raw pine ceiling, slightly angled toward its peak, following the cant of the roof. Now, however, it appeared flat. The boards were no longer one-by-fours; they were at least eight inches wide. And there was what looked like a huge, rectangular appliance hanging from it.

I was completely confused. One moment I had been lying in bed. I'd heard a rustling noise, opened my eyes, and found myself in a situation so totally different from what I had expected that I was simply silenced.

I lay there staring blankly at the scene before me. After a moment I realized that the big rectangular object had a woman stuck to it. I had the horrible feeling that the whole thing, woman and all, was about to come off the ceiling and fall on me.

Then I realized that there was a quilt on it, and sheets. Our quilt, our sheets. Beside the woman there was an empty place.

The scene resolved itself. It was our bed; the woman was Anne. Beside the bed was a table, and on the table were my lamp, radio, and book. I understood that I was no longer in bed. But what in heaven's name had happened?

Was the bed now on the ceiling? Or—

I comprehended that what was on the ceiling was me. *Me.* I had somehow been pulled up against the ceiling.

Immediately I started trying to call Anne, to wake her up. But all I could manage was a sort of whisper. My vocal cords wouldn't work. I hissed and gasped, but she is a heavy sleeper and she just lay there like a stone.

Then I began to be lifted higher. I would rise up, seemingly right into the ceiling, and a light of appalling brightness would come down into the periphery of my vision.

Once I went up, twice, a third time. Each time it was as if the wood around me became like a sort of warm wind, and this overwhelmingly bright light would seem almost to come down and consume me from behind and above.

The light seemed thick, the density of water. But it was so incredibly bright. It felt like the truth must feel in the heart, an overwhelming, wonderful, painful brilliance.

I also had an impression that there were people near me, but I could not see them. I was struggling, but I seemed to be restrained in some manner. I couldn't move my arms, legs, or torso. The only motor control I had was over my face, and that was limited.

A short time later I went spiraling down to the bed, moving through the air quickly and landing softly. As always seemed to be the case with these experiences, instead of waking my wife and telling her excitedly what was happening, I fell asleep instantly. I recall a normal night's sleep, uninterrupted.

I had not been unconscious when this took place. I had not been asleep. There was no amnesia and no confusion. I was aware of the fact that I had risen up to the ceiling, remained there for a period of time, and then floated back down to the bed. But surely that was impossible. Things like that don't happen. I am certainly not going to make an argument that they *do* happen. What I can say for certain is that I have reported exactly what I perceived.

2026 Update

I no longer have a direct memory of this event, but in June of 2025, something quite similar happened to an individual who is working on a creative project with me, one that is of interest to the visitors.

She was abducted from a home in the Hollywood Hills. While this was the first time somebody working with me was ever abducted while fully conscious, it was far from the first time people in my life had met the visitors. She was not injured but was frightened, of course, although not as terrified as I and so many others have been. What is germane here is that she was grabbed by the wrist and dragged up through the ceiling of her house. She remembers rising toward the ceiling, then everything goes blank until two hours later when she finds herself in a heap on the floor of her bedroom with the dawn light just starting to come in the windows.

Even though I no longer have a direct memory of the events described above, I do know quite certainly that such things can happen.

1988 Narrative Continues

Even the next morning I did not feel normally heavy. The mere act of walking fast produced in me the impression that I might just take off again.

When I told Anne about it, I found that it had yet another dimension. We discovered that when she asked me questions, I would hear a voice, very distinct, beside my right ear, which would give answers.

I will reproduce the initial dialogue, as I remember it.

Anne: "Why did you come here?"

Voice: "We saw a glow."

Anne: "Why are you doing this to Whitley?"

Voice: "It is time."

Anne: "Where are you from?"
Voice: "Everywhere."
Anne: "What is the earth?" Voice: "It's a school."

2026 Update

Over the years, I cannot count how many times I have told this story. The "It's a school" comment is pretty much a truism these days, although I do wonder, if our planetary bio-system collapses, if it won't come to seem more like a prison. For years, I thought that the prior comment, "we saw a glow," had to do with them seeing the lights of cities from above, and becoming curious. But now I know that it had an entirely different meaning.

After Anne died, as I have said above, she spoke to numerous people, telling them to contact me and by so doing convinced me that she was still present. As I reported in After-life Revolution, there was another instance of her speaking to someone, and this one not only shed new light on that comment, it revolutionized my entire life.

A few months after she passed, I went to a conference in Nashville hosted by William Henry. At these conferences, he would show slides of one beautiful painting after another and explain their inner meaning. His eloquence and scholarship were both impeccable, and Anne and I loved attending events at the Scarritt-Bennett Center. We had held our Dreamland Festivals there. So I went to his conference.

During a break, a woman came up to me very hesitantly and said she had just heard Anne's voice in her ear. I asked her what Anne had said. She replied, "Tell Whitley I can see him when he's sitting in the chair."

Every night at about eleven, I would do what I then called the "sensing exercise," which is a matter of directing one's attention to body and splitting the awareness between the flow of thought and physical sensation. To do this, I would sit in a chair in the living room, which I had been doing more-or-less nightly at that point for 47 years. She couldn't mean anything else. And then I remembered "we saw a glow." I already understood that the visitors see the world in the same way that our dead do—in fact, that they are far closer to them than they are to us.

'Of course,' I thought. 'It was me. I was the glow. And that's why Anne can see me and why she can still interact with me. She can see the glow when I do the exercise.

Shortly after I returned home, as I also reported in Afterlife Revolution, an invisible presence began waking me up for an additional session in the very early morning, a period known to Hindus as Brahama Muhurtha Time, a period when the mind is more open and the world is more quiet.

Ever since, I have dialogued during this time with whomever on the other side of life who is advising me. It is not channeling. I do not receive mental downloads. Rather, it is very much a discussion. I consider these sessions to be at least as important to my writing process as the implant, the functionality of which I have described before. In the late 80s, though, it seemed more like channeling.

My relationship with the visitors and probably my wife as well, has come a long way.

At first, I thought that what was meant was the glow of city lights and so forth, but now I know that it was something quite different.

1988 Narrative Continues

After this the voice changed dramatically. No longer was it a distinct sound, heard as if it were coming from a small speaker just to the right of my head. It became much more thoughtlike. I suspect that it was very much like what some people hear when they channel.

It has been about seventeen hundred years since channeled voices were a commonplace experience in our civilization. During the whole classical period they were an accepted part of life. The oracles at Delphi and many other places in the ancient world were channels answering questions in trance.

Among intellectuals of the classical era, contact with the Logos was eagerly sought, as this voice was believed to embody truth in its absolute form. It was through contact with the Logos that the classical world developed the philosophical underpinnings that animated it and gave it meaning. And the Logos was often quite literally a voice that one heard in one's head.

With the rise of Christianity the voice died, to be resuscitated occasionally in the form of miracles, such as the voices heard by Joan of Arc, and the voice of Mary at Lourdes and Fatima. Other, more private guides, such as Philemon, to whom C. G. Jung turned during his meditations, have played a role in modern culture.

So the voice I was hearing, as also the voices heard by modern channels, was possessed by an ancient and lofty human heritage.

I point this out to stress the fact that even at this apogee of perceptual strangeness, I was still well within the tradition of human experience.

As far as the levitation itself is concerned, that also has a long history among human beings. Recently, physical levitation has been associated with a number of UFO contact cases, most notably that of the anonymous French physician "Dr. X," a well-known medical official in southern France. Dr. X encountered two UFOs on the night of November 1, 1968, at his home. He experienced the healing of two injuries, had a triangular rash appear on his abdomen, as did his eighteen-month-old son, and afterward had numerous experiences of telepathy, instances of affecting clocks and— like me—electrical circuits, and at least one episode of levitation. To this day Dr. X periodically experiences an eruption of the triangular rash. It has been thoroughly examined by dermatologists and its origin remains unknown.

Except for the rash, his symptoms and mine were virtually identical.

In January 1988 I met another person who has had the visitor experience and lives in my neighborhood in Manhattan. We talked over lunch about our experiences. When she finally felt comfortable with me, she told me the thing she considers strangest about her encounters. "I levitated," she said with a defiant expression. "I'm sure I did."

Two months later, a woman had a levitation experience strikingly similar to mine. She, also, was not asleep when it started. She was lifted up to the ceiling of her bedroom and turned until her feet were facing out the window. She then experienced a blank hour. When she regained consciousness she was returning to the bed. She frantically tried to wake up her spouse but could not do so. Her next clear memory is of the morning. About a week before this happened her husband and I had had dinner together. I had been struck by the combination of fascination and fear that he exhibited toward the visitors. Somehow I was not surprised when he and his wife became involved. And I had learned not to reject testimony of levitation.

The visitors may represent a force of great power, operating at a level of scientific knowledge well beyond our own understanding.

I also found that instances of levitation were not confined to people who have remembered visitor encounters. A very pious young man, St. Joseph of Cupertino (1603-1660), had a habit of levitating, especially during mass. He was a religious extremist, given in his adolescence to the wearing of hair shirts and self-flagellation. In 1625 he became a Franciscan and soon started to fly.

Once he drifted over the altar during mass, and was set afire as he glided through the candles. So distressing was this event to his superiors, it was thirty-five years before they dared let him appear at a public mass again. His later encounters with altar candles were less traumatic: After that first disaster they no longer set him afire even though he sometimes drifted through their flames. He once flew up into an olive tree and had to be rescued, as he could not fly down again.

His levitations were witnessed by many people, among them Pope Urban VIII. He died quietly at an advanced age. The Church has thoughtfully made him the patron saint of airline travelers.

St. Teresa of Avila was also a levitator. She described her experience as "a great force" lifting her up. She did not care for levitation and used to ask her fellow nuns to hold her down during the attacks ... but as often as not she ascended before anybody could get to her.

In all, more than a hundred Catholic saints have been associated with levitation reports. From my experience it would seem that sinners can also rise on occasion.

During the nineteenth century a controversial medium, Daniel Douglas Home, astonished many men of science with his remarkable feats of levitation, even at one point drifting out one window and in through another in full view of many witnesses— but none of them saw him while he was outside the window. Maybe he "levitated' his way along a ledge. His levitations produced an absolute storm of controversy. The

British satirical magazine *Punch* lampooned them. Some scientists suggested that they were hallucinations, others that they were fakes. It should be noted that Mr. Home levitated before the emperor and empress of France, but insisted on doing so in total darkness. The imperial couple was convinced by the fact that the empress reached up and felt Mr. Home's shoe about a foot above her head. Mr. Home would have had to take further steps to convince me.

My levitation seemed totally real to me. It was real. It had to be real. And yet, it was *levitation.* How could it have been real?

I suspect that whatever happened to me on that night, I was once again in the presence of this amazing and confounding force that has produced every unexplained apparition from the visions of Apollo that haunted the woods around Delphi to the massive UFO that was seen by Japan Air Lines pilot Kenjyu Terauchi and his crew near Anchorage on the night of November 17, 1986.

This force levitated me in order to continue its work of shattering my belief in the accepted paradigm of reality. And it succeeded very well.

Something was done to me—something that was caused by a very real natural force, be it the higher technology of visitors or some other cause. As such, mine was not a "paranormal" experience but simply an unusual one, proceeding as all experience must from the continuum of possibilities that define our world.

The morning after my levitation I had a strong feeling of the presence of the visitors. While the "radiolike" voice was answering Anne's questions, it really felt as though they were in the same room with us. Even after the voice stopped, Anne continued to ask questions. The answers now came sort of like wind whispering in my mind, a soft, breathy whisper.

We went for a drive into town to get some groceries. All the way there and back Anne questioned me. As I drove through that sparkling summer morning a whole, hidden life unfolded in my mind. I vividly remembered being part of a "children's circle" where I would go frequently. I visualized it as meeting in a round, underground room. Often I brought tremendous feelings of guilt to the circle, because I had ensnared the other children. But they invariably comforted me.

I can remember the sharp, darting faces of the visitors as they spoke word after word, observing my emotional response to each one. I had been somehow altered for the purpose of the "experiment," so that all of the resonance of each word expressed itself fully in my heart when I heard it spoken. Thus the word *love* rang with longing thoughts of my mother and father and sister, of my grandparents and my friends, of my dog Candy and our cats, and of the smells and sights of our house. And the word *fire* conjured terrible images of being burned, of being trapped in burning rooms, of hearth fires and death fires, on and on ...

I thought that perhaps a record had been made of me during those sessions. Looking back on them, they seem like a remarkably effective test of my personality and responses. They also married me in a deep way to words. To me words have always been potent talismans, not just bland carriers of information. Maybe my awe for words stems from this experience. Maybe also, my writing career stems from it—and thus the books I have written about the visitors.

We returned to the house in the afternoon and put our groceries away. I felt a mixture of elation and relief. For the first time, really, I'd had some clear and extensive memories from childhood. I'd imagined that I might have had a few brief episodes of contact, but it was now beginning to seem as if I'd lived a virtual double life.

I wondered if what I was remembering was something special, exclusive to me and a few others, or if it was my way of understanding a much more universal human experience.

We ate dinner on the deck beside the pool, and lay on the warm boards watching the first stars come out.

I reflected that I had been given the liberty to imagine things I'd thought beyond imagination, to think in entirely new ways about the nature of our lives and our world.

The night of stars and shadows had been transfigured. No longer did I see constellations and planets in their serene orbits. I saw mind sailing free, and thought perhaps that the human brain has not generated its mind-stuff at all, but captured it as Prometheus did the fire from some higher source.

Perhaps the visitors are that source.

If so, then we can assume that they know more, by far, than we do. They know, for example, one thing that we cannot know, not just yet: the true nature of the plan they are unfolding in our lives.

2026 Update

At the time I wrote this, levitation seemed completely absurd, and yet the dream had been so vivid. Given what I know now, I wonder about that dream. I mention Joseph of Cupertino, but there are many more religious ecstatics who have levitated. In his groundbreaking study of the levitators of the Medieval and early modern eras, *They Flew*, Carlos N.M. Eire, while never advocating for the reality of the phenomenon, makes a powerful case that it can actually happen. He does this by analyzing thousands of pages of witness interviews and reports of levitation events amassed in Spain and

Italy by the Inquisition, which took an intense interest in such events, as it sought to determine whether or not levitators were being lifted by God to inspire the faithful or by Satan to lure the unwary.

What is consistent across all the cases he cites, but which he does not himself discuss, is the fact that the levitators entered ecstatic states so intense that they lost any sense of self, or ego, entirely.

When the ego is no longer in control, apparently other, unknown, forces can make changes in the body that seem to be completely impossible—which, if correct, has quite complex implications. The first question would be, 'who controls it?' and the second, 'why is it done?'

Did it happen to religious ecstatics because some higher force wanted to make an example of them to encourage, perhaps, greater piety? Or was it something done by them for inner reasons that they themselves were not outwardly aware of? Or something entirely different?

Understand, I suspect strongly that it is real, and I also think that its existence suggests that we do not know ourselves—really do not know ourselves at all.

In modern times, there have been mediums who seemed to levitate, and, in one case that I know of, a young woman who levitated out of a wheelchair while undergoing an exorcism in a mental hospital, as I reported in *The Fourth Mind*.

Does all this mean that my levitation actually happened, or was it a dream? This is one of the few stories in *Transformation* that I don't currently remember very clearly at all, so I'm unsure what to think of it.

But if it was a dream, it might have been inspired by an event that took place when I was about three. All I remember about it is that I was playing with a purple toy car on a flagstone walk in our front yard, then I was in the electric wires that stretched from the utility pole at the curb to a spot just above the kitchen window. To this day, I can recall looking down at the window and seeing my mother looking at me with enough of a frown on her face to make me fear that I was in trouble.

I am told that the gardener came with a stepladder and got me down, but I don't remember this.

The fact that she told the story, though, and that the wires were thirty feet up, to me suggests that I might have levitated.

I'll conclude by saying this: I hope that levitation is real, and we someday master this skill. It would mean that we had learned something about ourselves that is at present very hidden, but is obviously terribly important. And wouldn't it be fun? I think it would be such fun.

CHAPTER EIGHT

LONG-AGO SUMMERS

As the days passed, I remembered a few more things about my past. When I was being hypnotized by Dr. Donald Klein on March 5, 1986, I had spontaneously regressed from a memory of being with the visitors on December 26, 1985, to being with identical creatures in the summer of 1957. The doctor told me that victims of child abuse sometimes spontaneously shift from one memory of an assault to another, earlier one committed by the same individual and long forgotten. The trigger appears to be that the same abuser is involved both times.

I knew nothing whatsoever about this effect when I regressed. I was as surprised by my sudden shift to that long-ago summer as was the doctor. It took place because the being I had encountered on December 26, 1985, and the one I saw twenty-eight years earlier were identical.

What had my past been like? What had *really* happened?

I began to try to answer these questions, but it wasn't easy. It has been a quarter of a century and more since those young summers, and I never expected to want to recapture them by days and hours.

After that hypnosis session I tried to put the past back together, and thought that I had been relatively successful. I reported on the results in *Communion*.

I could not know or imagine what had really happened. At that time it was simply beyond my capacity to understand the depth or extent of my involvement with the visitors. The memory of the children's circle, which clarified itself after *Communion* was finished, hinted that there was more than I had realized. It was no more than the briefest of recollections, but it was as distinct and clear as any other real memory.

I sat in a circle of ten or twelve children during these gatherings. We met in a round room. I would usually feel very guilty and apologetic to the other kids. Some of them were very, very frightened.

Maddeningly, I could remember nothing else about the circle. Not a word that might have been spoken. Not a gesture. I didn't recall the presence of visitors.

The exercise of trying to remember was incredibly frustrating. My mind was filled with a mixture of real memories of ordinary life, fragmentary memories of the visitors, and screen memories that masked frightening experiences. It would have helped to be able to tell the difference between the real memories and the false ones, but I had no standard by which to judge.

Memory is a strange and poorly understood phenomenon. The mind seems to load conscious memories on top of one another. As they get older, some of them sink deep into the dark formative matter of self and others disappear altogether. During certain types of brain surgery, incredibly vivid memories from a person's distant past can be evoked, implying that at some level the whole of life is captured as if in amber.

The memory can play spectacular tricks. I once read of a woman who under hypnosis related vividly detailed past-life memories which were eventually traced to an obscure historical novel. This novel had been in her aunt's library when she was a child. She had done no more than page through it years before the hypnosis—and somehow captured its contents at a powerfully absorptive unconscious level of memory.

The mind is also good at covering traumatic or incomprehensible memories with amnesia. Victims of rape and abuse must often be hypnotized to enable their minds to release memories too fearful for them to address voluntarily. Sometimes, when a traumatic event is repeated many times or is of such a long duration that amnesia will not cover it adequately, the mind will resort to imposing a false "memory" over the real one. This is what I have called a screen memory. It is a familiar problem to those who investigate cases of child abuse.

I suspected that I had a lot of screen memories, but I had no way to tell the difference between what was real and what was not. What was the flavor of a screen memory? How would the feel of such a memory differ from a real one? Or would they be indistinguishable?

I searched and searched for some bit of memory, some witness statement, some fragment of knowledge, that would put my past into focus.

Was my whole life a screen memory? I halfway believed that I had been with the visitors nightly for years. That was certainly how I felt.

But there was one incident that could determine for me the way a screen memory differed from a real one.

In *Communion* I reported, contrary to my earlier assumptions, that I had not been present on the campus of the University of Texas on August 1, 1966, when mass murderer Charles

Whitman opened fire and killed fourteen students from the Library Tower. For years I'd remembered being there but hadn't been able to find witnesses who could place me. At the time I was writing *Communion* I concluded that this must be another screen memory.

Since it was my intention to be as honest as possible in *Communion,* I carefully reported that I hadn't been there even though the memory was so realistic that I had actually given interviews describing the event in detail. I could have simply hidden the discrepancy, but I felt that candor was absolutely essential to *Communion.*

The fact that my memories of the Whitman incident were so vivid interested and concerned me. If screen memories could be this vivid, then I was lost. I would never be able to understand my past.

I became obsessed with finding out where I was during the Whitman incident. If I hadn't been on campus, then where *had* I been?

I carried out an extensive investigation. I found that I was not registered in summer school on the Austin campus of the University of Texas, where the incident had taken place. Since I lived in San Antonio at the time, I needed a motive to place myself in Austin. Had I gone up to see friends? To take a test? That was possible; I was enrolled in a couple of courses by mail.

I discovered a reason for going to Austin on August 1. It was the hundredth anniversary of Sholtz's Beer Garden, a popular UT gathering place. Like hundreds of other students, I could have been up for the centenary celebration.

If so, though, I thought that I would have been seen by somebody. I couldn't find a soul who could place me on the campus. However, I remembered seeing one friend, James

Bryce, standing in the doorway of the student union during the sniper attack. He stepped back just as I ran forward and threw myself down beside a low wall. I asked Jim where he had been during the incident. He reported that he was in the student union and had spent a short time in the doorway. He hadn't seen me.

But I had managed to remember the exact location of another person who was there. Thus I must have myself been present. It is not surprising that others who were there did not remember me, in view of what I did right after the police brought Whitman's body out of the Library Tower.

Nobody could place me on the campus because I hadn't been there long enough to encounter friends. I'd driven up, parked, and was walking past the student union when the attack started. The experience was terribly traumatic to me. I'd seen people go down, heard the wounded shrieking, seen others get shot when they tried to help. It was a nightmare. After the incident was over I left in a state of shock. I went back to where my car was parked, got in it, and drove all the way back to San Antonio. I remember hanging my head out the window of the car at seventy miles an hour and screaming myself hoarse. Later I sat on the enclosed porch at my grandmother's house and stared at news reports of the incident.

Not until I really struggled with my memories did I recall all these details.

The actual events of the shooting have always been extremely clear. They were never cloaked by amnesia or covered by a screen memory. My recollections were and are vivid. I could be sure that this was a real event, accurately recalled.

2026 Update

The controversy about my contradictory reports of what happened at UT on that day continue to dog me. Budd Hopkins, who was angry at me because *Communion* had sold more books than his own *Intruders*, spent a good deal of time trying to paint me as a liar because of my confusion.

During periods of high stress, bursts of cortisol and adrenaline flood the hippocampus, which is responsible for the initial collection of memories. This causes fragmentation, time distortion and other forms of confusion. Terrifying events are not always remembered as they happened. Memories may be distorted or incomplete, and high levels of cortisol can cause a failure to transmit information that results in amnesia.

In my case, I remember both being there and not being there. But now that I know I had a motive for being in Austin, I am rather sure that I was indeed there.

For years, I remembered seeing a young boy on a bicycle get shot on the West Mall. This has been seized on in some venues and called an outright lie. In fact, the boy was called Alek Hernandez and he was shot in the femur while delivering newspapers near the West Mall entrance.

Had I not been there, how could I have possibly remembered a detail like that? Budd did me a great disservice by seizing on this in the way he did. It dogs me to this day. This is from a response to a Twitter post I made on September 7, 2025: "Didn't you get caught lying about being present during the 1966 University of Texas shooting, even going so far as to say you saw a kid's head get blown off in front of you? And then you were forced to admit you lied? You're that guy, right?"

The effects of trauma did cause me to misremember what happened to Alek. I probably heard him cry out and saw him pitch forward, and under the stress misremembered this as him receiving a head injury.

I am explaining this carefully here because I want it all in the written record. The incident took place 60 years ago, but it is still being used as a way to discredit my entire body of work.

1988 Narrative Continues

I had other memories, though, that were not nearly as vivid. In fact, some of them were full of bizarre contradictions. With the Whitman incident as a benchmark in reality, I hoped to be able to differentiate between the true and the false ones.

My first suspicious recollection dates from the summer of 1947, when I was two.

I had been on the porch at my grandparents' country home north of San Antonio. This was a large house on a hill, with a huge porch that faced east into a broad and peaceful view. It was built in 1906 by my great-grandmother, who had designed its enormous rooms and tall windows and sited it so that it nearly always enjoyed a breeze, even in the fierce Texas summers. It was truly a place of peace, although at the age of two I doubt that I was aware of it on that level.

My memories of the incident I am about to relate are spotty. There is no sense of narrative or continuity. My mother, however, also remembered it in part and I used her recollections to fill narrative gaps.

It was late afternoon, about five-thirty or six. The family was on the porch. My grandparents and parents were having drinks, and my sister and I were playing on the floor in front of them. The porch was wooden, and ended in an unprotected three-and-a-half-foot drop to the front yard.

I remember that they all suddenly got up and filed into the house, leaving me alone on the porch.

I was afraid and felt lonely. But then somebody called to me and I looked across the front yard and saw what I perceived to be a group of big gray monkeys coming up over the brow of the hill. There was a huge disk in the afternoon sky that looked to me like the moon.

The next thing I remember is seeing my grandfather standing motionless in the window with his head bowed as if in concentration. My mother said that they went in to listen to the news. I have confirmed that they could have picked up a broadcast from any one of a number of San Antonio radio stations.

But why would they all suddenly go inside, taking my four-year-old sister but leaving me to the risk of falling off the porch? My parents were conscientious people. It is very, very strange that they did that.

I ran down the porch, trying desperately to get my mother's attention. Then it is black.

My mother says that they all came back outside to find me sitting in my grandfather's chair saying that I had seen the moon come up over the valley. She reports that there was no moon. My grandfather's highball glass was empty, and they assumed that I had drunk it. But my mother did not remember my subsequent behavior. Had I seemed drunk? Slept, perhaps, until the next morning?

My grandfather made his drinks with a shot and a half of bourbon. I consulted a pediatrician about what this much alcohol would do to a two-year-old. His conclusion was that the child would be "frankly inebriated," displaying erratic behavior, an inability to walk, probable nausea, and a definite tendency to sleep. He also felt that such a large quantity of alcohol could pose a health hazard for the child. Mother did not report any dramatic aftereffects.

It is strange that the sequence of memory would include both gray figures and a disk. Could it be that this was an early visitor experience? I had no way of knowing. It was incredibly frustrating to attempt to grapple with a memory like that, not knowing what it actually meant.

If I'd been having these encounters throughout my life, then what had I become? Why were my visitors so secretive, hiding themselves behind my consciousness? I could only conclude that they were using me and did not want me to know why.

2026 Update

The memory of this event remains vague but constant. I drank the highball. I can still remember how nice it tasted and smelled. I also remember the moon over the valley, but unfortunately there is no way to determine exactly when the event took place. As I cannot prove that there was no moon, I cannot be certain that this isn't what I saw, and all I saw.

And yet, I also recall the dark figures. Did they abduct me?

I think it's possible that this memory represents an early meeting with the grays, but I cannot be certain, not in this case. I do wonder, though, given my sister not being able to remember me on the boat and all my talk as a child of spacemen taking me. Looking back, I think that I was asking for help, but not being understood. How could anyone understand, though? It must have like the fears of an imaginative child, although maybe not to my father.

I often wonder what he knew. Did he consult with his brother, my uncle, or did he have amnesia about what was happening, as so many do.

And much later, Anne said while being interviewed under hypnosis by Dr. Robert Naimen, "Whitley goes. Sometimes he just goes."

1988 Narrative Continues

What were the visitors' motives? *Communion* had become a number-one best-seller. What if they were dangerous? Then I was also dangerous because I was playing a role in acclimatizing people to them. And if they were benevolent? Then the agonizingly difficult task of bearing witness to their reality would turn out to be worthwhile.

My desperation increased as I searched across the years of my past, seeking answers.

I did not use hypnosis because Dr. Klein and I both thought that it had, for me, become an unreliable tool. I could no longer tell whether my mind was filling in the blanks in memory with imagination. The mind fights to preserve amnesia around things it doesn't want to remember. The early hypnosis sessions, when everything was fresh, were probably accurate. Now, though, I just couldn't be sure.

I returned in my mind to the children's circle. What had it been? Where had it taken place? My first thoughts about it came from the fall of 1951. I remember that distinctly, because in October I contacted a mysterious disease that rendered me susceptible to every conceivable form of cold and flu. I was out of school for three months, and it was during those months that thoughts of the children's circle began to recur in my mind.

I was tested for everything from mononucleosis to a gamma globulin deficiency. This last test had to be performed at the army's Brooke General Hospital because none of the local civilian hospitals were equipped to do it.

An immune-system deficiency was found, but it faded as inexplicably as it had come. I was eventually returned to school and the episode was forgotten.

2026 Update

I had completely forgotten what I am going to describe now, and never would have written these words had not something happened that was so suggestive of the reality of these memories that I feel, now, that I must do this.

In *Solving the Communion Enigma*, I discussed how I had found myself at the South Gate to Randolph Air Force Base in San Antonio while returning home from an animal exhibition my brother had invited us to. I had no idea why I had turned off the main highway and gone down the side road that led to the gate. It was, I think, buried and very troubling memories of things that had apparently happened there in my childhood.

When I wrote the material above, and also when I wrote *Solving the Communion Enigma,* I had no corroboration and was not sure that what I remember had even happened.

In the ensuing years, things have changed. I do now have corroboration.

I don't remember much, just being taken, starting in the summer of 1952, to Randolph on Thursday evenings for classes. I believe that my sister and one of the neighbor children, Mike Ryan, may have been taken to these classes also.

I recall a lot of noise, perhaps shouting, and being in a dark place. In October of that year, my immune system collapsed and I was taken to Brooke General Hospital for Gamma Globulin injections and isolated at home for the rest of the semester. I was removed from the Thursday evening classes.

A few years ago, I mentioned these memories to one of the best friends I have in the world. We are very close and have been since we were teenagers. He and his wife and Anne and I spent many wonderful times together, and I still meet them at least three or four times a year. (We live in different cities.)

He is an immensely successful man in his chosen field, and has represented the United States in sensitive negotiations with international impact. His reputation is beyond reproach, as is his integrity.

He has read every book I have ever written in manuscript, and I consider him my most valuable reader. Without his advice, I doubt that I would ever have become a published author.

We helped each other decide on the women we were to marry, and both of us have had long, joyous marriages. (His is still going strong.) He said to me after meeting Anne, "Whit, don't let this one go." Anne would always say, "When I heard he'd given me the imprimatur, I knew I was in." She was exactly right.

Some years before, he said to me that he was going to ask his intended to become engaged. I said, "Are you sure, because she'd be crushed if you changed your mind." We talked it out, and he asked her. Also a wise decision.

So we are as close, I would think, as two men can be.

To my surprise—no, astonishment—when I told him of the Randolph memory, he said that he was also recruited, but his parents refused when they heard that the "accelerated learning program" involved their child being placed in something called a "Skinner Box."

This was apparently a variant of an operant conditioning device developed by psychologist B. F. Skinner in the 1930s to train animals by rewarding repetitive responses. Skinner later developed human teaching devices that also used operant conditioning, but did not involve the placement of the subject in a box, but whatever was being done at Randolph did.

He recalled being in the living room with his parents when the recruiters came to the house. I do not recall the meeting with my parents. I assume that I was not present. My sister did not remember it either, nor did she remember the trips to Randolph. For that matter, I didn't, either, until I made the inexplicable detour to the base, and fragmentary memories returned.

Whatever was done, either intentionally or as a side-effect, it seems that it led to the visitors appearing in my life at around the same time.

After my mother passed away, we found a little box of memorabilia she had kept from across her whole life, from letters she'd sent home from summer camp to her teenage years and through her marriage. In this box was my report card from my seventh year, with all the absences from October through December recorded in the nun's neat hand.

She had only kept that one report card.

Unfortunately, my sister had control of the box and refused me access to it beyond that first look. I don't know if the materials even still exist, as she has passed away.

That my mother would keep that card to me indicates that whatever happened was important to her, and quite memorable, far more so than would be explained by a child's illness. It was as if she wanted never to forget what had befallen her little boy.

In any case, the childhood memories that I detail in *The Secret School* all come after the age of seven. While some of the stories in that book cannot reflect factual events, I believe that some of them probably do. I feel sure that there was a secret presence in the life of a little boy who was telling everybody who would listen that "spacemen" were taking him.

Could it be that somebody knew that this would happen—that what was done to me at Randolph was intentional, and designed to somehow prepare me for the entry of the visitors into my life?

There was a lab on the base run by a Dr. Hubertus Strughold, a Nazi scientist brought to the United States as part of the Paperclip Program. At Dachau, he had participated in experiments that involved placing Jews in tanks of freezing water and observing how their bodies reacted and how they died. He also placed Jews in pressure chambers and slowly drew out the air in order to observe the ways that reducing air pressure and oxygen caused confusion and then death.

Once in San Antonio, Dr. Strughold became the first professor at the School of Aerospace Medicine at Randolph, where he used the knowledge he had gained at Dachau to advance similar research here—but without killing anybody, one would hope.

I recall my introduction to the individual who would take us to Randolph from mid-July until I was withdrawn from the program in October.

I was in summer camp at Jack Tolar's River Ranch Day Camp. Each afternoon, one of the counselors would carpool myself, my sister and a number of other campers home in the camp's station wagon. One day, she did not let me out at our house, but told me that I would spend some time at her house instead.

When we got there, we went into the living room. A moment later, a man in a white guayabera shirt came in. I did not like the look of him, or anything about the situation. I was scared. Where was my sister? Why hadn't I been left at home?

When I did not see the counselor, I ran through the house looking for her. I found her lying on her bed with her back to the wall and her hands behind her back. She looked tied up, and very frightened.

Terrified now, I raced back into the living room and tried to get out past the man. All I remember is that he blocked the door. There, my memories end.

I assume that this happened after my recruitment, and that my parents knew that I wouldn't be home that afternoon. But why was it handled so poorly? Why not have him come to our house and be introduced?

I can only assume that whoever was in charge did not wish for him to be seen by parents. I recall that he spoke with a very odd combination of Spanish and German accents. Growing up in the Texas German community, I was, of course, familiar with both, but not in the same person—except for him.

Peter Levenda, whom I had heard of from Norman Mailer (He did research for Mr. Mailer on *Harlot's Ghost*, his novel about the CIA.) had become a friend after I took over Dreamland from Art and Ramona Bell and was looking for guests. I thought Peter might be interested, which proved to be true. He was, and is, an expert researcher into often very obscure topics, and he did find an Antonio Krause who had, after World War II, led a school in Colombia for German children who had left Germany with their parents after the collapse of the Third Reich.

Such a man might have had a mixed accent, but we were not able to trace any connection between him and Randolph.

So, there the story now ends. Somehow, I speculate, my exposure to whatever stresses were placed on me during that period deepened the involvement of the visitors in my life, which continues to this day.

1988 Narrative Continues

I could remember convincing certain children to come to the circle and then seeing them in extreme terror. I remember a boy screaming and screaming. But there were no *details*—no times, no places, no dates. I do remember a few specific people who were in the circle, but so far none of them have come forward. I feel conscience-bound not to approach them in any way lest I prejudice their memories. If they do remember, I hope that they will one day make their experiences known.

A woman approached Canadian documentarian David Cherniack in June 1987 with a story of being in a children's circle. I spoke to her, but could never be entirely certain that our memories coincided. According to her story, she had seen me while she was in the company of a number of other young children. I would have been about seventeen when this happened, and she around five. She remembered holding my hand and looking up at me. I do have a fragmentary memory from my late teens of helping a group of children in a gray, vaulted room. One of them was a little girl and she did hold my hand, but I cannot confirm that this woman was that child, or even that my memory is related to the visitor experience.

In addition to the memories I reported in *Communion,* I have recalled a number of other strange incidents.

In the early summer of 1955 I was walking home at night when I saw a huge light come down out of the sky. It dropped down to a point just above the kitchen porch of our old house on Elizabeth Road in San Antonio. I was standing a few feet away, struck with awe and fear. It hurt my eyes. At the time I thought that it was something alive, a being of fire. I remember every detail of that experience—the June bugs pounding on the screen door, my chest heaving from the scary run I had just made from a neighbor's house, the light rushing like a living thing into my eyes.

I remember it all so well. But what happened next? There is only another blank.

In the summer of 1956 my father, my sister, and I went to Port Aransas, Texas, to spend a few days at the beach. My mother did not care for the coast and remained in San Antonio. I believe we stayed at the Tarpon Inn.

One day my father chartered a boat and had the captain take us out into the gulf. I suppose that my father intended to fish. I remember getting on the boat and eating peaches from a bag Dad had brought. A storm suddenly blew up. There were terrific waves. Then I remember being back in the hotel. I have no intervening memories at all.

My sister also remembered the incident, and wrote me as follows:

"I don't recall much happening on the actual fishing trip, except a sudden storm, with wind and high, rough waves. I don't recall any rain with the storm, nor do I recall our having to shelter from it, so I am inclined to think that there was no rain associated with that storm. What I find even stranger is that I can see myself, Dad and the boat captain on the boat and on the dock but I don't see you anywhere. After the boat was docked an emotion seemed to pass between Dad and the boat captain, an emotion that said to me, 'This will never be spoken of by either of us.' For that reason," she continued, "I knew that I could never ask Dad anything about what had happened."

So, where was I? How is it that I disappeared from a boat in the middle of a storm miles out to sea but didn't drown?

2026 Update

I must remember here my dear sister Patricia, my best friend and protector during my childhood. She was eighteen months older than me and would always stand up for me and speak out in my defense when, as happened quite often, I had done something that had annoyed our parents.

I cannot say that, because she didn't remember me being on the boat, that I was mysteriously abducted from it. I recalled enough of the excursion to have asked her about it, so I was there at least part of the time.

As to the other memories recounted above, they have not stood the test of time as well. I no longer have a direct recollection of being in the vaulted room and holding the hand of a little girl. Does this mean, therefore, that it didn't happen? What it means is only this: over the years since I read the proof-pages of *Transformation* in 1988, the memory has faded. I cannot advocate, therefore, on behalf of it being the result of actual events, but equally I have no way to certify it as imaginary.

As to the boy "screaming and screaming," I do recall that, but I do not remember where it happened. Did it happen at Randolph? I have no idea whether or not I, Mike and Patricia were the only ones involved. Why would we have been?

1988 Narrative Continues

San Antonio reporter Ed Conroy began an exhaustive investigation of my past in 1987. He interviewed dozens of people who had known me when I was a little boy back in the fifties. Among them was a neighbor who had been one of my closest friends. He remembered what I had been like after returning from a train trip to Madison, Wisconsin, in the summer of 1957. During hypnosis on March 5, 1986, I had spontaneously recalled this trip. On it I'd had a spectacular visitor experience that involved seeing a room full of American soldiers in battle dress, all lying on tables and being touched by a tall, thin being with huge black eyes and a copper rod in her hand. (This was reported in detail in *Communion*.)

In a taped interview my childhood friend told Mr. Conroy that I had talked excitedly about "seeing soldiers" after my trip. My friend had not read *Communion* at the time of making that statement.

He and I had been together in my front yard in the summer of 1956 when we had seen a huge fireball shoot across the sky. A moment later an old black sedan went racing down the street in the direction that the fireball had fallen.

Mine is not the only case involving fireballs or black sedans. They are both common to many visitor experiences.

2026 Update

The friend mentioned here was called Mike Ryan. Mike was four years older than me, and the hero of my boyhood. We spent many happy hours together, continuing until he reached about the age of fifteen and left even its last vestiges behind. When he got a moped and I was too young to have one, we drifted apart. But I remember him with great fondness. We had many adventures together, including very nearly blowing up the neighborhood a couple of times with our pyrotechnic experiments. We did manage to burn down his room, much to the annoyance of his parents. (That ended the pyrotechnics.)

He did not remember the fireball that went across the sky that evening, or the speeding black car. But I do think that the event happened. It seems that it didn't make as much of an impression on him as it did me.

As to the bizarre memory of being abducted from a train with my sister and father, I can only say that some sort of encounter seems to have taken place. Whether or not the details are as I remember them, I cannot say, but I recall so vividly the moment I was reliving the experience under the guidance of Dr. Klein, and I said confidently to my father, "It's ok." When he replied to me, "No, Whitty, it's not ok," I relived the terrific chill of fear that went through my body upon hearing his words. There is nothing in the literature that suggests that hypnosis might elicit an emotion like that without prompting from the hypnotist, and Dr. Klein was far too skilled a psychiatrist and hypnotist to do anything like that. What happened was that I relived the fear that I had actually felt in that moment. To me, this means that the moment happened. But where? I do recall on that trip I became fantastically ill, vomiting again and again for hours, to the point that my father found a doctor on the train to help me. I don't remember what was done.

1989 Narrative Continues

A classic example of this phenomenon was related by Mary Sue Weathers, the mother of Patrick Weathers, who has had a number of visitor experiences. When Patrick was a child in 1957 or 1958, Mary Sue was driving him along a road near Meridian, Mississippi, when a fireball suddenly came down out of the sky and nearly hit the windshield of the car. They were engulfed in a flash of light, and then, as Patrick relates, "The thing went back up into the sky." Mrs. Weathers reported the encounter to the police, and was told that it must have been a meteor, even though the incident took place in daylight and the object didn't behave like a meteor.

My sister encountered a huge moving light on a summer night in 1967. She was driving home from a dance near Comfort, Texas, when she saw something she described as "a swiftly moving light" that looked to her "like a very large meteorite." She continued, "It went in an arc from right to left across the road, into some trees. It was quite a distance off the road, but close enough for me to feel that I should have heard something hit the ground. I had the car window down and I slowed almost to a stop, however I heard and saw nothing more. A short distance down the road, an owl flew across and into the car lights. Interestingly enough, it also came from the right to the left."

Like deer and other large-eyed animals, owls seem to be a familiar motif in repressed visitor experiences.

Right after New Year's Day in January 1987 my nearest neighbors in upstate New York heard a strange howling sound and saw a light hanging over our house. They went outside and observed this for a short time. Then the light went out and the howling stopped. Inside the house we noticed nothing, but I was having powerful visitor experiences during the ten-day period before and after this took place.

A few weeks later some other neighbors saw a huge fireball pass over their house and dip down into a meadow overlooked by their large living-room window. The fireball went to the center of the meadow and disappeared. My house lies just behind the woods that border this meadow. One of these same neighbors saw a bright light hanging over the woods on December 20, 1987, at two o'clock in the morning. As she watched, it darted away to the north.

Fireballs and strange lights haunt people who have the visitor experience. The more I studied my past, the more I became convinced that the visitors had always been a part of my life.

Another old acquaintance, David Nigrelle, also remembered what I was like when I returned from Madison. At the time I told him something that he describes as being "beyond science fiction." It disturbed him so much, he pretty well broke off the friendship. He remembered me saying something about "a being."

Mr. Conroy also interviewed Lanette Glasscock, the mother of one of my childhood friends.

Lanette remembered that I had often talked about being kidnapped by spacemen, and that this had so frightened me, on occasion she'd had to take me home from sleepovers.

It took me some time, but I finally recalled one such sleepover. What had frightened me was the clock in Lanette's son's room. It was in the shape of an owl or a cat and it had big eyes that moved back and forth. I remember looking at that face, and thinking how it looked like something else—what, I did not know. I got sick with terror and demanded to be taken home. I know now that the visitors have large, staring eyes. Is that why the clock scared me so much? Apparently I told Lanette that I wanted to go home because I was afraid of spacemen.

My fear of being taken by spacemen also predates by a number of years *any mention* of such a possibility in media that would have been available to me. In the mid-fifties I had access to ordinary newsmagazines, newspapers, and, at school, *Our Little Messenger*.

The classic case of the abduction of Betty and Barney Hill did not appear in *Look* magazine until 1966, by which time I had already suppressed and largely forgotten my own fears, so much so that I do not remember even noticing the article. I have since discovered that it was prominently featured in the October 4 and 18, 1966, issues. By that time I was twenty-one and I did not remember a thing about the "spacemen" of my childhood, nor was I interested enough in such things even to read a prominently featured magazine article about them.

I journeyed back into the past, seeking out old friends, trying with increasing desperation to understand what had happened.

Friends wrote or answered telephone queries with statements like, "You were really a little scary. You talked about aliens all the time." One wrote that his mother remembered me as "a strange child" full of peculiar ideas about spacemen.

He continued "I want to suggest that you have—either intentionally or not— misperceived your past." He went on to say, "I remember that you were always fascinated with the unusual and 'unreal.' One of my most dramatic memories of you was your recounting a set of experiences which I believe you attributed to your uncle. You reported that your uncle was driving near Lubbock when a large flying machine of some sort descended onto the highway in front of him, causing his car's engine to stall." He added, "My mother remembers you as a very odd kid who was always into strange things and talking about strange and obscure stuff...."

He also wrote, "Perhaps a lot of us in those days were beginning to pick up on science fiction images as the potent conveyors of mythic intuition." He sometimes imagined himself a space alien, other times a religious mystic. Far from being rare among the children in my neighborhood, I was participating in what appears to have been a general pattern of "alien" mythologizing.

Did it come from exposure to science fiction, or was it real? Perhaps there was an entirely real experience of a quite incomprehensible kind taking place, which we were interpreting through the science-fiction mythology that was available to us. Had we lived a few hundred years earlier, would we have been frightened of gnomes and fairy mounds instead of aliens and spaceships?

I discovered that the "uncle" that my friend remembered as driving near Lubbock was not an uncle but the late Leon Glasscock. His son and I had, with Mr. Glasscock's help, gone so far as to write to an organization called the National Investigations Committee on Aerial Phenomena in 1957 or 1958 seeking to report the incident.

There also returns a series of dreams that I've had since I was about twelve. I have a name for these dreams: I call them "the dark neighborhood." They are all the same, and they go like this: It is the late fifties. I wake up in the middle of the night. My body is filled with tingling energy, and I get out of bed, throw on some jeans and a T-shirt, and go downstairs. The house is dark, full of the thrill of the night. I go out to the storeroom, get my bike, and ride out into the darkness of Elizabeth Road.

The streets are empty, the houses dark and silent. I ride with almost preternatural speed up Elizabeth and across El- don, then down Terrell Road to Broadway. As I go down the hill I am sailing beneath the blinking stoplights like a ghost, until I am again in the darkness of the side streets, pumping along Patterson Avenue until I reach a certain spot, a curve in the road. There I stop and take my bike onto a path.

This path leads into a substantial wilderness area in the center of north San Antonio called the Olmos Basin. Most of the basin is a flood plain. It is totally uninhabited, a place abandoned at that hour of the night.

I ride down the path. My front wheel bounces on stones. Suddenly I am surrounded by total, absolute blackness.

I generally wake up from the dream of the dark neighbor- hood in a sweat. I cannot remember anything about what goes on in the dark part, except that it frightens me terribly.

Back in my adolescence I was drawn to the basin for an- other reason. I remembered a specific spot on a creek where there was an oak tree and the ruin of an old mill ... it was a spot that I identified with the greatest peace and tranquility I have ever known.

I used to try to take girls to that spot, but I could never find it. On discussing the place with others, I discovered that my brother remembered it too, and with the same associations, but he could not find it either.

In the fall of 1987 a man who also had some memories of the past in San Antonio wrote me a letter saying that he had some interesting things to discuss.

Upon talking to him in the company of Ed Conroy I dis- covered that he'd seen an unidentified object flying over the

Cambridge Elementary School in Alamo Heights, which is a bedroom suburb bordering Terrell Hills, where I lived. He had seen this object in 1957. His impression was that it was heading toward the Olmos Basin.

As it passed overhead making a sound and looking as if it were rocket-powered, he "heard" three thoughts. The first one was: "We are being observed." The second followed at once: "We must not be seen." And then a third came: "We must leave." The device sped away.

There was a large UFO observed over north San Antonio on November 7, 1957, according to the *San Antonio Express* of November 8. The reporters who observed it were adamant that it was no ordinary device, neither a plane nor a balloon.

2026 Update

The stories recounted here would go into the writing of *The Secret School*, which I decided to do after returning to Texas in 1994 and visiting the home of a beloved childhood teacher, Texas Poet Laureate Aileen Carter.

Mrs. Carter was also a dedicated amateur astronomer and a deeply religious woman. She lived in a mansion in downtown San Antonio. Among other things, it contained a chapel and on the roof an observatory. The chapel had a low, arched doorway, forcing adults to bow their heads on entering. Inscribed in the arch were the words "Be Still and Prepare to Meet Thy God." Around the circular interior of the small observatory are the words, "Lord, when I regard thy heavens..."

When I went to Mrs. Carter's house as a boy, it was partially made into apartments, but she still had the main rooms and the observatory, where she taught astronomy lessons in which I participated eagerly.

One of the reasons I decided to write *The Secret School* was how vividly memories returned when I went to her house, which was then just as she had left it on her death. I opened a chest at the foot of her bed, and the clothes she had worn all of her life were there, and also the scent of her perfume.

This unexpected discovery took me back to those days. I wish that I could now say that they no longer remain a mystery, but that is not the case. My childhood is destined to remain exactly that, I regret to say. Almost everybody I knew in those days has passed on, all the parents and most of the children, including Mike, Patricia and so many others.

I eventually found the tree mentioned above. It does indeed stand beside a creek in the Olmos Basin. I also found, behind it, the ruins of some benches, which are the ones we sat on. A short distance behind them in those days stood the Sisters of the Incarnate Word Retirement Home.

Although I continue to remember crossing the Olmos Basin from Patterson Avenue in Alamo Heights to the tree, a distance of about three quarters of a mile, I think that this must have been impossible for a child. And to ride my bike late at night from Terrell Hills to Patterson—I just don't believe I could have done it. I was a small boy, aged eleven or twelve, and I was uneasy in the dark. It simply doesn't ring true.

And yet the tree and the benches are there, so what may have happened? I think that the key lies in the close proximity of the old sisters home. I still think that the secret school took place, but I would be willing to accept that it involved an elderly nun, probably a science teacher, who enjoyed gathering a little class of eager children from time to time to teach us wonders that we would not be learning in our ordinary classes.

I was a keen student, especially when it came to history and science, so if a call had gone out through the Catholic school system for children who might enjoy such classes,

I would not be surprised that I ended up on the list. When I heard that the class would cover geology and astronomy and archaeology, my hand would have shot up immediately.

The figure was hooded in black. The Sisters of the Incarnate Word wore a black habit like that in the 1950s. It was dark, so maybe the class took place in the evenings after school, or even on summer evenings.

I wish I could have enquired of my parents, but both of them had passed by the time the possibility of the Secret School came to mind.

If I did indeed go to it in the depths of the night on a bicycle and then cross the basin, well, then it happened as I remember it. But I'm keeping my options open. I think it happened. I'm sure it did or I wouldn't have remembered the bench and the trees. Maybe it even happened as I discuss above, and more extensively in *The Secret School*, but I can only assert that looking back on those days, I still feel the thrill of discovery and the wonder of those classes. Whoever was in those black robes was a wonderful teacher.

And so the events of those days pass into the shadows, into memory and into the mystery of the past.

1988 Narrative Continues

For a subtle reason, the account offered by my correspondent was given added credibility. He was unaware that the dialogue he repeated had a tripartite structure familiar to me from my own experience and study of the visitors. It was sometimes as if they actually spoke according to the ancient law of three forces. According to this law the universe if fundamentally divided into a positive and a negative force, and the reconciliation of these forces expresses change into the world. This simple law is a truth of nature. It is friction between opposing forces that causes the light and heat upon which all life is dependent.

I doubt that the witness was aware of the hidden structure in the dialogue he reported. It is not likely that he would have happened to invent it in just that way. The first statement, "We are being observed," was a positive expression of a fact. The next, "We must not be seen," expressed its negative implications. The third, "We must leave," reconciled the two into a creative action.

He also went on to say that he'd had the feeling in those days that there was something going on in the Olmos Basin, perhaps even something alien living there. He also remembered the spot with the creek and the ruined mill. Unlike me and my brother, he was able to find it and took Ed Conroy to see it.

My correspondent's testimony made me wonder about the dream of the dark neighborhood. Perhaps there had been nights when I actually rode that sleeping neighborhood, racing along real streets on a very real bicycle—toward a rendezvous in the Olmos Basin with the visitors ... and, just maybe, with the other members of the children's circle.

Throughout all of Western folklore there are stories of people flying to meetings with supernatural beings. The experience was a commonplace of witchcraft, and was believed among the ancients to involve the journey to a meeting with the god Dionysus.

Does it really happen?

Is there someone waiting for us in the night and forest?

PART TWO

LIFE IN THE DARK

"Every angel is terrible...

If the dangerous archangel took one step now down toward us

from behind the stars our heartbeats

rising like thunder

would kill us."

—RAINER MARIA RILKE

The Duino Elegies, "Second Elegy"

CHAPTER NINE

THE LOST LAND

While it was easy to find people from my childhood who remembered me talking about aliens, by the time I was in college I spoke about such things only infrequently. I had some discussions with friends about the possibility of extraterrestrial life, but nobody remembered me talking about being taken by visitors.

A number of unusual events occurred, especially in 1967, but I was by then very far from blaming spacemen.

By 1968, when I was living in London, even talk of outer space had ceased. I have reviewed my unpublished writings, dating from about 1964 onward, and there isn't in the whole body of work—which consists of eight full-length novels, forty or fifty short stories, and hundreds of poems—a single direct mention of UFOs. Because of the existence of this material and the witness testimony from earlier in my life, it is possible to conclude that my childhood was full of alien-abduction fears, but that these had receded so completely by the age of twenty that they didn't provide the theme for any of my creative output. They were, however, present in a deeply symbolized form. Indeed, these fears are as implicit in much of my unpublished work as they are overt in books like *The Wolfen,*

The Hunger, and *Catmagic,* which all contain references to intelligent and predatory nonhuman beings.

The first real narrative I was able to construct from my adulthood came from an incident that took place in 1968. I described the events that led up to it in *Communion.* Throughout 1986 and into 1987 my memories of this incident gradually increased until I was able to fill in a good bit more detail. The memories were startling.

In 1968 I was living in London. During the summer I spent between two and six weeks on the Continent, and have been unable to account for most of that time. As reported in *Communion,* I crossed to the continent on a ferry and took the train south to Italy. On the trip I met a young woman. I remember her name and her nationality but I have not been able to trace her. We went first to Florence and then to Rome. In Rome something happened that terrified me. My screen memory is that I got lost in the catacombs under the Vatican.

Whatever happened, I literally rushed back to my pensione and threw my things into my suitcase. Something I saw in the room horrified me. I have tried to recall what it was, but all I have been able to find out for certain is that I told a friend at the time that I had seen "a dried owl" somewhere in the room. If that is indeed what I saw, I am not surprised that I ran!

I made an unsuccessful attempt to extract more of this memory via hypnosis, but my feeling is that the material that emerged was not correct.

I know now that owl imagery is persistently connected to the visitor experience. Seeing an owl is a characteristic screen memory, reported by many people. My sister and I have both seen owls in unexpected contexts, and there was a period of time in my childhood when we were haunted by a very weird owl. More recently, a man had a frightening confrontation with an owllike apparition in a house near mine in upstate New York, a confrontation that I will record on later in this book. I commented on the long magical history of the owl in *Communion,* recalling that it was both connected with wisdom and was the symbol of the goddess Athena, and of the "eye goddesses" of the Middle East who preceded her. It was especially important to the ancient mother-city of Mari.

I rushed off to Rome's Termini station, where I jumped on the next train out. As it happened it was going north, and I stayed aboard as far as Strasbourg. There I left it and hopped another train, again choosing it because it was just starting to leave the station. This one took me all the way across southern France to Port Bou, where I got a Spanish train bound for Barcelona. I remained there in a back room in a hotel on the Ramblas. I only went out at night.

In *Communion* I reported that the rest of this memory was "a jumbled mess." After much thought I believe that I can now reconstruct it in some detail.

I was hiding in my little back room one night when a woman arrived with what she described as a ticket on Egyptair. This was not as impossible as it sounds; in 1968 Nasser had organized an enormous number of student flights, and Egyptair had many European destinations on its schedules. These usually turned out to be almost total fiction, as most of the flights weren't actually running.

I took the ticket, but I have no memory of going to the airport. My next clear memory is of the interior of the plane, which I had entered through a door in the floor. During the flight I became nauseated. Someone I perceived to be a nurse or stewardess dropped three drops of a clear liquid out of an eyedropper onto my tongue.

The air in the plane smelled nasty, and there was a continuous bone-rattling hum and a great deal of sharp jolting around. I can remember a large blond man in a white uniform sitting beside me. He described himself as my "coach" and he read aloud from what looked like a book made of limp cloth.

I left the plane through the hatch in the floor and was taken out across a broad expanse of concrete by four men in dark-blue uniforms. They were small, considerably shorter than me. At the time this did not seem at all unusual. In appearance they were identical to the men I encountered on April 1, 1986, and who carried me from my room on December 26, 1985. I now know that they have also been seen by many other participants, and are in fact one of the most commonly encountered types. They are usually much more friendly than the beings with the large, slanted eyes, and they sometimes display a considerable sense of humor.

In retrospect, I wonder how I ever could have just dismissed these memories as "a jumbled mess." They are absolutely fantastic, and now that I have looked at them clearly and calmly they do not seem to be jumbled at all.

Who was the "coach?" What stewardesses give you drops on your tongue, and what plane smells like a sulfurous privy? And since when do passengers enter and leave a plane by a hatch in the floor?

I returned to London sometime later. It could have been days or weeks. I wound up standing in front of the St. James hotel at dawn, absolutely exhausted. I have no really clear idea about how I got there.

Friends who knew me during that period reported only that I was gone for a good stretch of the summer. There aren't any records, so I can't be sure how much time passed.

2026 Update

I think that the young woman I met on that trip was apparently a nun on the lam. I have now remembered quite clearly what I saw in the pensione. For the three days we'd been traveling together, the young woman and I had enjoyed a very nice time. We'd kissed but not performed any intimate acts. We'd talked and talked in the way that young people do, and she'd taken me to meet some friends of hers in Florence.

When we got to Rome, we took a little pensione near the terminal, and the next day set out to tour St. Peter's. It was there that things became odd. She seemed to turn into another person, until finally she was stalking along, her face twisted into a furious glare, unresponsive to my efforts to reach her.

It was clear that something was terribly wrong with her, and I decided that it would be better to get my things and leave the pensione.

When I got back, I paid off the proprietress. The young woman had very little money, and I wasn't about to stick her with the bill. I then threw my things into my bag and started to leave.

But I was curious. Could I find out anything more about her if I looked in her case? Perhaps she was an escapee from an insane asylum and needed rescue, or was running away from home and perhaps should be coaxed back, or at least given some emotional support. We'd been having a fine time, so maybe I shouldn't just run out on her.

Her case was unlocked, so I decided I would lift the lid. When I wrote *Transformation*, I still had not clearly recalled what happened next. The dried owl was not 'somewhere in the room,' it was in the case, and beside it was a folded nun's habit.

The owl was smashed, it's beak pushed to one side, it's eyes shriveled. The habit was folded, but I could see the white of a wimple.

I realized that I was looking down at a nun's habit and a dried owl. Of course, it could have been something else, something entirely innocent, but it was what propelled me straight to the station and onto the next train out of Rome.

After a long and aimless journey up to Strasbourg and then across a wide swath of Southern Europe, I ended up in Barcelona where I wired my father for money and waited in the hotel for it to come in while the staff became more and more uneasy about the bill I was running up.

Finally the money came in and I got myself to the airport where I took the awful flight back to London. I think that my 1988 description can be interpreted in a more prosaic way. I may well have been on some sort of Egyptair flight for all I know, in which case it would have been a Russian plane, which would account for why it seemed strange to me. In fact, it was probably an Antonov AN-24 turboprop, which was flown by Egyptair in the 1960s. Being of Soviet construction, it would have had minimal soundproofing and would have done a great deal of buzzing. I did get sick and, although the rules are different now, in those days of bumpy flights and air sickness bags, the flight attendants might well have been prepared with anti-nausea drops. The door wasn't a hatch in the floor but a rear door, which the Antonov's did have. It is also perfectly possible that attendants in blue uniforms might have met the plane at Heathrow, which was where Egyptair (United Arab Airways) landed. Given that I had been dosed with something, I'm not too surprised that my perceptions of leaving the plane seem so distorted, or that I assumed looking back in 1987 when I was writing *Transformation*, that I would have perceived my memories through a screen of alien contact.

The one thing about the trip that cannot, to my mind, be explained is how I knew to go to the St. James's Hotel when I arrived back in London. For one thing, I was wrong in *Transformation* about the name. It was and is St. James's Court.

How I knew to go there I have no idea. It was a pricey hotel and not one I would normally have stayed in. The oddest thing was—and I remember being surprised about this at the time—not only did I not quite know why I'd gone there, I found that I was expected. As soon as I said my name, the desk clerk said yes, we have your room ready.

Of course it could be that they had rooms available and he was simply being cordial, but that was not my impression. I then went to the room, spent the night and returned next day to the International Student's House where I had been staying prior to leaving for my trip in June. I had previously arranged to pick up my things and move to a boarding house in Hammersmith where a friend had a room. From there, I went on a search for a flat and eventually ended up in a bedsitter in Pimlico, where I lived for the rest of the term.

The night at the St. Jame's Court hotel has always mystified me. Even if I had no reservation and the clerk was being polite, how did I know to go there at all? I was living on a student stipend from my father, and it certainly did not include nights in costly hotels like that. Why didn't I just go back to ISH? I could have taken a room there for a few shillings. Oddly, I have no memory of paying the bill, either. In those days, of course, there were no credit cards, or if there were, I had never heard of them and had none. So how did I pay? Or was the room prepaid? I have also wondered if anything unusual happened to me while I slept that night, but can remember nothing.

I believe that the young woman I met on the train probably was a nun, and a very unhappy and disturbed one. As to the dried owl, I have found an obscure folk tradition in England and other parts of Europe that involved nailing a dead owl to a barn door to ward off evil. As the young woman was Anglo-Irish and obviously a bit eccentric, she might conceivably have put a taxidermied owl into her luggage to scare thieves away.

I wasn't planning to steal from her, but the owl certainly scared me away.

My bottom line here is that I met a beautiful but disturbed young woman on the train and left her behind when I realized my mistake. Except for the mystery of St. James's Court, the rest of it can be summed up as the struggles of a young man leading a very strange double life trying to make sense of it all.

1988 Narrative Continues

In 1972 a number of vivid thoughts surfaced that I now realize were connected to that summer. They involved a journey to a great desert. This desert had a tan sky that was so bright it was difficult to look at. It never really got dark there.

The little men took me into an oasis-like setting that was bordered by tall, very thin trees and crossed by a narrow lane. Over this lane there stood an enormously high arch. One of the men with me—who seemed very jolly and gay—said that the arch was to commemorate "the achievements of the scholars." Ahead I saw a completely tumbledown building. It was on a cliff at the edge of the oasis and was so old that it seemed almost to have blended with the stones themselves. Beyond and below it I could see the tremendous desert.

I was told that the building was a university "a million years old." I was really very excited to go inside. We approached the building and I said, "Is it in ruins?" The reply was, "No, but the scholars aren't much good at maintenance." There was an imposing entrance, but I was taken around to a side door that was reached by clambering over sharp volcanic rocks. These stones were fearsome, and for years afterward I had a recurring dream of climbing through them and trying very hard not to cut myself.

As we approached the door we encountered two taller, thin men with gigantic, black, almond-shaped eyes. They were not nearly as friendly as the small men in blue. In fact, when they stared at me I felt naked. It was hard to be in their presence. One of them said, "He isn't ready yet." This deflated me. Things had been going so well; I'd felt very much approved. Now there was a sense of desperation. Why wasn't I ready? I wanted to go in.

The two tall beings left. One of my guides announced, "They said you weren't ready, but now they're gone." So in we went. I found an absolutely featureless corridor made of what seemed to be dark-green stone. The floors were dusty and felt like packed earth. There were doorways, and light shone across the floor from each. I was taken into the first room. Its floor was etched with a circle, and there was a large window looking out over the desert.

When I went into the circle I wanted at once to dance. There was no music, but when I danced I felt a sensation that I cannot describe. The best way to characterize it would be to call it a movement that led at once to great loneliness and great excitement. When I danced I found myself for moments inside other people and other lives. I was walking up a narrow, curved road. A portly redheaded man was running toward me. He was wearing a white toga, and my impression was that I was seeing something happening in ancient Rome.

The dance took on great passion and intensity. Round and round I went, sailing through armies of lives, places familiar and unfamiliar. It was as if my soul had hungered for this. I sailed round and round and round, going faster and faster. I don't know how long I danced, but it was glorious.

Reluctantly, I left the university and was taken to another building. This building was a three-story adobe structure down the lane from the university. In it there was a room for me to live in. It was unfurnished. I slept on the floor. Once I woke up to hear somebody talking loudly in English. Two men appeared, both of them normal-looking. They were wearing khaki clothes that looked military. I had the impression that they were Americans. One of them had a Bell & Howell movie camera, which he pointed at me. They were standing outside the door to the room behind a white tape. The one without the camera said, "Why are they keeping you outside of the enclosure?" I replied that I didn't know, and he looked absolutely furious.

Next I was with a woman who was so pale that even her lips were without color. She handed me a piece of fruit that looked like a giant fig. She told me to eat it. I said that I didn't care to eat it. She replied that I had to.

Feeling very dubious, I bit into it. At once there was a terrible bitterness, and it seemed like my head was going to split open.

I was aware of a group of people, some with tears in their eyes, watching me from behind the line of white tape as I went off on my own. I found that the grass was very soft and fine, and I sat in it for a time. Then I started to return to the university, but one of the tall beings who'd said I wasn't ready was there. He waved me away and I thought it better not to go. I went instead to an area of shacks made of what looked like adobe and dried tree branches. They were very rough and simple. In them I would find things like a single wooden bowl, or a discarded blue uniform. Some of the small men were there, and I was so surprised at the simplicity of their dwellings that they laughed aloud at me.

There isn't any more than that.

Among my masses of old poems I found one that seemed strangely related to this memory. It was written in the summer of 1968, shortly after I returned to London from the strange trip. It was entitled "Barcelona." In part it reads:

We seem to see so many things,

The ships that never were,

The fairies at their ebat ...

Once upon a midnight we danced in circles beneath the waning moon,

the blood-red moon of the Mediterranean ... We flew when we danced—

We danced a long time ago ...

I remember so well dancing that lost wild dance, a journey across the essence of time. It feels as if the best of my life has been lived in secret, and is lost somewhere down a labyrinth. All I have left are confused memories, flickers and flashes, and a few snatches of verse to suggest the wonderful journeys I have taken and the magical things I have seen. I hope and pray that it will one day be given to me to remember.

I have, however, discovered a few most interesting things about the 1968 memories. In December 1987 I was given proofs of Jacques Vallee's new book, *Dimensions: A Casebook of Alien Contact,* in order to write a foreword. I was fascinated to see that the traditional journey to Magonia, or "the land of the fairy," often started with three drops of liquid being placed on the traveler's head or face. Vallee mentions that a young woman who was taken had her right eye soaked in "a green dew," whereupon she could see many wonderful things. Another had "three drops of precious dew" dripped on her left eyelid before making such a journey.

The "nurse" gave me drops on my tongue. I have always known that. The screen memory was that she was a stewardess and I was on an airplane. A stewardess would have given an airsick passenger a Dramamine tablet, if anything. It would also have been the only time I have ever been airsick in a passenger plane.

In addition, the journey back from the world of the dead has in many traditions, such as the Greek, been preceded by the eating or drinking of a bitter substance that induces amnesia—the ancient Greeks called it "the milk of forgetfulness."

I was made to eat a bitter fruit just before leaving that strange, lost land. Before I returned home during my abduction of December 26, 1985, I was forced to swallow a milky substance that left a horrid taste in my mouth. On May 20, 1950, a French woman was abducted. Shortly before being returned she experienced a "sickening, metallic, bitter taste ..."

Were these drugs that made us forget? And if so, then what is the drug that induces the voyage to Magonia? Is it a powerful hallucinogen, or something that acclimatizes the body so that it can slip across space-time to another world?

I had to live with the fire of the question inside me. My mind drifted back to that tumbledown university on a desert cliff so far away. Across many summer nights my mind retreated, to the light of other skies. I will never forget the moment I entered that door and saw the glow of that distant sun falling across the floor. I remember the dust rising from my footfalls in that sacred and mysterious place. Was I in an annex to the golden city, some ancient corner where the very light shines with truth?

Was it really so far away, or is that place part of the memory and heart of every human being?

2026 Update

The journey to the ancient university remains among the most profound events of my life. Was it a real, physical journey or something else? For a long time, I tried to narrow down the possibilities, but I could not manage it. All I can say about it is that it seemed physically real, but I just don't see a mechanism for it. It happened overnight, which means that I would have had to move faster and farther than Santa Claus. Of course there's the idea of the warp drive, but what that entails is drawing two widely separated parts of the universe together for a brief moment and crossing from one to the other. The obvious fallacy here is that it must take more energy than the universe contains to bend it, so I doubt that even advanced aliens are going to be able to do that.

The event seemed physical, but I don't know how it could have been. On the other hand, I have been out of my body a few times, cleanly and provably. On four occasions I have been seen by other people, and on one of them conversed with the individual who was observing me, which he remembered vividly.

We don't know the rules of out of body travel. I can say that I once moved 1,500 miles from Petaluma, California to Wilmington, North Carolina in a few seconds, and observed enough detail to convince some professors from the university who were with me at a conference in Petaluma that I really had been to their campus, a place I had never seen before.

So maybe you can go a lot farther or even into other universes when separated from your body, and perhaps that's the explanation for this marvelous experience.

When I talk about the experience in the media and at conferences, which is often, I describe only the visit to the university and then being told I could not enter, and how that made me feel. For years, it was a continuing source of disappointment—a university a million years old, what might I learn in such a place! And worse, I was thrown out before I even got to start.

There is a telling detail in the description above that I did not understand at the time, but that I do now understand. It is the reference to dance.

First, I enter a corridor with a floor of "dark green stone," then pass into a room with a circle in the middle of the floor. When I enter the circle, I feel a tremendous desire to dance. Even after all these years, as I write this my whole body seems to vibrate with the furious, fertile energy of a great and powerful dance.

Ancient myth is mostly discounted nowadays as the silly imaginings of primitive peoples, but only by the ignorant. Those more adept at understanding the texts see, for example, that Genesis addresses not just the creation of man, but also the evolution of consciousness as it proceeds from the immortality of plant life. In the university, this is symbolized by the green floor in the corridor. Then I go into a room and experience an overwhelming urge to dance. This room is the space where consciousness left the timeless bliss of the parthenogenic plant world and ventured into movement.

When I wrote *Transformation*, I did not understand the possible meaning of my journey into the ancient university, like the city I traversed earlier, a place where the truth is known.

In the little poem I included—without quite knowing why—there occurs the phrase "the fairies at their ebat." But what might this mean? Ebat?

In French, "ébats" means frolicking, and when used in the phrase "ébats amoureux" can have the connotation of a sexual frolic. (As any reader of my work must be aware, there is a deep sexuality present in the contact books. It has been thoroughly snickered about and sneered at by many a fool, God knows.)

Interestingly, the word also works in Turkish, where "ebat" (without the accent) is derived from the Arabic word for "dimensions."

So, perhaps the meaning is something like 'dancing in the dimensions.'

In this room, then, I felt the energy of the dance of life itself. I knew it, too, but not consciously. It was without knowing why that I included the little poem in the text, which hides within it the secret of the dance.

Ancient knowledge sees Adam's creation as the evolution of animal life out of the plant world of Eden. "We danced beneath a waning moon, a blood-red moon." That is to say, consciousness left the thrall and stillness of the plant world and became able to move at will, propelled by the power of oxygenated blood. And the fourth and fifth days passed, and the creatures of the sea and the land began to move about, and this was Adam before he and Eve discovered themselves. And then they ate the fruit of self-knowledge and became human. They became us. And at that moment, mirroring the larger event in my own little life, I was driven from the university. I left Eden and entered life.

My initiation began on the porch at my grandparents' country home, when I drank of the cup of knowledge and saw racing toward me actualized versions of the unknown that I was to face for the rest of my life.

It continued at Randolph, where all my expectations about what reality was were stripped away. The little boy, now desperate in ways he could not articulate, began crying out to anyone who would listen that "spacemen" were after him, as indeed they were.

My dad was involved, but in what way I do not know. As my sister noted in her memory of the event in the Gulf of Mexico, it was understood that we were not to speak of it.

And what of her and what of Mike? They both led hard, broken lives and were broken people. Why? What broke my wonderful sister and my brilliant friend? What unseen presence lurked in the shadows of our lives that they could not bear, but which I could?

> *"Once upon a midnight we danced in*
> *circles beneath the waning moon,*
> *the blood-red moon…"*

And yet again, the story is shot through with accounts of tasting the bitter drug of forgetfulness, the Milk of Nepenthe, a derivative of opium that brings the deep sleep that cleanses us of all memory and lands us back in this strange lost world of ours, crying out to any god we can imagine, begging for some help, some release.

But it's up to us, and we can do it, all on our own. Our souls can dance, and when we do dance, and dance truly, this exquisite frequency that we call consciousness and the dance and the blood and the body become one. I have seen this in a Sundance I witnessed on the Lakota Sioux Reservation, felt it in the Gurdjieff Movements I participated in as a young man, seen it again when I watched Dame Margot Fonteyn and Rudolph Nureyev dance "Swan Lake," and seen it in a friend's garden when her children were "dancing dancing," which I remembered in a poem in *A Hidden Garden,* my book of poetry. I have seen it many places, in Sufi dance and at Studio 54 a long time ago, where wild music and drugs and sweat and sex drew the great will itself into innocent bodies, bad kids touching wonder all unknowing.

And in the end, we will dance us free. I know we can. I live for that, dancing always inside myself, in my secret heart.

CHAPTER TEN

SECRET KNOWLEDGE

recognized that I was going to have to face an unpleasant reality. No matter how hard I tried, I was never going to be able to sort out my past. It seemed as if I had indeed led a double life. But I could never know the details.

What is hideous about this is that I have always thought I had a very reliable memory. It has been one of my most useful tools. Books like *Warday* are based on detailed and meticulous research committed to memory and then woven into the fictional narrative. I have always felt profoundly *in control* of my understanding of who I am and where I come from.

I am not the only mystery walking this earth. Every one of us is a mystery. We do not really know who we are, not one of us. Every past is full of contradictions. Still, I was avid with curiosity, and I kept feeling that there must be some small, perfect breakthrough that would open the fortress of remembrance. But the breakthrough did not come.

I returned to the present, sadly conceding yesterday to its own devices. In any case, there was another important field of endeavor, that of the memories that began with October 1985. I had them well organized. In January 1986, when I realized that what was happening could be important, I began to keep a detailed daily journal.

Ironically, just when I had given up on the past, the present proceeded to give me a fascinating possible insight into the events of 1968.

In early August 1986 an unusual houseguest arrived at our cabin. Unfortunately, I was asked to disguise this person's identity. A noted documentary filmmaker, Linda Moulton Howe, came to visit us with him. We had a small houseparty: Linda, the scientist, Dr. John Gliedman, and our family.

Linda had been in the area, heard from the friend of my experiences, and wanted to meet to compare notes.

In the early eighties she'd had a very unusual encounter with a man who identified himself as a member of the air force. Their meeting was held at an air force base in connection with a documentary she was preparing. She was allowed to read a briefing paper concerning crashed disks and retrieval of the bodies of nonhuman beings. She was specifically informed that she was being shown this paper at the direction of superior officers.

The document and the agent's statements had naturally been of great interest to her. The whole experience had left her with a lot of unsatisfied curiosity.

The typed pages which she had read were titled "Briefing Paper for the President of the United States." There was no specific president mentioned, and she didn't remember a specific date. She was not allowed to take notes on the spot, but recorded her recollections later in detail. The controversial document surfaced in 1987, and her memory proved to be accurate.

The document describes a series of crashed UFO disks at Aztec and Roswell, New Mexico, at Kingman, Arizona, and a crash in Mexico. Nonhuman bodies had allegedly been taken from the craft and had been examined in laboratories. The creatures were described as about four feet tall, gray-skinned, and hairless, and having large heads compared to their smaller, thin bodies. Their faces were flat without ears or nose, and had a slit for a mouth. They had large eyes. Because of their skin color they were referred to as "grays."

The paper also described direct contact between government officials and a survivor of one of these crashes. This being was called Ebe, an acronym for "extraterrestrial biological entity." The officials were told that the gray beings had carried out a long-term intervention in human affairs, manipulating mankind's biological, sociocultural, and religious evolution. The being had eventually died of unknown causes.

The paper outlined the government's efforts since the 1940s to ascertain the origin, nature, and motives of the beings, and, presumably, to gain some sort of control over the situation, or at least some insight into it.

The agent told Linda that she was being shown the document and given the information because the government intended to release to her several thousand feet of film taken between 1947 and 1964 showing crashed disks and extraterrestrial bodies as historic footage to be placed in her documentary.

She never received the footage. Had she been shown a real document, or was she the victim of some sort of complicated disinformation scheme? When the promised footage didn't materialize, the company she was working for became disillusioned and dropped its plans for the documentary, which she believes was the real outcome desired by the air force.

Over the years she did more investigation. She came to my house to find out if there were correlations between what I knew about the visitors from personal experience and what she had read in the alleged briefing paper and been told by the agent and other sources.

When I first started grappling with the visitor experience, I would have dismissed a story like this out of hand. Crashed disks? Government cover-up? Plain nonsense. But I have run across some information that strongly suggests otherwise.

2026 Update

Obviously, with the testimony of people like Lue Elizondo, David Grush, Jake Barber and others now being a matter of public record, there is no further reason to speculate about their being materials and biological remains in the hands of the U.S. Defense Department.

1988 Narrative Continues

In *Communion* I reported that a prominent scientist and defense consultant, Dr. Robert Sarbacher, had written a letter to a UFO researcher that said, among other things, "materials reported to have come from flying saucer crashes were extremely light and very tough." He went on to say, "I still do not know why the high order of classification has been given...." Dr. Sarbacher died in 1986 after a long and distinguished career. He was the author of a dictionary of electronics and engineering that is considered a fundamental contribution to science; a consultant for the navy, the air force and the Defense Department; the former dean of the graduate school of the Georgia Institute of Technology; and a director of the General Sciences Corporation.

Linda had also heard this story, and knew some of the people who had met Dr. Sarbacher. One of these was Stanton

Friedman, a noted UFO researcher. I got in touch with Mr. Friedman in the fall of 1987.

He directed me to some extraordinary information collected by himself and researcher William Moore about an event that seems to have taken place in Roswell, New Mexico, on July 2, 1947.

The air force originally announced that a flying disk had crashed on a ranch near that town, and that it had been collected by a Major Jesse Marcel, a crack intelligence officer attached at that time to the 509th Bomber Group, the world's only atomic bomber wing.

Major Marcel had in 1979 contributed a videotaped statement to a documentary entitled *Flying Saucers Are Real.* In his statement, the major was absolutely unequivocal. "One thing I was certain of," he said, "being familiar with all air activities, was that it was not a weather balloon, not an aircraft, not a missile. A lot of the little members had little symbols which we were calling hieroglyphics because they couldn't be read.... It [the metal] was not any thicker than the tinfoil in a pack of cigarettes, yet when I tried to bend it, it would not bend...." Major Marcel added, "The reason that this story has remained hidden from the public for over thirty years is that General Rainey released a cover story at that point." (The general claimed that the debris had been identified as coming from a crashed weather balloon.) The major's statement was made after he had retired from the air force with an honorable discharge a few years before he died.

Also through Mr. Friedman I met Major Marcel's son, Dr. Jesse Marcel. He has a successful medical practice in a western state. Dr. Marcel remembered the crashed-disk incident vividly. He was eleven years old at the time. One day his father brought home some unusual little I-shaped objects. They were very light and were covered with strange violet symbols. Major Marcel explained to his son that they were from a flying disk.

Friedman and Moore have documented interviews with dozens of people connected with the incident that took place at Roswell. Many of these people were direct firsthand witnesses. The two researchers have all but proved their case, and yet the press remains highly skeptical.

I believe that I discovered why this is. *The New York Times* reported on February 28, 1960, that Admiral Roscoe Hillenkoetter, the former director of Central Intelligence, had said, "Through official secrecy and ridicule, many citizens are led to believe that the unknown flying objects are nonsense." He continued, "To hide the facts, the Air Force has silenced its personnel."

Given "official secrecy and ridicule," the press has been put in a hopeless position. Who are they to believe, ordinary citizens with wild stories or government officials and highly educated scientists?

More than that, I suspect that the government *itself* may be in a position at least as difficult. CIA Director Hillenkoetter actually joined a UFO organization, the National Investigations Committee on Aerial Phenomena (NICAP). He resigned from this committee in 1962, saying that he believed the air force had done all it could and the only alternative was to "wait for some action by the UFOs."

Whether or not the visitors somehow compelled the United States government to keep their secret, the fact remains that they themselves could easily make their presence known at a moment's notice. But they remain hidden.

2026 Update

Much has changed since I wrote what appears above. Things that were then speculative are now accepted in many authoritative quarters to be true.

First, the filmmaker mentioned was not a "he," but rather Linda Moulton Howe. Neither of us can recall why she wanted to remain anonymous at the time, or if she did. I could have become confused because the scientist who was with her certainly did. As I cannot find him anymore, I will leave it that way.

I would like to turn now to the matter of Dr. Sarbacher. I talked to him on the phone in July of 1986 and sent him, at his request, a document describing my experiences. This was the first thing I ever wrote about them. In those days, we were still on typewriters and I did not, unfortunately, keep a carbon.

I sent it to him via UPS overnight, at the time a new service and the only overnight that was available near our cabin. The next morning, I received a call from the delivery person saying that Dr. Sarbacher had died, specifically that he had fallen off his boat. I had become aware through talking to Bill Moore that people who talked too much had been assassinated from time to time. In recent years, Lue Elizondo, the author of *Immiment* and a person making disclosures under the Whistleblower Protection Act of 1989, was retaliated against by the Pentagon, which spread a lie that he had no official role in UFO research. David Grush, who made disclosures about the existence of materials and biological remains from off-world in the possession of the Defense Department was retaliated against by having his personal medical records released.

I have also been a victim of this sort of retaliation. On Sunday, June 11, 1998, *Parade Magazine* published a story in their "Personality Parade" column to the effect that I had admitted that I had temporal lobe epilepsy and had made a contribution to the Epilepsy Foundation. then a newspaper Sunday supplement with a circulation of 37,000,000, making it one of the largest magazines in the United States.

My book *Breakthrough* had been published on June 1, so this was clearly intended to harm the sales of the book. I wrote *Parade* in protest, and they published a correction in the same column on July 11. I talked to Peter Van Haverbeke, the Epilepsy Foundation's director of public relations who said that my name was not on any list of celebrities distributed by the foundation. This contradicted what *Parade* said.

The editor told me that he had relied on his recollection of information about me in the book *Seized*. But there is no such information in that book.

I thought that the *Parade* article, being published when it was and for no apparent reason, might have an origin somewhere in the intelligence community. I discovered that *Parade*'s publisher, Carlo Vittorini, had been a member of the Army Reserve. Was he prevailed upon to plant the article, then? Recently, I was unable to find any direct connection between him and the Air Force in his online biographical material.

There has been much more of this sort of character assassination, of course, but at least I have not been driven to my death as was Paul Bennewitz, a physicist who was interested in UFOs and terrorized into committing suicide, or possibly done to death, as Dr. Sarbacher may have been. The UPS deliveryman who called told me that he had fallen off his boat. He did die in Florida, but all I have ever been able to determine is that it is recorded as natural causes.

As to the reasons that the Department of Defense is willing to go to such lengths to deny the reality of UAP and the presence of an apparent nonhuman intelligence, I think that there are two fundamental ones.

The first is the fact that the Air Force is responsible for protecting the population from threats from above, which, in this case, it cannot do. This is probably the primary reason that I have been attacked. Like it or not, I am the poster boy for alien abductions. Just for the record, I have never asserted that this is what happened to me. While I can prove that the implant in my left ear has unusual properties because it has been recorded on videotape doing impossible things, I do not have any similar proof that nonhuman beings are physically real.

Given the information I have now, in particular the detailed information about the alien bodies that were whispered to be at Ft. Detrick in Maryland for years, and the analysis of them that appeared from a biologist on social media in 2024, which I wrote extensively about in *The Fourth Mind*, I do now believe that an actual, physical alien presence is a probability. As to what that word "physical" means in this context, there is no way to be sure.

Regarding why they did what they did to me, and have done to so many others, I think that the explanation is a little beyond our present understanding of what the world is and what we are. There is an energy that we cannot yet measure reliably, which I think is conscious. I also think that the answer to the motive behind the abductions will be found when we do understand it. Right now, though, our science and along with it most of the western intellectual establishment and our upmarket media, actively deny that there could be any consciousness outside of the physical body, just as they deny that nonhuman beings could be here on Earth.

For me personally, the result of this, when combined with the machinations of the Department of Defense, has been total isolation from the intellectual discourse. I am, effectively, a nonperson.

It was not always like this. When *Communion* was published, the *New York Times* gave it a good review, and did the same for a few of my subsequent books. No longer. I don't believe that I've had a review there in more than 20 years.

Fortunately, the world has changed so much that such reviews don't matter as much as they did, and I still have a thriving readership.

The second reason for the secrecy is more esoteric and also more uncertain.

As I have reported and discussed elsewhere, I was told by one of my uncles and by his friend Gen. Arthur Exon that they had been at the Air Materiel Command at Wright Field in 1947 when the debris and biological remains were brought in. The general informed me further that he had been liaison to the scientific committee that was studying the matter for more than 20 years, and even as late as the 1980s was still going to Wright to advise the committee on the subject and contents of meetings that had not been recorded. (I discuss this extensively in *Them*.)

He also said something about them changing our perceptions that was rather vague, but which he seemed to think was terribly important.

I have since pieced together what I think this is, and, if I am right, then it could be another reason for the secrecy. It is the fear that they cannot enter our reality unless we, as a species, let them in by becoming convinced that they are as real as we are. To me, this suggests that they are not part of reality as we perceive it, but that if we became certain that they were real, this would trigger their ability to enter our world, in effect through the door or our own minds.

Given that the door is in the mind, the tripping point that would unlock it could be an official admission that there are real aliens here. Once we knew that for certain, we could never 'unknow' it. There would be no going back, and if the fear that their mere presence would alter the way the mechanics of how the world works, or would, at the least, cause us to see it as much as or more through their eyes as through our own, the result would be the most dreadful disaster in our history, and probably the last one.

No president, on being confronted with an issue like this, is going to admit anything that might trigger such a thing.

I can never be absolutely certain about any of my memories, but, as I reported at the beginning of *The Fourth Mind*, I am beginning to realize that they may be more reliable than I have supposed.

One such memory speaks directly to this issue.

It was sometime in 1996 or 1997. We were living in the little condo we had in San Antonio, where we had moved after losing our upstate New York cabin. I was awakened in the night by a punch on the shoulder. I got up and went immediately into the living room.

Now, the memory changes. Exactly how the change works is hard to explain. It is not that such memories become more dreamlike. Something else happens to them, and I am not sure we have a word for it. It is as if the input that the brain is receiving is perhaps moving at a different frequency. That is the best way I can explain it.

What I saw were four dark blue figures sitting on the floor. They looked human, although quite small. They had Hispanic features. I squatted down in front of them. I was not three feet away. The room was lit from the streetlights outside. I looked directly into their very dark but human eyes. I said, "I can see that you have quite a history, too." They continued looking at me with obvious dislike.

Then one of the gray people was there. I felt that it was the one whom I had known, at that point, for at least ten years.

When this took place, the room changed its appearance. There were now what looked like small black insects racing in patterns on the walls. The corners were not straight. The furniture looked like something put together by a child.

In retrospect, I have come to understand that I was seeing what she saw. I had been enveloped in her version of reality.

We then took a walk in the neighborhood. The sky was a dull red color. The trees seemed odd, but I cannot say how. The buildings, mostly condos, looked shabby and badly constructed. We passed through to the corner of Eldon and Geneseo Roads where a house still stands where an acquaintance had lived in the 1950s. There were pecan trees there, and we gathered some pecans.

It is about 2 miles from where our condo was to the house, and I don't remember how we got that far, seemingly almost instantaneously, or why we went, except perhaps because she wanted the pecans.

I remember it as a quiet, rather contemplative time together. There was nothing exchanged between us. She seemed sad, and I believe it was because we had lost the cabin, and she knew that our relationship would never be the same again, not without that private space to conceal her comings and goings.

So I would agree with this second fear: close proximity to them may change the way the world appears to us. But I am not so sure that this is as much of a disaster as it might at first seem. My impression is that I was experiencing reality in a more true way.

Nevertheless, I cannot imagine a president daring to open a door that could lead to such uncontrollable change, especially as it is in the mind, and therefore can never again be closed. And I can see that, in a world as unprepared as ours, the chaos would be, at least at first, fantastic.

If this is all correct, then no administration is going to allow full and complete disclosure. But something may come. Perhaps it will be admitted that there are materials. I have been saying for years that, if we have an intact disk, it belongs in the Smithsonian.

I stand by that.

1988 Narrative Continues

The secrecy means that the individual citizen is left alone, ignorant and entirely helpless when they appear in his home. It also means that he can, if he is able and inclined, rise to the challenge, and acquire in the process knowledge and strength that will be deeply his own, and his to keep. No ordinary social institution, no matter how well intentioned, can make such an offer.

It would seem to me that CIA Director Hillenkoetter's UFOs are taking action. And that action—fantastically—is to come into contact with us not as a society but as single individuals, and not in our ordinary state of mind but in a profoundly different state where we are at once more vulnerable and perhaps on a deep level more capable of understanding.

Both Linda and I felt that the briefing paper had been some sort of trick to confuse her attempt to get at the truth, that it had been a clever mix of fact and fiction. By comparing her recollection of its contents with my own memories, we hoped to separate the truth from the lies.

She and I spent about eight hours talking together, comparing notes. Some of her information coincided with things I remembered.

She described what she had been told about the "planet" of the grays: a desert, with a glowing tan sky and adobelike buildings. This was startlingly familiar to me. My experience in 1968 had involved a place of tan skies and adobe structures. Outside the immediate area of the buildings it was a harsh, ugly desert as well. I also remembered that it never really got dark there. Because the planet of the grays was orbiting a binary star system, it also was said to be perpetually light.

I could not believe that I had actually *been* to another planet orbiting some unimaginably distant star and returned in a single summer. I could easily think, however, that I had been taken on a very realistic simulation of such a journey using a combination of hallucinogenic drugs and hypnosis. After all, my trip really began when the mysterious "nurses" placed three drops of liquid on my tongue.

We also found that some of the beings I had seen in my various experiences and the ones described in the paper were quite similar. Since *Communion* had not yet been published, Linda had no idea of what I had seen. And yet she described the small, gray beings and their home perfectly, using her data from the briefing paper and other research. In late 1987 the briefing paper itself emerged, released by researchers William Moore and Stanton Friedman. Its contents were very much as Linda recalled them. The paper was declared a fraud by a number of authorities. One who took the trouble to research its authenticity was Dr. Roger W. Wescott, a recognized expert in linguistics with a very high reputation indeed. In a letter dated April 7, 1988, concerning the paper and some other documents allegedly authored by Admiral Hillenkoetter, Dr. Wescott commented: "There is no telling reason to regard any of these documents as fraudulent or to believe that they were written by anyone other than Hillenkoetter himself." He added: "This statement holds for the controversial Presidential Briefing Paper of November 18, 1952." Coming from a forensic expert in linguistics and style of Dr. Wescott's stature, this is stunning support for the authenticity of this incredible document.

According to Linda' filmmaker's information there are two basic types of visitor. In addition to the small beings with large, black eyes there are taller ones, fair-complected and more humanoid, who generally do not induce the same sort of fear in people that the grays elicit.

I had seen these two types of visitor as well as others, including the small men in the blue uniforms I have previously discussed and the white beings who have had such a powerful transformative effect on me.

The best description of the gray beings came to me from a correspondent whose experience was unusual in that it started during the day. Although she ended up with hours of lost time, when she first saw the beings it was broad daylight and she was fully conscious.

"Two of these beings," she wrote, "looked the same and one was taller and thinner. The two short fat ones were about four to four and a half feet tall with broad faces and black enormous eyes but only a hint of where a mouth and nose might have been, almost like a pencil drawing.... I instinctively knew these were workers and were male. The other one was female and about five feet tall. She had a very elongated face. Dark piercing huge eyes and once again just a hint of where a nose and mouth may have been."

After our long conversation, Linda and I felt frustrated. We had, we felt, made some progress, but it was only in the direction of informed conjecture. The description above, however, is very exact, and other things about my correspondent's experience suggest strongly that it was entirely real and has been accurately reported.

As evening fell Linda and I finished our conversation and went down to dinner. Since early morning it had been rainy and dense with clouds, and it was now drizzling quietly.

I was disappointed because I had wanted our guests to see the magnificent night sky at the cabin.

After dinner we were going to watch an old movie on the tape machine when I suddenly heard a voice quite clearly, like a radio near my left ear. It said, "Go outside." I went out on the deck, and beheld a beautiful and awesome sight.

The clouds were leaving the sky, opening like the door of a great observatory. I called the others, and together we watched as the whole cloud mass slid from north to south as if being pushed by a giant ruler. This was literally like a door opening. The line of clouds was perfectly straight.

We stood there watching the stars. Later we went into the hot tub. John Gliedman, who is an amateur astronomer, observed a dim star make some odd maneuvers. It came in from the west and stopped in the constellation Lyra. After remaining for a considerable period of time near Vega it suddenly vanished. To him this was completely inexplicable.

An hour later the clouds came back. The next morning the houseguests left.

Things got very quiet at the cabin. My eagerness to learn about the visitors faded into uneasy fear. We were alone again. The visitors seemed more real to me than they ever had before.

I felt totally vulnerable.

CHAPTER ELEVEN

THE TERROR OF THE REAL

Two days after the guests left I decided to take action on my own behalf. There was only one logical thing to do: confront my fear.

I knew how to go about it. I just didn't want to contemplate what I had to do!

When night fell in the country the woods seemed to rise up around the house and clutch it with avid fingers. There was often a powerful feeling of presence. People would hear footsteps on our decks or porch, see lights shining in the windows, hear strange whistling noises in the sky above the cabin.

The one thing I could not imagine doing—the worst thing— was going outdoors at night. I could barely stand to go near the windows, let alone leave the house. I sweated out each night behind a wall of security devices.

I could not dispel my fear. I'd already determined that not one human soul knows a single certain thing about the visitors. Nobody. And the more knowledge an individual claimed, the more inwardly afraid he would usually turn out to be.

I couldn't get any reassurance from the visitors. I couldn't get even the breath of a promise—let alone a guarantee—that they wouldn't hurt me.

What I had to do was to challenge the whole situation—my fear and the visitors themselves. I could deliver my challenge by the simple process of going out into the woods alone in the dead of the night.

On the night of Friday, August 22, 1986, I attempted to walk out alone.

2026 Update

When I started doing that, the beings eventually responded. They have been in my life ever since. I cannot really imagine what life would be without them. Given that it led to this outcome, the *Communion* experience was profoundly initiatory, insofar as it overturned my entire understanding of the world and our place in it, and revealed to me that it was actually a very different place than I had thought, far more mysterious and exciting than I had ever imagined that it could be.

By going out into those woods alone in the night, I said to them, "yes, I want to do this. I want to have a relationship with you." And they agreed.

In 1989, two people I saw clearly—part of a larger group I heard but did not see—put the implant in my left ear. To this day, I am uncertain about whether or not it has anything to do with nonhumans. But it certainly has to do with the vast human reality that isn't supposed to exist at all, namely our dead. For years, I couldn't tell if it was doing much of anything. Then, in August of 2015, Anne passed over and a few months later it began to function. A slit opened in my right eye and I could see words racing through it as if there were somebody typing them at blinding speed. My work began to become richer, more complex and more insightful. At one point, I asked it, "who are you?" The typing slowed down and it said, "It's me, Anne."

I was visited by two men in the late night of September 27, 2019, two days before I was due to have a CT scan of the implant at the request of an interested doctor in the official world. They were concerned that I might have it removed, and proceeded to explain to me how it works.

It turns out that the words I see racing past are memories that are too deep in my brain's filing system to be accessed directly. The implant brings them to the surface, and adds depth and nuance to my creative process without interfering with it. The implant can also transmit, but I was not told what it emitted.

They told me that it was invented by a man called Konstantin Raudive. He was an expert in something known as electronic voice phenomena, which involves picking up transmissions from the dead over radios and sometimes even television.

Amazingly enough, the only other person who appears to have an implant that functions the same way, creating a slit in his visual field with typed words racing through it, is an expert on Konstantin Raudive.

I think that Anne and others work with me through the implant, which gets me to another discovery that has evolved greatly in recent years. This is that nonphysical human and non-human beings work together. In fact, there might not even be any meaningful way to differentiate between them.

None of this would have happened had I not started going out into the woods alone at night. Sometimes I would spend the afternoon being mocked on some radio show, then go out later that night to encounter the visitors. It was just amazing.

1988 Narrative Continues

It was ten-thirty. I had purposely waited until Anne and Our son were asleep. I went to the side door. It opens onto the deck that overlooks our pool. The water was gleaming softly with light reflected from the house. Beyond there is a low hill, and behind that the woods.

The trees were silent. The quiet that settles over that place at night is amazing in winter, but this was summer and I was somewhat reassured by the singing of the cicadas and the crickets.

I looked toward the dark path that leads into the woods. Dimly I remembered being carried down that very path, struggling, trying to shout.

Slowly, I walked along the deck. I could barely manage to move. My mind was whirling with images of them, faces and hands and whispery, gabbling voices.

The part of my mind that needs to understand soon became full of questions and fear.

The visitors were goblins. Soul-eaters. And I was going into the dark to tempt them.

I stopped at the gate that leads from the deck into the back-yard. My hand pulled, but not hard enough. I didn't open it.

And I wasn't going to. The truth was that I couldn't go into my own yard at night, let alone along the path to the woods.

I stood there for a long time, staring into the night. To be frank, the intensity of my fear was greater than I had imagined possible. My throat was cracking dry. I was queasy. I was shaking so hard I almost couldn't control myself.

I'd never witnessed such terror in myself. My mind was frightened, but some other, deeper part of me was literally beside itself. The visitors brought terror to the blood and muscle of me, to the reptile that crouches at the bottom of every human being.

Why? Did my unconscious know something about them that my conscious mind was just beginning to admit?

Finally I turned around and went back into the house. So much for a walk in the woods. I hadn't even made it off the deck!

The next night came, and again I got stuck at the gate, unable to make myself go through it. The eyes of the visitors were so startlingly, amazingly *conscious*. No wonder I dreaded facing them.

As the days passed I told some of the scientists I was working with of my attempts to go out at night. It was interesting that not one of these men, not even the most skeptical, thought this was a good idea. My most brutal critic said, "My God. That's the most terrifying thing I've ever heard in my life." Another one added, "If you're walking in those woods and you see something that looks like the Wolfen—no matter how ephemeral it is—get the hell out of there."

So much for scientific objectivity. Understand, these were men who claimed to be *sure* that there was a prosaic explanation for what was happening to me.

If the mind is not afraid, then the heart is afraid, and if the heart gains courage, then the blood is afraid. In my case, everything was afraid.

And I had good reasons. All of the *what if's* connected with the visitors arrayed themselves against me. If I made the least gesture of assent, I worried that they would come and steal me away. Or perhaps they would kill me and eat my soul.

I wondered what my scientist friend had really meant when he cautioned me against my own Wolfen.

I reviewed my writings. Except for *Communion* and one recent short story there is nothing that relates directly to the UFO phenomenon. But the whole corpus of my work seems to reflect some sort of attempt to cope with an enormous, hidden, and frightful reality.

My early poetry is full of references to being lost in time and dancing by night, to a very different view of life than fits convention: "God is wild; I am tame.... Night falls and an age ends.... We call and are answered through the thick foliage, by voices too strange to be our own...."

The Wolfen were gray, hid in the cracks of life, and used their immense intelligence to hunt down human beings as their natural and proper prey.

Then there was Miriam Blaylock, the vampire in *The Hunger*. She drank blood, and extracted from it the stuff of souls. They were the source of her immortality. And when her human consorts died, their souls remained forever trapped in their bodies, for all eternity. Like the Wolfen, a part of nature, Miriam describes herself as belonging to "the justice of the earth."

Black Magic is a novel about secret psychic research and mind control.

And *Night Church:* Again the issue was a force that could consume the soul.

Was the force I had written about again and again my mind's way of dealing with suppressed horror of very real visitors? Only in *Catmagic* had the force emerged in anything like a positive light, and in that book the "fairy" had been responsible for manipulating and controlling human society in such a way that the flowering of souls would be the outcome.

I gave up my attempt to walk in the woods—and I hadn't even left the deck.

The next morning, of course, I had no trouble at all. I walked freely in the sun. Blue bachelor's buttons danced along the sunny paths. The deeper woods were fragrant with pine. Tall hickory and maple trees hung over the little brook that borders my property. I could see fingerling trout lurking under stones. The water sounded happy and young and confident.

All of a sudden I felt exhausted. Abruptly I sat down in the middle of the path. I was ready to cry but I did not. I watched a bumblebee amid some clover.

And then I got up and I told myself that I would go into the woods that night. I would do it without fail.

At eleven, I once again went outside. I was in a state of preternatural awareness.

Slowly, like a nervous rabbit, I crossed the deck.

I thought to myself that I was being a real fool. You don't tempt a tiger.

I kept on, though. I concentrated on putting one foot in front of the other.

I reached the gate.

I could smell the grass, hear the rustling summer leaves. My legs felt like pillars of stone. I was freezing cold. My heart was thundering; I could hardly breathe.

To help myself I did what I had learned in my years of meditation and inner work. I took my attention and placed it firmly in my center of gravity, just below the navel.

Then I walked down the steps and out into the yard. Every puff of breeze, every crack of twig, set me to vibrating in an ecstasy of dread. I barely managed a circuit around the edge of the grass.

Going into the woods was again impossible.

When I returned to the house I poured myself a brandy. I needed it to calm down, and I felt as though just venturing beyond the gate called for celebration.

The night I slept pretty well, better than I had in some weeks.

The next day was one of quiet and contemplation for me. Again I walked through the sunlit woods, thinking about the difference between dark and light. During the day there was no question of fear. It was at night that I grew afraid.

The mind peoples the shadows of the night with demons.

At about eleven on the night of August 27, I again went outside. It was as hard as it had been before.

I had once again waited until Anne had gone to bed. She and I had discussed these midnight walks, and she had agreed that I had to face them, even if there was an element of danger. She understood my need to confront what frightened me.

I tried to walk up the low hill that leads into the woods. When I got to the top of the hill and stared down into that darkness I was almost paralyzed. I could hear the little brook running, and the faint rustle of an occasional falling leaf. I could not walk into the shadows, not even down the same path I had walked a few hours before in sunlight.

Once more I went around the edge of the yard. At its far end the land drops off into a tangle of brush, and when I got to that point I looked back at the house. The lights were warm, the line of the roof lonely and stark. The cool stars swam above. A meteor streaked across the heavens. I assumed it was part of the Perseid meteor shower, which comes annually in August.

I returned to the house, took a shower, and then went downstairs to do some reading. Dr. Gliedman had given me his essay "Quantum Entanglements: On Atomic Physics and the Nature of Reality," and I had been reading it. I sat in a chair by a window and picked up the manuscript. A glow came around the house, but it was so brief that I ignored it.

It became very quiet. I was awake and alert, perfectly normal in every way. Anne and Our son were asleep. My cats were sitting on the couch nearby.

The cats both got restless. The Burmese sat up. The Siamese began pacing along the back of the couch.

In his book *Catwatching,* Desmond Morris reports that research has shown that cats are sensitive to earthquakes, volcanic eruptions, and severe electrical storms. It is not known if they are sensitive to vibrations or to a buildup of static electricity. It has also been demonstrated that they are extraordinarily sensitive to the earth's magnetic field.

The Burmese was crouched, staring up at the back wall of the room. The Siamese was walking slowly along with his entire tail stiff and puffed up like the tail of a raccoon.

I called to him and he looked at me with fear in his eyes. It was quite uncharacteristic of this bold, friendly cat.

The cats' fear didn't make sense to me at all. I decided that there must be some animal outside, perhaps a deer. I returned to Dr. Gliedman's essay.

I read the following sentence: "The mind is not the playwright of reality."

At that moment there came a knocking on the side of the house. This was a substantial noise, very regular and sharp. The knocks were so exactly spaced that they sounded like they were being produced by a machine. Both cats were riveted with terror. They stared at the wall. The knocks went on, nine of them in three groups of three, followed by a tenth lighter double-knock that communicated an impression of finality.

These knocks were coming from just below the line of the roof, at a spot approximately eighteen feet above the gravel driveway. Below the point of origin of the knocks were two open windows. Had anybody been out on the driveway with a ladder I would certainly have heard their movements on the gravel.

In addition, to get a ladder to that point they would have activated the movement sensitive lights. But it was dark beyond the windows.

It would be next to impossible to stand on the sharply angled roof that covers the living room of the cabin. While the angle of the roof above the upstairs bedroom is almost flat, this roof is extremely steep. What's more, I would certainly have heard anybody crawling around on the roof. There would have been creaks and groans from the boards, and there is no question but that I would have noticed the sounds, given the profound silence of the country night.

I am absolutely dead certain about the reality of the knocks. They were not made by the house settling. Nothing but an intentional act could have produced such loud, evenly spaced sounds. They were not a prank being played by neighbors. In the summer of 1986 I had not yet told my neighbors about the visitors. What's more, the prank explanation was hopelessly impractical.

To reach the place from which I heard the knocks it would have taken at least a twelve-foot ladder and a long stick. A ladder that size weighs a lot, even an aluminum one. The people carrying it would have had to go down my driveway without turning on the motion-sensitive lights, and they would have had to place the ladder in gravel without being heard by a man sitting a few feet away from an open window. I ascertained by experiment later that this was not possible.

I cannot emphasize enough that there was and is no way to explain the knocks, except as something done by the visitors. They were not like the vague tappings associated with spiritualism. These were hard and strong and totally real, and their spacing, in three groups of three followed by the lighter double-knock, was precise and regular.

The cats were beside themselves with fear. The Siamese was walking stiff-legged on the dining-room table. The Burmese was staring at the wall, her eyes wide.

Then they both darted away. The Siamese went to my son's room. The Burmese hid on a shelf of linen in the bathroom. When we got up the next morning she was still hiding there. She did not even come out for water until nine-twenty the next night, when she suddenly rushed out and into the cat box.

The moment the knocks ended I had glanced at the clock on the videotape recorder. It read 11:35. The cat remained in hiding for nearly twenty-two hours after hearing the sound.

There was something about the sound that had a significance for her that it did for me. There must have been. Unlike Coe, the Siamese, Sadie is not a fearless cat, but she had never hidden like that before.

To me, the knocks were an absolutely clear indication that something entirely and physically real was present and that it was taking an interest in me.

This is exactly what people who are afraid of the idea of visitors don't want to hear. But I am not lying, I am not confused, I am not mentally ill, and I do not have organic brain disease. In any case, a manifestation like the knocks cannot be put down to disease. Such a thing is not a symptom. My cats would not have reacted to something happening in my mind. I am reporting a true event. It was the first definite, physical indication I had while in a state of completely normal consciousness that the visitors were part of this world.

They were responding to my attempts to develop the relationship and accept my fear by making their physical reality more plain.

The stunning event of August 27, 1986, strengthened my wavering resolve to keep the matter where it belongs, which is in question. It is an awfully serious business, and it cannot be removed from question except as we learn more facts. Should we decide to believe something about this that is not true, we will ruin it for ourselves. We will form yet another mythology around the visitors, as I suspect we have been doing throughout our history.

The moment after the nine knocks I thought to go outside. I also thought, *You're not ready yet. You just go up to bed.*

The next morning I thought that was exactly what I had done. But there was something wrong. While the knocks were taking place I was unquestionably in a normal state of mind. As soon as I began to move from the chair, though, I feel that I may have entered another state.

Unfortunately, I did not remember that something may have happened after the knocks until weeks later. On the morning after, my immediate thought was that I had failed miserably. The visitors had come, had knocked—and I'd just sat there, too scared even to open the door!

I therefore don't know whether I concocted the subsequent memories to make myself feel better, or if they were hidden by a more prosaic screen memory.

One day I glanced at the clock on our videotape machine and suddenly remembered seeing it when it said 2:18 A.M. An instant later I recalled that I'd seen it reading that time as I went upstairs on the night of the nine knocks. But they had come at 11:35. I thought I'd gone upstairs a few minutes later.

Had I lost nearly three hours of time on that night?

It seemed to me that I had two completely different sets of memories superimposed on one another, both covering the same time period. I could remember sitting in the chair for a moment, putting down the essay, and then going up to bed thinking that I wasn't ready yet to see the visitors face-to-face.

I *also* vividly recalled going to the door, struggling to open it, and finally getting it open.

I went out onto the deck and looked around. There was nothing. I started to look up but noticed movement beside my right leg and looked down instead. There was something gleaming at waist level: three sets of large, black eyes barely visible in the dim light.

The next thing that happened was that my deck and pool dissolved into a magnificent vision. In this vision I was standing before a field of yellow flowers that rose up a low hill. The sky was black and full of stars so large and bright that it seemed as if I could reach up and touch them.

Even though the sky was dark the flowers were bathed in bright sunlight. As I watched I felt a wind blowing around me from behind. Suddenly children of all ages and sizes were running past me and out into the field, running and laughing through the sunlit flowers and up the low hill. They ran in a dense column, laughing and waving, and I felt an anguish to join them.

They ran up the hill and right into the sky, a glowing column of children, and when they reached the top of the sky they exploded into new stars.

A voice said to me, "This is the field where the sins of the world are buried." I wanted to go out to it but I could not, and that was painful, but I was filled with joy just to know that it was there.

Both the memory of going upstairs and the one of this vision covered the same time period. Frankly, the second memory sequence seemed more real, although it was far more extraordinary than the first.

Later I told my brother about this experience, and he said "The odd thing is that I've had a private fantasy of a field of yellow flowers all of my life. When I'm relaxing I often imagine that field."

The following spring we were to make a lovely discovery at the house. After an absence of three or four weeks we returned to find that there actually *was* a field of yellow flowers where I had seen one the previous August.

It turned out that the landscape architect had planted the area with bulbs in October—without, of course, knowing of my vision. I had not even known that she had done the planting, let alone what kind of bulbs she had used.

By coincidence she had chosen yellow daffodils.

CHAPTER TWELVE

FIRE OF THE QUESTION

In the days after I heard the nine knocks I was shattered, overwhelmed. I remembered their eerie precision—three groups of three perfectly measured, exactly spaced sounds, each precisely as loud as the one previous. And then there had been a soft double-knock, completely different in tone from the others. It had communicated a distinct sense of finality, and seemed by its lightness of tone not to be a part of the group. The nine knocks were a sort of communication. The tenth was punctuation.

I tried everything to duplicate those knocks. We tossed stones at the house from a distance. I clambered up on the roof and tried to lie down and do it with a stick. In those days there wasn't even a gutter in which to brace one's foot. I tested the sensitivity limits of the automatic lights. There was no way to get to the windows without turning them on. I had people creep up to the house with ladders. No matter how quiet they were, I heard them easily. And once they did get up to the spot where the knocks had come from, nobody could even begin to duplicate what I can only describe as the terrible accuracy of those sounds.

I had people tap from different locations on the wall, thinking that perhaps I had misread taps that had actually been produced from lower down. But it was easy to tell where the knocks had come from. I even called the Audubon Society to find out if there was any species of bird that might peck the side of a house at night. No woodpecker makes sounds like that. What about squirrels, rats, mice, coons? All as unlikely as an insomniac woodpecker, because of the extraordinary precision of the sounds.

I also experimented a little with the cats. At exactly 11:35 a few nights later, using a ladder that I had placed in the afternoon, I went up and repeated the knocks as best I could. Sadie hardly glanced up. Coe didn't notice at all. My knocks were as loud as the ones the visitors had made. But the cats remained indifferent.

I finally sat myself down and told myself to face facts. The knocks had been real, physical events. They had been made by something that was part of the physical world. Whatever it was must have been observing me carefully, watching me try to overcome my fears. It had responded to my struggle.

This went beyond everything I had imagined or anticipated. If only I hadn't hesitated in the moment after the knocks, would I have met the visitors in full and normal consciousness? What would have happened if I'd gotten up and gone outside at once?

Thoughts like that tormented me.

The nine knocks made me struggle even harder to understand. And I did not understand. But I had a few ideas.

It was as if I had discovered an unknown world that has always been around us, that may be an even greater reality. I remembered that in the golden city there had been all of those strange stadiums, lit with amazingly bright lights. I'd had the impression that they were jammed with observers, that the streets and buildings were empty because the inhabitants were all in them. But there had been no sound and I had been unable to rise high enough to see within. When I finally rose above the city, the light in the stadiums was so bright I still couldn't see.

What was happening down inside them? Had I been able to look, would I have seen our lives there, our struggles being enacted before silent angelic audiences?

During this time the nature of my fear changed. Previously it had contained an element of the abstract about it. Somewhere inside myself I had been assuming that I would be able to wake up even from the worst, most fearful visitor experience.

I realized that they must have been aware of my attempts to walk in the woods. I felt more than watched; I felt entered and observed from within.

The fear of kidnapping resurfaced. I twisted and turned on the horns of the dilemma. How could I protect my family? What would I do if they actually took Our son—or me, or Anne, or all of us?

The sense of helplessness was appalling. Who could I call? The police, the FBI? Like this whole society, these organizations are victims of the process of denial and ridicule described by CIA Director Hillenkoetter. Officially they ignore the visitors. Unofficially, they laugh.

There was no hope of help at all. Even the most well-meaning of our friends and supporters could not really understand the situation we were in.

I and my family were facing the hardest, most terrifying and remarkable thing, and we were facing it by ourselves. Or, more accurately, I was facing it. My wife and son were insulated from the full impact of the thing, because it wasn't happening to them directly.

It would have been beyond my ability to endure this had there not been something about the nine knocks that offered me the promise of new understanding.

I will not lie and say that I overcame my fear. I did not overcome my fear. They were *physically real*. This meant that all of my clever speculation went by the boards. What was I to do? Where was I to turn? The strength of religion, the power of intellect, sheer physical courage, all blew away like so much dust.

During the seconds that the knocks were taking place I had not been particularly afraid. More shocked and amazed. The fear reasserted itself afterward, and it was still very much with me.

Every time I thought that I might not have gotten up and walked out of that house on my own I agonized. Why was I so fearful? Why couldn't I overcome the primitive parts of myself and show a little courage?

I was suffering with such thoughts when I suddenly realized that the nine knocks had a very special and wonderful meaning for me.

Back in the early seventies a man whose intelligence and commitment to spiritual development I respected very much, Gurdjieff teacher Joseph Stein, had given me a set questions to ask when I was really at sea about something.

There were nine questions. Just as the knocks had been, they were divided into three groups of three.

The nine questions are as follows:

GROUP 1

What is the nature of the substance or problem?

What is its origin?

What is its composition?

GROUP 2

What is its function?

Who possesses, controls or causes it? What is my opinion of it?

GROUP 3

What is my relationship to it?

What are my expectations of it? What is its destiny?

Perhaps the nine knocks were organized into three groups of three for reasons I knew nothing about. But they had jogged my memory, and I could use the nine questions to clarify things for myself.

I understood that the only thing now standing between me and helpless panic was my ability to ask questions.

The trick would be, though, not to jump on definite, final answers. Simple answers close doors. And I did not want to close them, I wanted to open them wider!

I sat down and began to work with the nine questions. I worked with the desperation of the possessed. At last I had a tool. The questions could put borders around things, define limits, perhaps suggest new directions for me to take.

From my journal:

"What is their nature? I am thrilled by their power. Also, frightened. Curiously I want them with me, to care about me. At the same time, I'm so darned scared. Why? Control is the issue. I don't want to give up control, but they are very con-trolling. They feel like something that is both deep inside me and far away.

"Their origin? Oh, people say this and that. Some that they are from Zeta Reticuli. Others that they are from another star system, or even from Mars. If they are from another planet, it does not seem to me that they just got here. Are there cities somewhere, swarming with them, street corners where they are commonplace? Do they have libraries and restaurants and names? Why do they all dress alike? Why don't they laugh? Is there any place I know they are from? I know they are from the night.

"Composition? That's impossible! I can't even begin to answer that. Skin, flesh, blood, bones? What would it be like to kiss them? Are they warm? Why do I think of their hands? Cool. Yes, and I remember they have a smell, pungent, organic. I want them to touch me. I want them near me. But they act like predators.

"Function—not as far as they are concerned, as far as I am concerned. They are not only functioning in my life to terrify me. They have another function. They are forcing me to grow. Stressing me so much that my mind is evolving. Rats—there were tests of rats in the seventies. Stress tests. Rats were stressed with electrocution. Day after day they were made to suffer for long periods of time. They grew stronger, their brains got larger, they became better rats.... I think this is mentioned by Joseph Chilton Pearce in *Magical Child*. Dora Ruffner told me about the book.

"And suddenly a voice—a tired, young voice says as clear as day: 'Thank you.' Them. *Their function is in some way to make us evolve*. And now at last I know a little something.

"Who is in control? Obviously, them. But no, that isn't true at all. Who walked out into the night? I did. Who wants them to come back? I do. And that is the truth.

"How about my opinion? So unsure. Maybe they are the best friends I could ever have. Friends with the courage to be hard on me in order to help me grow. But they are so terrifying. They come across as very negative. But the whole universe exists because of friction between negative and positive.

Atomic friction causes the heat and light of the stars. Positive and negative forces battle perpetually. This is simple, physical reality.

"Does that make negative forces evil? No, essential!

"Words of Jesus, from Matthew: 'But I say to you, Love your enemies, bless them that curse you, do good to them that hate you....' Oh, Jesus, you knew, didn't you? You knew how to work with a force like this.

"Relationship. Yes, a big relationship! I actually have a real relationship with you, and you are real! Have you been our demons all along, tempting us, tormenting us, laboring through the ages on behalf of our growth? Is that why you sound so tired? What promise there is in this relationship, a new world!

"Expectations? Do I have them? I'll say I do! Thousands of them! Now that I am beginning to work on these questions, I expect to grow. Still, though, I sense deep inside a raw, primitive terror that doesn't even have access to words.

"Destiny—a word full of the wind and the night. When I think of destiny I think of huge fleets sailing off the edge of the world. Destiny is a child laughing suddenly in the middle of the night. It is the hardest hour, when dawn is just coming and I lie unable to sleep, feeling the lives of those I love like sand in my fingers. It is toxic wind overspreading the earth, dioxin on a summer breeze. It is the smiling old sun. It is the peace that we all are seeking, that is perhaps the deep, true reason that life emerged in the first place."

The nine questions helped me enormously. In reminding me of them the visitors gave me a marvelous tool. Suddenly I was no longer the victim. Armed with good questions, I was a partner in my experience, and possibly its master.

Before the nine questions, the visitors seemed to be in total control. They were terrible, implacable predators.

Now I knew a truth: I loved them, wanted them, needed them, chose them, and called them.

I was responsible for the visitor experience becoming a part of my life. I was not being randomly oppressed by them.

I saw us on our little blue planet hanging in the dark, and suddenly I felt loved and cherished by something huge and warm and incredibly terrible.

We and the visitors were together seeking our truth and our destiny. Pressing us from every side was the night.

The golden city floated into my thoughts. I knew now the meaning of the towers of white light that blazed there: In the golden city night has no end. But neither does that light, for it is the eternal fire of truth, and also the light of any ordinary human heart.

2026 Update

Let me try to unpack this extremely complex set of perceptions. When I wrote *Transformation*, I had not yet had enough experience with our visitors' ability to manipulate and control memory. I am beginning to understand how their current thought processes relate to the way we used to use our minds before we had evolved what we now call logical or rational thinking.

This is not the only form of thought, and only arose slowly with the emergence of writing, which was originally invented not to communicate thought but to record lists of property and records of trade, which appear in Sumer (modern day Iraq) and Iran, and more-or-less simultaneously in Egypt.

This chapter begins with one of the most purely physical experiences I have ever had, but then it changes into something very different. I think the later material is both imaginative and real at the same time, almost as if there was a real experience there, but one that was probably so strange that my brain had no way of processing it, so it attempted to give it meaning by linking it to imagery and ideas that it already possessed.

Before I discuss that, I would like to talk about the physical experience.

At this point, I had made my willingness to continue on together clear with the late-night walks. And now here they were, offering not only more relationship, but *physical* relationship. I cannot tell you how many times I have looked back on that night in sadness. After the nine knocks, there was a period of perhaps thirty seconds of silence, then a quick double tap that seemed to communicate an end.

Still I sat there, frozen, amazed, disbelieving and believing both at the same time.

Ever since, I have felt certain that they have a place in the physical world. There are many theories about them being 'imaginal,' but beings that are fundamentally part of the imagination don't leave you with injuries, and they are a common part of the abduction experience.

To this day, I find myself thinking if I had gotten up and stepped outside, what would then have happened?

But I could not know the answer to that question and I was afraid, and I will regret that forever—except...what if I made the right decision? The cats certainly wouldn't have gone out.

While, these 37 years on, I still remember every single detail of the moment of the nine knocks, the only thing I recall of the imaginative material that follows is the impact that the vision of the field of yellow flowers had on me.

I think that the material is an assembly of bits and pieces taken from a part of the mind that sees the world as we did in the youth of our species and as we do when we are babies. This way of understanding the world around us predates the way we think now, which developed along with the invention of writing.

What, then, was behind the visions and the imaginings? Was there anything concrete that existed outside of my dancing neurons?

I know, now, that there was, because I have engaged with the visitors many times since in this same way, and even learned to communicate with them in symbolic imagery that cannot really be translated into words.

Language is a group of sounds that are associated, by mutual agreement, with our acts and the world around us. It can be captured in writing in many different ways, ranging from simple lists and numbers to the most subtle poetry. I remember that other language like one might remember a journey to a land where everything is a secret, and the horizon of knowledge, like a *fata morgana*, fades endlessly into longing, loss and the vast distance.

CHAPTER THIRTEEN

THE JOLT OF THE TRUE

was changed by those nine knocks, but the people around me weren't. It seemed to me that nobody could really grasp that they meant the visitors were a physical reality. The reason, of course, was that I had been the only person who had heard them. To me this pointed out the fact that people had to participate personally in the visitor experience if they were to feel its full impact. No amount of description, no level of sincerity, no proof, could equal the awesome jolt of the real thing.

In August I had sent the manuscript of *Communion* to my brother, Richard.

Like my sister, he'd had a very complicated reaction to the book. Both of them had certain memories that were hard to explain in normal terms, my sister more than my brother. Was the visitor experience, then, the explanation for things that had happened to all three of us?

Richard tended to take an uncommitted view of the matter. He felt certain that something had happened to me. But he was not comfortable with either the psychological explanation or the conventional UFO explanation.

Back in the mid-seventies, he and his friend Ann Cotton had been traveling in West Texas when they had seen some unusual lights beside the road. They were in an isolated area, and had just passed through a town. A short time later they found themselves passing through the same town again, going in the same direction. At the time it happened Richard mentioned this incident to me. Neither of us thought of it in terms of a visitor experience.

He was concerned that my manuscript implied too strongly that the visitors were a physical reality. When I told him about the nine knocks he listened with interest, but the story seemed to have little real impact on him.

He decided to come up to the cabin over the weekend of September 12-14. He'd never been there before and he was eager to see the location of the story, and to discuss it with me in more depth.

The day before he arrived, a small but important incident took place in New York City. My wife saw, in the middle of a clear afternoon, a silver disk move from south to north across the city. It was going fast, and we decided that it must have been some sort of helicopter, because we could not imagine such a thing passing through city skies unnoticed.

Much later, in January 1987, I discovered how open the city skies really are to the visitors. Some friends saw an object over the city at night. They observed it hovering for about half an hour, and even saw a helicopter take evasive action. One of these people is a star marksman, and he was able to describe the object with such care that I could not doubt that it had been one of the large boomerang-shaped UFOs that have been reported so often in the Hudson Valley region north of New York. As an experiment I called the relevant police precinct to report it. When he heard "UFO," the duty officer said, "Let 'em come," and hung up the phone.

The visitors are certainly capable of penetrating to the center of cities. Our society has so completely dismissed them that they have free reign here. Because of all the debunking and denial they can come and go as they please and do what they want, and be confident that they will be ignored. It is ironic that those who deny the existence of the visitors are actually doing their work for them.

I noted Anne's sighting in my journal and did no more about it. At the time it seemed a small but interesting fact, nothing more than that.

On Friday, September 12, we picked up Richard at the airport and drove up to the country. In addition to myself and Anne and our son, Richard and a family friend, Denise Daniels, were with us. Saturday was a beautiful day. At about eight in the evening we all went for a walk to the meadow that lies beyond our woods. As we moved through the woods I was feeling quite proud of my place and of the best sellers like *Warday* that had enabled me to buy it. Perhaps I was doing a little too much prideful explaining to my younger brother.

Suddenly I heard a loud, very old, and low voice say, "Arrogance! I can do what I wish to you."

I practically jumped out of my skin. The others had gotten ahead of me on the path, and their total lack of reaction told me that they hadn't heard a thing.

When we reached the meadow we could see the moon coming up over the line of trees on an easterly ridge. There was a beautiful star beside the moon that I assumed was Jupiter, which would have been rising that night in that approximate position.

A few moments later Richard said, "That star is moving." All five of us observed this phenomenon clearly.

The bright star proceeded to move toward the moon, disappear as it crossed its face, then reappear on the other side. Gathering speed, it curved around under the moon and dropped lower. It seemed to get larger and come closer to us. Then it stopped. After a moment it moved off, gathering speed again. For a moment it disappeared, seeming to flash off. When it reappeared again it was moving really fast, speeding. Then it disappeared again, this time for good.

The next moment it seemed to me that there was a light fog around us in the meadow. I had the impression that three people were coming out of the woods toward us. I called to my son, momentarily confused as to his whereabouts even though he was standing right beside me. My brother stared fixedly at the woods.

Later he said that he'd also felt the impression that there were three people standing where I had been looking, and had fought an almost overwhelming desire to walk toward them into the woods.

We had all seen the strange moving star. There was no question about that. It did not have a disk shape. In all respects it appeared to be a star. It wasn't a plane or a meteor because it had remained stationary for too long beside the moon. Even if it had been coming directly toward us, it wouldn't have appeared to be motionless for so long. It couldn't have been a satellite because of its odd maneuvers. It wasn't Jupiter because it flew off. And its speed was too high to be explained in any ordinary way.

We returned to the house, feeling rather shaken. I reported the voice I'd heard, and as night fell my brother wondered if we were going to have a peaceful sleep.

Despite the event, though, we all slept well and were not disturbed in any way.

Both Richard and Denise were changed by what they saw. No rational person could attribute the sighting to a known source. Now my brother listened to me with new interest. Denise went from believing the standard debunking scenario to realizing that there was actually something quite astonishing taking place.

As we drove them to the airport on Sunday afternoon they both commented on their change of perspective. I reflected on how much this had depended on the visitors themselves. Reading *Communion* had not changed them. Hearing my experiences had not done it. But seeing a light in the sky, completely impossible to explain as anything but a UFO, had done it.

No doubt that is one explanation for all the brightly lighted objects that are seen, the visitations that take place, the constant sense of intrusion into our lives. Rather than approach us through the medium of our social institutions, the visitors have chosen to come into contact with us on an individual basis, reaching us soul by soul.

After Richard was gone I began to wonder about the voice. Nobody else had heard it, but it had come to me only minutes before we saw the strange light in the sky. Was I stretching things to think that the two might be related? As usual, there was no final way to answer the question.

It had been so loud and so real—and so incredibly stern. "Arrogance! I can do what I wish to you." *Was* I getting too arrogant? I didn't feel particularly prideful. One doesn't, I suppose, when one is.

The previous Friday I had made a large transfer of funds from one bank to another. This represented, as a matter of fact, all the cash I had. Without it I would not have been able to meet my obligations and would have been forced into bankruptcy.

Late Monday afternoon my accountant called to tell me that the money had disappeared. My agent told me it was a computer error of some kind. Nobody could understand what had happened. I was frantic. Beside myself. But before I could get a fuller explanation the banks all closed for the day.

I sweated through Monday night in a state of terrific upset. I possessed only what was in my wallet. If that money wasn't found, we were going out into the streets. On Tuesday morning it developed that an inexplicable computer error had caused the money literally to evaporate into electronic oblivion. Sufficient paper records were eventually found, so that the sum was recovered. Nobody at the banks had ever seen anything like it.

As I put down the phone after being told this good news, Anne came into my office. She'd seen *another* disk, going in the same direction as the first, at just the moment that the call had come through.

It was like a period at the end of a sentence.

My frame of mind was such that I became convinced that the visitors had just made a show of strength. It was like a lesson in humility, expertly designed and managed, and incredibly effective. After seeing all that money evaporate before my eyes, I was a chastened man.

Whether the visitors caused these events to come into my life I will never know. I think that there was a relationship, mainly because of the theatrical nature of the lesson. I was learning that demonstration and theater were the primary means the visitors were using to communicate with me. Compared to the demonstrations, the voice communications were minor.

In the past three weeks, because of these demonstrations, I'd seen my experience enter a new level of realism. I had heard them at my house when I was wide awake. And now I might well have had a taste of what they could do to me unless I admitted my arrogance and made an effort to change.

September passed, the summer lingering and softening into fall. Late in the month we moved back to the city. I was still struggling in a desultory way with sweets, but the visitors seemed to have become silent about the issue, and then to have retreated from the center of my life. I was beginning to think that I could at last forget.

2026 Update

When, on September 18, 2025, I asked my brother what he remembered about the UFO sighting, I got quite a shock. His recollection is vivid and much more detailed than what I recalled even a few months after the incident, when I was writing *Transformation*.

He first saw the star in front of the half moon, and asked how you could see a star there. It then came down to treetop level and skimmed along just above the trees. It was not a star but a UFO, and it shone, he told me, with "an extraordinarily bright bluish-white light." A few moments later it shot up into the air and disappeared among the stars.

This is an interesting illustration of how two people can stand side-by-side and observe the same thing but come away with two entirely different memories. Even more remarkable, it was not until all these years later that we even thought to compare notes.

The taking of my money as punishment for arrogance, which is exactly what it was, marked the first open and obvious lesion that I would receive from the visitors. Looking back, I see it as an essential lesson for my future life.

In the following years, I would be disparaged by many people, but also supported by those whose lives had been changed by the visitors. I learned from that, and later from seeing how people live who are closer to the grays than I am, to minimize my involvement in the material world and always to see all others as equally important, and as my equals. As Paul puts it so eloquently in Galatians, "There is neither Jew nor Greek, slave nor free, male nor female, for you are all one in Christ Jesus." (Galatians 3:28.)

As to the relationship of the grays to demons, angels and us, I see them as teachers. I once asked the lady on the cover of *Communion* what I could give her. The answer was, "Child, you are so poor. What could I possibly want from you?"

When you look past the fears, many of which are expressed in this book, and the dark manipulations of sinister and secretive forces in the human community, what you see is not an evil and dangerous presence, but a harried band of dedicated teachers who are here trying to do the impossible, which is to prepare mankind for entry into the great choir of conscious and intelligent beings who are spread like faint sparks in a vast darkness, across the endless reaches of space.

CHAPTER FOURTEEN

DISTANT WITNESS

As summer turned to fall, they entered my life again.

The last weekend in September was mild. We were in the city and were having a lot of fun enjoying the Saturday afternoon crowds and the shops along Bleecker Street. We'd taken our son to a comics shop where he'd hit the jackpot, finding four favorites that he hadn't read. Anne and I had gotten some books and records we'd been wanting.

The world seemed incredibly real to me, and yet also distant, as if it were all reflected in pools of new rain.

This was an afternoon far from the visitors. The sky was blue, the air was warm, and I was entirely surrounded by other people. Safe. I walked along licking an ice cream cone.

All of a sudden a young voice cried out to me, "Can you stop eating that!" I turned, expecting to see a child, but there was nobody beside me. It sounded exactly as if a child of about eight had shouted in my ear.

I remembered the visitors' admonition about sweets and decided, experimentally, to toss away the cone. The moment I discarded it, three young voices shouted in unison,

"He threw away ice cream for us!"

This sounded totally real, but so close to my ear that it couldn't have been generated by somebody, say, hanging out of an apartment window or standing across the street. I had never heard disembodied voices before the visitor experience started.

They made me uneasy, because they are a classic symptom of schizophrenia. I could not claim that these voices were not of the type that schizophrenics hear; I'd read extensively in the literature of the disease and knew that schizophrenics hear every imaginable sort of voice.

However, this was my only symptom. Some paranoids hear voices, and often these voices give them commands, but what I was hearing lacked a quality of grandiosity that seemed to me to be associated with paranoid imaginings. There was something very ordinary about these voices. They sounded like people, and they weren't commanding me in grandiloquent terms.

They were also incredibly spontaneous. Nowhere, not even far back in my mind, was there the feeling that I was manufacturing them. If somebody had put a small radio in my ear, the voices would have sounded exactly as these did. There was even the slightly tinny quality that one associates with small speakers.

What was more important to me, though, was the total absence of other symptoms that would be associated with psychological disease.

In subsequent weeks I got a number of similar messages, some of them about sweets and some about other foods. I ended up eating a more-or-less vegetarian diet, drinking no caffeine, and really struggling with the sweets.

I struggled so much and the voices were so persistent that I finally asked them, in thought, why I should stop eating sweets. The reply was immediate: "We will show you."

Thus began the first of a series of theatrical communications that were extremely revealing of how the visitors chose to transmit information.

What they did was breathtaking.

I was sitting quietly in my apartment office on the afternoon of October 1 when I asked the question, and the quickness of the reply suggested to me that I should wait right there.

I waited an hour but nothing happened. Then I got annoyed, went out to the kitchen, and got a Dove Bar from the freezer and ate it with relish.

On Tuesday, October 2, I lunched with Australian film director Philippe Mora. He had renewed the acquaintance we'd had in London in 1968 by inviting me to a screening of his new film, *Death of a Soldier*. Afterward we ate together and I told him a little bit about the visitor experience. He listened with a certain amount of interest, but the conversation went no further. As we parted, he mentioned that he was going to Australia to work on another project.

It was now October 7 (October 8 in Sydney). I was in my office when the phone rang. It was Philippe, phoning from Sydney. What follows is a close rendering of the conversation.

Philippe said, "Do you remember Martin Sharp from London days?"

I hadn't seen him in nearly twenty years, but I remembered Martin well enough. I'd been to his flat, the Pheasantry, on the King's Road in Chelsea during my year there. "I remember Martin."

"Something odd's happened to his mother. I thought you might be able to shed some light on it."

"What happened?"

"Well, last night she woke up and found something very odd. There were half a dozen little men in her room; men wearing broad-brimmed hats like Asian farmers' hats."

"Little men?"

"Yes. I thought you might be able to give us some idea of what happened, in view of that story you told me. They lifted her up to the ceiling, Whitley, and then put her down again. They didn't hurt her, but she's upset."

"I can understand that. Does she believe in fairies, ghosts, anything like that?"

"No."

"Does she take an interest in UFOs?"

"Mrs. Sharp is very conservative. I doubt if she's ever even thought about them.

What do you think happened to her?"

"I'm not sure. Is there anything at all that's unusual about her?"

"Well, she's quite ill. Probably dying. She's bedridden."

"With what?"

"One thing I know she has is an uncontrollable form of diabetes. Very bad."

A shock went through me. The visitors had been telling me not to eat sweets. I asked them why and they said that they would show me. A few days later here was this call: A woman indirectly acquainted with me had been raised to the ceiling by "little men" and she was severely diabetic.

Mrs. Sharp passed away in late 1986, dying of liver cancer and diabetes. Martin and Yensoon Tsai, a close family friend who had been with her the morning after the incident, wrote me about it in 1987. Yensoon, who is a very traditional Chinese, offered a transcript of the notes she had written for her diary shortly after the incident. The notes were taken from Mrs. Sharp's description of what happened. Yensoon interprets Mrs. Sharp's experience in entirely Chinese terms, thus offering a fascinating insight into the way cultural background controls our perceptions of the visitor experience—as it probably has throughout the ages.

Yensoon wrote:

"In the evening of the 7th of October, 1986, Mrs. Sharp partook of a bowl of Chinese herbs." (Note: The herbs involved would not have induced hallucinations even a short time after consumption, let alone eight to ten hours later.) "She was wide awake the following morning at 4 A.M. Looking up at the ceiling with her right arm raised in the air, she suddenly saw seven little Chinese men appear and descend from the ceiling. They were three feet tall, all of them wearing Chinese coolie hats with a round brim. Their bodies were round, each of them wearing a different color, red, green, blue and yellow. The yellow little man seemed to be the leader. He gave Mrs. Sharp a stern and icy cold look. As if a hole was bored into her heart and she shuddered. His subordinates were much more genial to her. They smiled at her and the blue little man touched her hand, murmuring words of comfort. She found that he had a slimy and soft body. The 'leader' motioned his subordinates to lift Mrs. Sharp up to the ceiling and then put her down onto the floor. She protested and ordered them to put her back to bed, but to no avail. In a trice, she found herself in a verdant park. The sun was setting. Although the surroundings were a joy to her eyes, no living things were visible, only the wind was soughing amidst the trees. It struck a note of desolation to her. She felt a sense of despair. The little blue man presented her with a blue silk flowing robe, which she happily put on because it was her favorite color. The moment she put it on the sun suddenly sank beyond the horizon and they lifted her up in the darkness, at which time she lost consciousness. Upon regaining consciousness she found herself to be in her own bed. After this episode, Mrs. Sharp's condition declined rapidly."

Yensoon also described the little men as being "like Chinese mushrooms," referring both to their shape and to the texture of their skin. Many people who have been close to the visitors have noted this skin quality. To my mind, this is a very exact description of one type of visitor. Their skin is clammy and they are small, round, and quite strong— very much in contrast to the taller ones, such as the being I depicted on the cover of *Communion,* who seem frail by comparison.

Yensoon also pointed out that the deceased wears a blue silk robe in a Chinese funeral. To me the appearance of this robe was another example of the way the experience alters itself to fit the cultural references of the people it is affecting. There was thus a message not only for Jo Sharp and me but also for Yensoon. It cannot be forgotten, however, that Mrs. Sharp was physically touched by the beings, and vividly described exactly the way this felt. It is all too easy to retreat from the idea that the visitors are physically real—at least at times. They effortlessly translated her from the physical world into another reality, one that seemed to be a sort of archetypal place of death.

Upon reading this account, I remembered my hypnosis session covering events that occurred on the night of October 4, 1985. During that session I had seen my son in a beautiful but strangely desolate park. I had thought him dead and had experienced emotional devastation.

Could there be an actual place somewhere, in some parallel reality, where the dead linger in sighing gardens?

If the soul exists, then it must in some way be a part of nature and so subject both to its laws and to the application of appropriate science. Perhaps Jo Sharp's soul was extracted from her body and she was given a vividly symbolized demonstration of what awaited her. One can imagine the strange, empty park, the wind sighing in the trees, the sun setting … the images of death abound, gentle and strange.

My own contact with the visitors was full of vivid demonstrations and symbols. The rich theatrics reported by Jo Sharp seem to me to be characteristic of one form of close communion with them.

Martin Sharp added in a letter, "Jo (my mother) was not a person to hallucinate … and though highly imaginative she was not a vocally spiritual person. Indeed, she would say, 'The only thing "up there" are possums on the roof.'" (Which there were.)

Later, when her death was approaching and she would lapse into a hypoglycemic coma, the doctors would feed her barley sugar to bring her out of it. During this period there were a number of episodes that Martin found upsetting. While she was in coma she would talk, taking on two different personalities. One of them seemed almost cheerful to him, and was cooperative. The other was duplicitous and strange, and resisted taking the sugar. "The other manifestation was positively sinister. She would appear totally collapsed … unconscious almost…. She, or rather 'it' would watch my every move through half-closed eyes. The 'unconsciousness' seemed a ploy because she appeared possessed by an alien, hateful intelligence—cruel, arrogant, despising help, strong. I would say physically strong. (My mother was very frail.) Palpably evil. The whole atmosphere of her room would change. It was most upsetting. Her doctor would sidestep the issue when I tried to talk about it. This entity would not take barley sugar, or would manage to hold the barley sugar in the mouth and not suck on it, spit it out, do almost anything to avoid the return of consciousness which the barley sugar would effect." He went on to say, "Jo would have no memory of these experiences when the 'invader' retreated after the sugar solution had its effect. I thought it was very important to discuss but no doctor would. If I'd known more about exorcism I think I would have attempted to do it."

Martin's interpretation of all this was that she had somehow been possessed by the spirit or essence of her disease. He wrote, "I believe that the spirit which possessed my dear mother in these times was using her as a window."

Even before I received Martin's and Yensoon's written descriptions of the events, I was aware that Mrs. Sharp's initial experience had been intimately connected with death. The beings had lifted her up as if in demonstration, and then shifted her—or her soul—into a symbolized representation of death. The message for me was crystal clear:

If I continued to eat sweets, I too would end up there.

The visitors had somehow sifted through the grains of my life and found the mother of a man I hadn't seen in twenty years, determined that she was diabetic, and done something to her that would get back to me through Philippe. It suggested extraordinary powers of observation, at the very least. They obviously had the ability to examine lives in detail, and then to find the most useful person to serve as the object of their demonstration.

This event led me to the thought that the visitors may have a far more sophisticated ability to enter our lives than we have even begun to suspect. More important, it was becoming clear to me, based not only on my own experience but on that of

Mrs. Sharp and others, that they appeared to be involved with what happens to man after death.

I was having a lot of trouble grappling with that concept, largely because it made me feel so helpless. I began to want very badly to understand more about the soul. At the time I was, like the great majority of people, very unsure about whether or not it even existed. I resolved to begin research into it. But at the moment it seemed to me that I was faced with an urgent mandate. Fulfilling it would be simple enough.

All I had to do was stop eating sweets. Again I tried, more seriously this time. I found that it was amazingly difficult. I ended up in the ridiculous position of pacing the floor over the fact that there was a box of Oreos in the cupboard.

I had thought of myself as being mildly addicted to sweets. But when I really tried to stop, my "addiction" became a devil!

My earlier thoughts about the meaning of sacrifice returned to mind. I had to admit to myself that I understood the principle of it. I understood very well. I just didn't want to do it.

In the early days of Christendom people used to go into the desert to emulate Christ with fasting and prayer. They would spend months, years, a lifetime, struggling to reach Christ through self-denial and privation.

I managed to go four days without ice cream, and then I bought a pint of Haagen Dazs vanilla and ate half of it.

I realized that I wasn't strong enough to deny myself. My consumption of sweets went back to my normal moderate level. I decided that this was a more sane way to live. I wasn't really interested in trying to copy even a small part of the lifestyle of crazed third-century hermits.

The visitors did not respond at once. Instead they moved slowly and carefully to the point of anger. Their restraint amounted, I suppose, to a kind of tolerance of my weakness. But their tolerance had its limits.

PART THREE

BEYOND THE DARK

"Our birth is but a sleep and a forgetting:
The Soul that rises with us, our life's Star,
Hath had elsewhere its setting, And cometh
from afar..."

—WILLIAM WORDSWORTH,
*"Ode: Intimations of Immortality
from Recollections of Early
Childhood"*

CHAPTER FIFTEEN

THE WOODS

Sooner or later I was going to have to go deeper into those woods. My relationship with the visitors was beginning to demonstrate to me that burying fear and coping with it were two different things. I had to face it, to taste it, to take its measure—and that was only possible when it was making my legs wobble and my mouth go dry.

I extended our time in the city. The lights seemed so reassuring.

I was now fully aware that I was in a relationship with physical visitors. I was consciously trying to deepen and enrich it even though I did not know if they were dangerous.

The more I challenged my fears, the more involved with me they became.

The cabin waited for my return. The woods waited.

I strongly suspected that they could have walked into my house and dispelled my terror of them in a moment. That they did not was probably an ethical act. By leaving me in the dark they were granting me the chance to surmount my fears on my own.

Time after time the fact of the relationship would hit me anew. I would be walking down a street, sitting in a movie theater, reading to my boy, eating breakfast, when suddenly the thought would come again, *They're real.*

I still didn't know who or even *what* they were. But those things didn't matter now. I would leave the solution to those problems to the future, or to the visitors themselves. They are clearly in complete control of the situation. It is probable that they could come forward publicly if they wished. But they don't. I doubt if anything we can do would change the plan by which they are revealing themselves to us. The point, for me, was not to worry about who they were but to make use of what they had to offer.

Instead of harming me, the visitors seemed to be daring me to transcend my weaknesses. I began to see an elegant and objective ethic behind their frightening manifestations and weird demands. If I could bear their presence in my life, if I could surmount my fears and my weaknesses, I was going to learn some extraordinary things.

At any rate, with the lights of the city around me, that's how I rationalized things. Why I considered the city such a safe haven I don't know. I suppose it just felt safe, because of all the activity and the people.

We went back to the cabin on September 26, 1986, arriving at about five. After dinner we watched an old movie on the tape machine.

When it was over I put our son to bed with a story and returned to the living room to read. At ten Anne went upstairs.

I waited until about midnight. I sat reading in the same chair where I had heard the nine knocks.

I would rather have gone out earlier, when my neighbors were still awake, but the sense of vulnerability and isolation that the late night brings seemed essential to a full experience.

There was absolutely no question in my mind about one thing: Whatever the visitors were, they could become physical. How deeply they could penetrate our reality—if they did not originate in it—I did not know.

Finally the clock struck twelve times. I got up, took a deep breath. As the chimes died away, absolute silence enveloped me.

I went over to the side door, opened it, and stepped out onto the deck. Everything was familiar. We had closed the pool and its dark-green cover loomed like a great shadow at my feet. I listened to the cicadas crying and the occasional thump of a bullfrog down in the slow water behind the house.

I was scared, of course, but I would not have been there if that was all the situation had to offer me. There was also the tremendous, growing wonder. The visitors were *real*. This was prime experience.

I felt that my previous attempts to challenge my fear had drawn them closer to me.

Would this attempt cause a meeting?

I crossed the deck. My hands were shaking, but I opened the gate into the yard without too much difficulty. It swung out with a creak. I looked up into the dark sky.

Then I took the three steps down to the backyard. I kept having the feeling that something was going to drop out of the sky and grab me.

I walked up the low hill that leads into the woods. I looked down into the dark, then turned around and looked back at my little cabin. There was only one lighted window. I imagined Anne and our son asleep in their beds. We are so small and new and confused, we human beings. And yet, a man *can* go into the woods at midnight.

As I descended into the blackness under the trees, I had to turn on the small flashlight I had brought. I could have taken a powerful torch, but I wanted only enough light to enable me to keep to the path.

Slowly, hesitantly, I went down the way a few steps. The woods seemed as still as a leopard waiting for me to come near.

I remembered racing home from the neighbors when I was a boy, my steps echoing in the empty street, the shadows lurching and twisting around me. I had been scared to look up at the sky for fear that I would see great eyes staring down at me.

Sweat was blinding me. I was shaking and nauseated. I decided that I wasn't going to make it. The path was too dark and the woods were too big and, God help me, the visitors were too real.

At that moment I thought to myself, *You can turn around and go back to the house and give up.*

But I didn't want to give up. I refused, absolutely, to turn back. I remembered being taken into these woods on the night of December 26, 1985.

My mind screamed at me, *Go back! Don't do this!*

Something slithered on the path. The cicadas stopped. The crickets stopped. In the menacing silence that followed, I heard what sounded like the whisper of leaves against soft cloth. It was coming up the path, this sound.

My breath began to choke me. My heart was laboring. I thought to myself that a man could die of fright. The Reverend Robert Kirk, who wrote *The Secret Commonwealth,* an early and brilliant treatise on the hidden life of the fairy, died of an apoplectic fit while walking on a fairy mound where beings had been seen a few days before. Ambrose Bierce, a great and very enigmatic horror writer who was deeply involved in occult work, simply disappeared.

The sound grew more and more distinct. I didn't know whether to run. You don't run from a menacing animal. But this?

The movements stopped. Now the path was like a bristling, hostile wall. I peered into the deeper darkness.

You go back, my inner voice said to me. *You don't have to do this. Go back, go to bed.*

But that was a lie. I did have to do this. It had fallen to me to do it.

No matter what, I was walking out into those woods.

Even though I wasn't sad, tears poured down my face. The inner man was crying. I felt like somebody was standing in front of me in the path, but there wasn't anybody there. There was no way for me to tell if I was really being menaced or if my imagination was running away with me. As a professional writer I use my imagination as a tool. I know it well. Still, in a situation as extreme as this I could not be sure if it was tricking me or not.

I put one foot out. Then the other. I reached ahead into the black, waved my arms. There was a hissing, sighing noise—blowing leaves, or them?

Pine needles crunched beneath my feet; the trees seemed so large, the path so narrow. My light was inadequate and I was soon struggling in confusion through the undergrowth. Then I found the way again and went on, down deeper and deeper into the darkness, toward the meadow beyond the woods.

I felt as if somebody was going to reach out and touch me. This sensation almost drove me mad with terror, it was so strong. My movements became jerky and uncontrolled. I was at the edge of blind panic.

It seemed an infinity of time before I came to the end of the tree-clad path. Then, quite suddenly, I was there. Before me stood the night meadow, a grand expanse in the darkness.

I remember how wide the sky seemed to become as I left the woods, and how the night was spread with the stuff of magic. I stood there for a short time, then faced the woods again.

As I walked I imagined a voice whispering eagerly, "He's coming this way." I stopped. At this point the path forks. One fork leads toward the house by an old road. The other takes a more roundabout way through the deeper woods.

There was a lot of fear, but there was also a thrill involved in this. The night woods were absolutely sensuous. The silence was a marvel.

I took the long way. I might as well have been in a cave, it was so dark. As I walked I kept turning around, listening, stopping. But I saw and heard nothing.

Once I got out of the deep woods I saw the house again. It looked so sweet and warm that I almost wept as I walked up to it. And then I was inside. It was over. I had finally done it.

I half expected to confront the visitors that night, but I did not. I learned something from that walk that I did not want to forget, not ever: Where the incoherent animal lives at the foundation of my being, I was literally sick with dread over the visitors.

That was where I had to do my work. I had to go down in there and shine some light. Change at that primitive core level was what I needed.

Change. Could there ever be real change in the heart of a human being? Truly, that would be an application of grace in this world.

I wanted so badly for the visitors to be benevolent that there was a possibility I would fool myself about them. The more deeply I explored myself, the more intense was the fear I found. I had the sense that I got closer to the visitors as I went deeper into myself.

On the surface I wanted very badly to love them and to believe that they were trying to help me. But down in the primitive parts of my mind, I was literally wild with terror. Stepping outside at night I became almost like an animal, listening, peering around, sniffing the air, feeling as if every shadow concealed some terrible being with great, black eyes.

I remembered how frightened the cats had been on the night of the nine knocks.

It was with a cold feeling that I asked myself if the animal within me might be the part that really knew the truth. I could look at what was happening to me either as a very genuine attempt to enable me to contact and cope with my fears on my own or as an extremely subtle effort to lure a free and decent human being into some kind of unholy trap.

I did not know which it was. I could not find out. There were no precedents, there was nowhere to turn. I had lost my assurance that this had happened to anybody else before. I don't think it has—not to anybody who returned to record the experience. I wondered if my time was running out.

2026 Update

Over the years, one comment from this chapter has become for me the central issue of our whole relationship with non-human intelligence: "I remembered how frightened the cats had been on the night of the nine knocks. It was with a cold feeling that I asked myself if the animal within me might be the part that really knew the truth."

The reason that their reaction remains important to me is they don't have a highly developed neocortex, which is where the intellect might take over from instinct, and look for positives that aren't actually there. We want all to be well. But cats can't do that. They can act only out of instinct, and instinct was obviously telling them that something was more wrong than what I was perceiving.

Over the three decades since the event, I have been turning this over again and again in my mind.

Times have changed, of course. The cabin has another owner, Anne has died, our son has grown up and has children of his own. Coe and Sadie are part of the long-ago.

I must mention them both and honor them, for they went through the contact experience, too, and faced the visitors and were afraid, too, and it killed Sadie.

As I reported in detail in *Afterlife Revolution,* she died tragically as a result of a contact experience that took place in the cabin. When this happened, I had gotten into the habit of sleeping with a camera on the table beside my bed. Cellphones had not yet been invented and home surveillance systems were also pretty much in the future.

Day after grinding day, I was going on TV and radio and not being believed. Because of this, instead of reaching people with this terribly important story, I was being marginalized, and I felt that this was a dangerous mistake—something that I am now certain is true. Little did I know, as I have since come to understand, that I had professionals in social engineering working against me from behind the scenes, as evidenced by what would be done to me using *Parade Magazine* some years later. In those days, though, I still naïvely believed that pictures would help, so when I woke up one night to find the entire cabin suffused with pink-purple light, I ran down the hall toward the balcony that overlooked the living room, which appeared to be the point of origin.

Hanging there was a ball of light or plasma emitting a purple-pink glow. Sadie was crouching on her stomach nearby. She looked as if she was edging toward it.

I instantly realized that if I got a picture of this it might help me get my point across. As this was before digital photography, people were not so ready to assume that a photo was faked. I thought I had gold in the form of a pink-purple plasma.

As I was grabbing the camera, the whole house was briefly suffused with pink-purple light. Then all went dark. Cursing my luck, I went downstairs to find no sign of what I had seen. Sadie was there, but she was now curled up. I went down and looked at her. She was wrapped in a little ball on the rug behind the couch. She seemed fine.

Disappointed, I returned to bed.

The next morning, as I was walking down the corridor toward the stairs that led to the kitchen, Sadie came crawling up to me on her stomach yowling.

I picked my little gal up and was horrified by what I saw. Visible in both eyes were misshapen pink-purple tumors.

The vet tried to save her, but there was nothing to be done and we had to have her put down. She was a lap cat by nature, an ideal companion for a writer, given that we tend to sit a lot.

Sadie wrote books with me, many books, purring softly in my lap while I typed away. I miss her and I feel so guilty that I wasn't more careful. But I tell myself, 'what could you have done?'

When, in 2013, Anne was found to have a complex and awful brain tumor, I have to admit that it crossed my mind that maybe she, also, had been a victim. In the British Ministry of Defense Condign Report, it was mentioned that the "plasmas"(read UAP) emitted a type of nonionizing radiation that was known to cause tissue damage. John Burroughs, who touched a UAP during the Rendlesham Forest Incident ended up with a damaged heart muscle, and it took a demand from Senator John McCain to extract his medical records from the U.S. Air Force, which had classified them. In *Afterlife Revolution*, I also theorized that all the CT scans Anne had received during her treatment for her 2004 brain bleed most likely led to the cancer, and I believe that this is the most likely explanation. It's hard to see how exposure to a brief flash of light in 1988 could lead to cancer in 2013, especially because in 2005 she had received so many CT scans.

When Sadie was destroyed, Anne and I discussed whether or not we should continue going to the cabin. We made the decision to cut back on our trips there, and made sure that our son visited far less frequently.

Subsequent occupants haven't noticed anything unusual there, but when I go back, as I now occasionally do thanks to the kindness of the current owners, I will usually take a few friends who have had close encounter experiences, and we sometimes meet the visitors there.

These friends are not simply interested parties. They are people who spend their lives as I do, in daily, dedicated pursuit of greater relationship with this unknown presence. We do not go to the cabin as tourists looking for adventure, but rather as associates of what also comes there from time to time, in pursuit of deeper and more fruitful relationship on both sides.

My impression is that the visitors do not enjoy being disturbed and do not welcome our presence. They will usually engage with us, though, but I don't think they like it. I do think that they gain from it, or why do it at all? We do, too, or we wouldn't go.

There are many people nowadays who "call in" orbs, but generally without any deep understanding of what they are doing. One highly organized group called Skywatcher spent a great deal of money doing this both by using what they call "psionics" experts and also broadcasting a certain signal. Both of these techniques worked, but then what? Video was made, but nobody apparently engaged deeply.

As the visitors are already cranky about being disturbed by us when we go to the cabin, I cannot imagine how they would react if we failed to open ourselves to the process of communion with them, which I think may be the only thing they enjoy about contact with us.

Is it dangerous, then? I wish I knew. We all do. But we have no intention of stopping.

This is a huge change from what it was like at the cabin when *Transformation* was being written. We got groups of people there—or rather, Anne did—and the visitors did show up. But we were not able to engage with them, no more than I was on the night of the nine knocks.

That is no longer true. Over the years, I have become more and more committed to our relationship. At this point in my life, I am deeply enmeshed with them, and have moved far from the western materialist paradigm. I am not talking about some sort of hypothetical or imaginary relationship. It is quite real. They can and do penetrate into the physical world in order to interact with me and at times I am able to project my attention into the frequency that they inhabit.

I have left conventional materialism behind. It's not that it's not real, but rather that it isn't real enough. My materialism extends into what I think of as frequencies that we cannot as yet detect with instruments. But we can do it with our minds and bodies, and the sensing exercise, performed consistently over years, may attract interest from presences that inhabit those frequencies, which include our visitors and our own dead. In fact, compared to that vast universe of awareness, the physical world is a scrap of a thing, a part of reality so dense and deeply embedded in the stream of time that those in other frequencies can hardly even detect it—unless, of course, it does something like explode a weapon so powerful that it disrupts more than the physical level, as likely happens with nuclear weapons.

Others have different experiences of contact. I don't think anyone should stop, not those who see beautiful ladies and space brothers and angels, nor those of us who see beings who have stranger appearances and more challenging ways. In defense of the short ugly ones that I know, I will say this: ten seconds with them is easily as powerful as ten years of meditation.

The lives of the close encounter witnesses are a map of the human future, all of our lives. Both those of us who are treated to the beautiful and those who are not are part of this story, and we are all going to have to work together to draw it into a coherent narrative, so that we can go down this road together, and deeper, and deeper yet, until finally and at last, what we are doing becomes consistent and understandable and, above all, true.

CHAPTER SIXTEEN

PASSAGE INTO DEATH

A few days after my walk in the woods we went back to the city. It had been a hellish effort, and I was already looking forward to another period of relief. No sooner had we gotten back, though, than I received a shocking call from my brother, Richard.

He had some disturbing and totally unexpected news.

Our mother was feeling a new loneliness connected with the death of her own mother the previous April. She needed me.

I was thunderstruck. "In three months' time you will take one of two journeys on behalf of your mother. On one of them you will die...."

The visitors weren't quite on time: It was nearly four months since that statement had been made. But I had told nobody about it. And suddenly I was taking just such a journey as they had described.

I could not say no. Of course not. Mother needed me and I had to go. Richard suggested that I fly down to Texas the next day, and I agreed.

I made my airline reservations. I never dreamed, not for a moment, that a prediction made by a strange being sitting on my bedside in May would actually come true. In May there had been absolutely no reason to suspect that my mother would need this kind of family support months later. She is a strong, self-sufficient, and very intelligent women. She had accepted the death of her mother. Now she was feeling grief, months later, and there was no question at all about my delaying. I had to be there.

I did not—could not—tell anybody in the family the secret of the two journeys. It was unthinkable to tell Anne. She certainly had no reason to suffer this with me. And as for telling Mother—that was obviously out of the question.

I had to get on that airplane not knowing which of the two journeys I was taking. Would it be the one that would end in my death, or the one that I would survive? Or did the fact that more than three months had passed mean that there was nothing to worry about?

On the morning of the flight I woke up wondering if it was to be my last day alive. What did death mean to me? Was it oblivion? A new level of being? Heaven or hell?

I wanted so badly to know, riding out to the airport in the still, silent predawn.

My hunger for life was intense. I had paused on the way out of the house to look at my sleeping child. Was I cheating him by even going on this journey? What was I to do?

Mother needed me. My son had a right to his father, Anne to her husband.

And in the middle of it all there was this distance, and this airplane, and this hard journey. I wanted to live.

My boy's face floated into my mind's eye. I heard his cheerful, confident voice calling me, "Dad!" And then this or that triumph reported.

My life belonged to him more than it did to me, to Anne, even to Mother. And yet here I was accepting this insane risk. I didn't doubt for a moment that the risk was real.

It felt darned real.

The flight was to leave at about. 7:30, and the terminal at La Guardia Airport was not crowded when I arrived at 6:45. My feet echoed on the floors. There was a softness to the morning that I had not noticed in a long time. The faint smell of coffee in the hallways, the voices of the early travelers, a man trudging along with a briefcase, a woman rolling a stroller ... and outside the windows the long, clean forms of airplanes.

The world around me seemed so unexpectedly sweet. I thought to myself as people passed me that we human beings close ourselves off from each other not because of fear but out of an excess of love. We cannot open our hearts to our real feelings about each other because we are afraid it would hurt too much.

I went through the inspection point and down to an airline club where I spent about fifteen minutes drinking orange juice and staring blankly out at the life of the airport, planes moving, men driving big baggage trucks, a catering van loading breakfast onto a plane.

I remembered how I used to take business trips with my father when I was a boy, going out to the airport in the hour before dawn and walking onto the field where a Trans Texas Airways DC-3 would be waiting. The romance, the wonder of sailing off into the dawn, had given way to the emptiness of jet travel, so far above everything that it became an eventless waiting between moments of life.

I was a nervous flyer. In the past I had gone through periods of absolute terror in the air, until I recognized that my real fear did not involve the reliability of the planes and crews but the idea of giving up control to others. To cure myself of this I imagined what the flight would be like if I were in the cockpit. I soon began to feel more comfortable realizing that my life was in the hands of people who knew what they were doing.

When the time came I went to the gate. I phoned Anne and told her good-bye. I was as cheerful as I could manage, and she suspected nothing of my true feelings. Then the boarding call came over the loudspeaker and I went to the plane.

As we rolled along the runway I reviewed my life and my relationship with my mother. I have always tried to be good to her—I love her very much—and I couldn't think of anything I had done that might have led me into the death journey.

Then again, we do not know what death is. Maybe *not* taking the death journey would be the real punishment. Perhaps this life is a sort of sentence, to be endured until the day and hour of completion and then to end in anguish and terror. Only afterward do we find out how foolish our fears were.

Or perhaps we go from a hard place into an even harder one, into some sort of oblivion that is worse than physical death. I thought perhaps we have a *potentially* immortal soul, but one that can be killed even after the body dies.

We took off, the plane roaring and shuddering its way into the sky as they always do. Modern jets do not float off like old planes did; they do not fly, but rather are thrust into the air by the sheer brute strength of their engines.

Neither can they glide. Should the engines fail, they drop like projectiles.

The engines are very reliable.

I listened to the plane, to the grinding sound of the landing gear coming up, to the rising scream of the wind as our speed increased. Far below I saw Manhattan dwindle into the morning. Another plane shot past like a leaf a few miles away. I imagined how it would be if we collided with another airliner, a glancing blow and then the long fall. Not too many months before a 747 had crashed slowly in Japan and some of the passengers had written last notes to their families. "The plane is twirling faster now...."

We flew on into the vacant world between places. A woman across the aisle, I noticed, was weeping quietly to herself. Behind me two children were traveling with their mother and they were full of excitement and wonder. The stewardess handed me my breakfast with a crisply professional smile. The plane roared along uneventfully.

Everything was absolutely, totally, and completely normal.

I read *The New York Times* and waited to die.

Staring at the paper didn't help. Eating an omelette and drinking orange juice didn't help either. The ground was far, far away. Every little sound the plane made spoke peril. A stewardess frowned. Had she heard a funny noise? Was this the beginning of the end? The captain came on the intercom to tell us how nicely everything was going.

Was it hubris? Would the plane burst into flames in another second?

A woman dashed toward the bathroom and I practically jumped out of my skin. My hands were shaking so much that I couldn't see the paper, let alone read it.

I felt faint. The plane was like the inside of a sealed tomb. I fought a sudden impulse to rush to the door. Descriptions of air disasters paraded in memory. A DC-8 that had caught fire and crashed in the Rockies—and one passenger had leaped out of an emergency exit just as the plane slid into a mountainside ... the Japanese 747, twisting and turning in the sky with its terrified mass of passengers ... the sad expression I had once seen on the face of a dead man on a street corner ... graves, funerals, tombs, children at gravesides.

Down I went, into the black places where we face death, where we cry out in the silence. There was nothing there, nothing! I thought of all the insects I have killed, of the cat I once ran into, of the snakes I killed when I was a boy in Texas, of the death of my grandfather, of the death of my father, of the death of my grandmother, of age and wisdom, and of the sudden, surprising silence that follows the death of a beloved.

The hours passed. I imagined my son in school, doing his reading at his little desk in the room festooned with drawings; and I thought of Anne working on her book, learning by slow degrees to be a writer, and of her hopes, her love, the simplicity of companionship.

I thought also of the visitors sailing the skies and the mind, so strange, so alien, and yet so very close. How could I ever have imagined that they were not part of me? Of course they were part of me—they were part of us all; to some extent they must have leaped out of us like butterflies out of the winter chrysalis ... and who knew if the shadow of the butterfly did not terrify the poor caterpillar as much as did that of the bird.

We managed to land in Dallas and take off again without incident.

I was so surprised when the plane landed in San Antonio that I practically kissed the elderly gentleman in the seat beside me.

Then we were leaving the plane. It was over.

I drove through the familiar streets of the north side of San Antonio remembering the old places, the ended days. Down Broadway I went past Pat's Drugstore, where I had gone to buy comic books on my bike, and Winn's, where we had gotten cap guns and kites, and St. Peter's Church, where I had

had my first great battles with the question of the soul, and the Broadway Theatre, where I had spent many a summer Saturday in dreams of darkness while the Texas sun blasted down ... and then walked home beneath the big trees of the old neighborhood with the lazy cicadas screaming.

And what else, what else? Why did I have such a powerful sense that so much of my life had been lost to me? Where did it go? What did those strange flashes of memory mean? What in the world were all those fireballs doing in my life, and who had come knocking on my door?

Then I was at Mother's place, and the door opened, and there she stood, and suddenly she was small and sad and I felt the unknown that surrounds the little light of our lives.

I hugged her and we went inside together and talked of the old days. We did not speak much about Granny's death, but rather the way it had been for us in San Antonio in the fifties. It was a much smaller city then, dreaming in the Texas sun. We spoke of hours we had spent together discussing the proofs we had sought for God and for our own immortality, of the summer nights and books we'd loved, of our obsessions with history and literature, and of the long conversations with Father Patrick Palmer over the sense of papal infallibility and the future of the Church.

Always the Church would return to the center of our conversations, what it meant to us and where we expected it to go in the future. We were then still involved in such things as not eating meat on Fridays and we believed that it was a mortal sin to miss mass on Sunday. The ritual of the mass was of enormous importance to us. We believed, if not in the sense of the words, then in the *mysterium,* the moment of *hoc est corpus* whispered over the pale bread, and felt the presence of Christ within us when we partook of the Host.

How far we had come since then. Neither of us attended mass as often as we had.

We were filled with doubts about the new pope, torn between a need for direction and the inescapable thought that some sort of failure had taken place to bring Catholics to the point of disaffection that so many of us had reached.

Mother needed to be cherished now and I lived far from home. I felt guilty about living in New York. But I could not imagine leaving now, or taking my boy out of the school that was serving him so well, or removing myself and Anne from the lives we had made.

Mother seemed so small. Had she always been this tiny? We talked of nights at my grandparents' country home, of watching the sun set across the valley, of listening to the cowbells clanging as evening overspread the farms in the valley below. We remembered our evening walks on the road and the time I'd almost stepped on a seven foot rattlesnake. And our dogs, Prissy and Sidney and Candy and Carnahan, a succession of passionate beasts.

Where does death take us?

Mother had become as pale and soft as a moth, she who had carried me. I felt her vulnerability, her desperation. Now that her mother and her husband were gone it was her turn on the frontier of the night. I was still well back in the light, still warm, but the wind was blowing her and she wasn't young and strong anymore.

We talked and talked. We went out to lunch together. Decisions were made that we hoped favored the future happiness of the family.

My few days in San Antonio ended, and I prepared to return to New York.

It hit me on the way to the airport that the trip back was also part of this difficult journey.

How miserable that the confrontation with mortality would have to happen all over again.

I am not in the habit of contemplating my own death. And our culture supports me. We think of death as a disaster. Our entire concept of medicine is built around staving off death. When it comes it is a defeat for doctor and patient and a source of grief for all concerned.

We don't really grieve for the dead; the living grieve for themselves. For the dead, the suffering, the waiting, the losses, all have ended and they have passed into a state about which we know nothing.

It seemed only an hour and my three-day visit was over. Mother was feeling better and I had a lot of work to do in New York.

I have never liked it that my family was so spread out, and it always hurts to leave her. She stood at her door waving. I will never really understand the relationship between mother and son. I will never part easily from her.

The streets were quiet. I drove slowly back to the airport. My mind turned to the being on the bedside. Was this to be the fatal flight? I remembered the softness of the white cloth against my fingers.

I felt so vulnerable and ignorant. How could such a thing as this be happening?

The flight back was on a new plane, a Boeing 757. We took off into a beautiful sky and the short hop to Dallas was easy. While on the ground there we were told that there would be a delay because of bad weather between Dallas and New York. I sat in the airport thinking of the storms that stood like a wall between us and the distant runway where we were supposed to land.

At last we took off. Seated beside me was a pilot returning to his home base. He had his wife and two small children on the plane as well. I was reassured; if anything did start to go wrong, this pilot would know instantly. If he didn't react to some rumble or screech, I wouldn't either.

The flight was very hard. Lightning flashed outside the windows and there was a great deal of bouncing around. I could hear the wind roaring around the plane and see by the lightning flashes that the tops of the clouds were higher than we were. Jets fly at great height, so this meant that these were really tremendous storms.

I peered out into the reefs and canyons of cloud, into the anger of a great storm system. The pilot in the seat beside me was looking at it too. The dim cabin of the plane became heavy with humidity. Despite all the air conditioning, the storm was seeping in.

We were rocked and tossed about. I saw gigantic fingers of lightning off the wing tips, and the miserable flicker of the plane's strobe lights against passing mountains of cloud.

Suddenly the PA system came on and the captain announced that we were moving to a different airway because "New York Control" was unable to get flights through the weather ahead. The pilot sitting beside had been getting quieter and quieter. Now he suddenly blurted out, "That means they've lost it." He laughed nervously. "I hate it when these new controllers start jockeying us between airways. They don't know what's going on up here. They can't handle it when we have storms."

This was the death journey. We were going to collide with another plane, or we were going to be broken to pieces by the storm or struck by lightning or blown off the runway when we tried to land.

Behind us the pilot's two kids were sleeping peacefully in their mother's arms. She was leaning against the window with a pillow behind her head, her own eyes closed. I thought of the other people on the plane.

I felt the most acute agony of longing to be with my wife and son. Who would put our son to bed, read to him, sing to him? He was only seven. And what of Anne? I remembered the recording of her voice, taken while she was being hypnotized for *Communion:* "He goes ... and it's lonely, it's so *lonely.*" She was alone a lot in her childhood, and she has so enjoyed the warmth and closeness of our relationship.

The sensation of being in a trap made me frantic. In my imagination I saw the visitors come dropping like bats through the ceiling of the plane, heard the people screaming, saw the wings collapse, felt the explosion—and felt my soul being carried away by a triumphant spiritual predator....

I wondered if I might not be in the grip of demons, if they were not making me suffer for their own purposes, or simply for their enjoyment.

Suffer, though? The man beside me was upset too, and he had his whole family in this plane.

Wives lose their husbands, children lose their fathers, essential people die all the time. But the world does not stop; life keeps drifting toward its unimaginable fate.

If I died on this night Anne would weep and then pick herself up and go on. And my little boy would nest his father in the pearls of his memory, and also go on.

This was the truth. What I had to do here was accept that their fate belonged to them and contemplate instead my own.

I had a lot to think about. Throughout all of human history we have had methods for dying. Every religion from Egyptian to Christian has offered a way to the soul after death, a system by which it would go toward its judgment and find its place.

In a reality made of energy, thoughts may literally be things. I suspect that in such reality a person who dies without a way is lost, unable to surmount the confusion that his own soul is creating around him.

What would be my way of death? What if in another moment there was a great roar and I found myself disembodied but still alive, hanging in the air of another sky? Where would my judges be, where my guardian angels? I would wander as helplessly as a cloud. I would drift, waiting for something to happen. But what if it was intended that we create our own realities after death? A man who dies with no expectations would be in danger of oblivion.

Maybe a lot of us die that way now, in terror and confusion, and perhaps the visitors are beginning to peek out from behind the curtain to see what is going wrong that we no longer require them as keepers of the gates of heaven. What if the modern plague of spiritual emptiness is really a symptom of the death of souls?

I could not invent a new cosmology for myself while waiting to die in a storm-tossed airplane.

The thing shuddered and wallowed and groaned. My throat choked up, my hands shook, my breath got short—and suddenly I changed.

I just changed. One moment I was a miserable, terrified little man, and the next there was this wonderful sense of freedom. It was simple and animal and real. All of a sudden I was like a colt in the morning, like a little boy seeing the ocean for the first time.

Death seemed a very different experience. Gone was my dread. Now there was a preciseness to death, a sense of absolute correctness about it. It did not belong to the dark at all. I belonged to the dark. Death was a part of the grace of nature.

My fear was gone. I accepted my situation. I was ready.

And then I saw through the clouds the warm lights of New York and the stewardess was telling us to put our seat backs in the upright position and fasten our seatbelts in preparation for landing.

The plane rocked as it touched down and then we were rolling, then coasting, then crawling along the runway. Before I knew it we had reached the gate.

A changed man, a profoundly changed man, left that airplane. I had been brought face-to-face with death.

I had been so scared and wanted so badly to live. But, the peace I touched was so incredibly, transcendently great that I also now loved death a little, or at least I accepted the truth and presence of it in my own life.

On that night I was freed from something that haunts us all: How will death feel?

What will I do? How will I be as I die?

I know how I will be. I have already died a little. The visitors have had the courage and wisdom to give me this gift, this singular liberty.

Love at its most true is not afraid to be hard.

2026 Update

This chapter illustrates a core method the visitors have of working on the inner self. Before I continue, though, please be reminded that we do not know who we are dealing with here. Are the ones who took me from my home in December of 1985 the same as the ones who gave me the life task that this chapter describes? That, we do not know. But I feel secure in saying that the 1985 encounter was a physical event. Less so in identifying who caused it. And I cannot say whether or not whomever did that also whispered the prediction in my ear that caused me to do a life review during the journey to see my mother. I do feel that the life-overturning shock of the close encounter opened my mind to noticing all that has happened since. It shattered my expectations about what life is, with the result that I have been noticing and engaging with things previously unseen ever since.

Once, I would have taken the prediction as literally true and not gone to see my mother. But by the time I was given the false prophecy, I was deep enough into life with the visitors that I did not immediately assume that it was absolutely going to come to pass as predicted.

The purpose of these predictions is not to reveal the future to you, but to give you a chance to reveal you to yourself. I have now seen this many times in my life, and always laugh quietly to myself when another close encounter witness announces the second coming or the end of the world or "the landing" on such and such a date. Then the date comes. Then the date goes. And another prophet bites the dust.

So it's important to understand that this is a teaching technique that is not so much present in our world. It compels the subject to go on a journey of inner discovering against the background of a threat that, at the time, seems very real.

When those storms came up on the way home, I was absolutely convinced that I was about to die. Even all these years later, the fear I experienced remains with me, and so does the place I came to, the reconciliation with my own death.

I have seen when my wife died and others, too, that strange *lessening* of the body that so distinguishes the final moment.

Anne was very ill, but the moment of her passing left her body so suddenly inanimate, as if something had literally left it, and in so doing caused it to become less than it had been just a moment before.

I think often of that moment, and with it comes, always, an awareness of the greatest blessing of this grand life of mine: I have been granted, on a physical level, the touch of the nonphysical world.

I know with the certainty of physical touch and observation that nonphysical beings exist.

I didn't know this then, though. But that night on that plane cracked just a bit the door that is wide open in me now, to the world all around us, that waits for each of us, every one, and for me.

CHAPTER SEVENTEEN

FURY

Life exploded around me in flowers of thought and talk. People seemed luminous, possessed of a sweetness and beauty I had never before noticed. Hard people appeared as innocent as children.

The streets of New York were suddenly full of magical beings, and the most ordinary of us now appeared charged with light.

In every single glance, though, there was also fear. We are all terrified of death, and not until that terror is lost can it be seen in others. Generally we ignore death, but in reality every one of us is facing it every moment. We are afraid all the time. The fear is even there in the startling seriousness of sleeping faces.

What a mystery people became, rich, strange, their faces etched by some dire and wonderful hand to a vividness that I almost could not bear.

The light falling across the breakfast table in the morning, the voices coming in through the windows of our city apartment, the roar of trucks, the angry, sullen cries, the laughter of kids down at the bus stop, all reemerged as part of something beautiful and quite inadmissible to language. I could not name it, but I could know it with a knowing that was so simple and so frankly true than not even the most subtle word could express it.

The least look from any eye seemed to contain the very essence of truth. I saw the laughable absurdity of the egotism that afflicts so many of us as our proud old civilization teeters toward its evening. We are all the same, literally so, innocent or experienced, foolish or wise. We are all little particles of something we cannot name, fiercely intelligent and full of overwhelming passion that emerges from the mystery that made us and lives within us—and *is* us.

I will not call it soul or God or Paraclete or essence or Christ-consciousness. It is old, I know that, but I will not diminish its potential by naming it before it consumes me into itself. I may die without giving it a name, but at least I will have surrendered to it enough to let it turn me toward the direction of its light.

When I would turn my thoughts to death I was like a child amazed by a field of daffodils.

Then I thought, *what happens afterward,* and I realized that I was by no means free from fear. The visitors had given me a great gift, but I had gone through hell to get it. And now that I had it, there was always the possibility that it would turn out to be an illusion.

I could not shake the idea of the soul predator. I took my midnight walks regularly now, and every time I reached the darkest part of the woods the thought would come whispering back.

I had no evidence that it was true. I just couldn't rid myself of the notion that there was something predatory about the visitors. I had terrifying fragmentary memories of them—

memories of leering visitor faces, of long, four-fingered hands, of recoiling at their touch.

Those moments remain as if sealed behind smoky glass. I couldn't tell where the memories came from. There were dozens, maybe hundreds of them.

Where were these images from? Reality? Imagination? Were they nothing more than my own frightened apotheosis of the visitors? Unfortunately, I could not know an answer to these questions.

Thus I was unable to put this particular fear to rest. But I was also unwilling to demean a relationship that was beginning to bear such marvelous fruit.

I decided not only to live with my fear but to plunge deeper, if I could, into the relationship. That seemed to me to be the only way to learn.

I asked them in my mind to do whatever I needed the most. I sat in my office at our apartment and whispered my request, repeating it over and over, feeling it from the center of my bones. "Do what I need the most. Do it!"

I set no conditions. I did not even try to think what I might need.

The next day I began to hear the voice yet again urging me to stop eating sweets. I was annoyed and disappointed. This was what I needed the most? What about the growth of consciousness? What about understanding the true nature of our relationship?

No, it was none of that. Instead I began to hear choking noises inside my chest every time I ate a Fig Newton or an Oreo.

I really tried hard to stop this time. I was amazed at the results. I all but sweated blood over cookies and ice cream! It was unbelievable, ridiculous, that I could hunger so much for something so trivial.

I just couldn't stop. I didn't have the strength. Two days after quitting them I was having dreams about cookies. What infuriated me was that this was such an innocent pleasure and it seemed so unnecessary to deny myself.

I understood the importance of what the great hermits like St. Anthony of Alexandria did. In turning away from the pleasures of the world they offered themselves to that which lay within. It was this act that freed them from the blindness of life and enabled them to see the very light of the soul.

When the visitors warned me about sweets they may have been attempting to lead me into an understanding of just how profoundly addicted I was to external life. Previous to this battle over sweets I had thought of myself as a person without addictions. I didn't smoke, drink much alcohol or caffeine, take drugs, or do any of the other things that are associated with addiction. But as soon as I attempted to deny myself a cookie I found out that I was just as addicted as the next person.

I discovered this intellectually, but it did not occur to me that it might also be literally true on the physical level. I did not really believe that there might be some sort of actual, physical state that the visitors wanted me to enter, one that could not be accessed without giving up sugar.

I did see that making this sacrifice would symbolize my surrender to the needs of the soul. But I didn't *want* to surrender. I wanted to enjoy the pleasures of being alive— sweets included.

In early November we returned to the cabin for a week or so. Over the course of the fall we had been back and forth many times and there had been no sign of the visitors. At about eleven that night I went walking in the woods. For the first time

I was completely unafraid. I had accepted even the soul-eater possibility. If that was our fate, then so be it. I wasn't being harmed right now. That was reality. That was what I knew.

It had not been easy to participate in the visitors' little theatricals—like those airplane flights—but the benefits to me were so enormous, I could not consider that they flowed from anything except a very considerable love.

I walked along in the night woods, my feet shuffling the new-fallen leaves.

As it was cloudy, the woods were very dark. I had to rely totally on my flashlight. I went down among the tall trees to the meadow beyond, reflecting as I walked on the beauty of the night and on how small these woods actually were. The real forest was a mile in the opposite direction. This place where I had been so afraid was only a congenial little woodland peopled by a few deer and coons. There was nothing to harm me here.

As I walked out into the meadow I saw something streak across the sky. It looked like a spark. As it was clearly visible under the cloud cover, it could not have been a meteor. But what kind of spark? Certainly it wasn't from a chimney; this particular spark had been moving against a rather stiff wind.

Then I heard a voice speak, the voice of a child: "Go to the middle of the meadow and look up."

I went a short distance and looked up. I saw nothing. The voice returned, telling me to move a little back, then a little to one side or the other.

When I looked up again I saw a round, dark shadow about the size of a quarter. It was absolutely stationary behind the rushing clouds. The stillness of the thing made it seem unreal. One is used to seeing movement in the sky, never stillness. Even a hovering helicopter moves. This was as still as a stone.

I watched it very carefully, observing that it was black and absolutely featureless. I also noticed that if I moved my head even slightly the object instantly disappeared! It was as if I were seeing it through a crack in a wall. I asked the voice to speak again. I listened. I waited. I started to get cold. Then the disk disappeared completely and did not come back.

Finally I returned to the house.

The next day, a Saturday, was cloudy and quiet. Autumn was giving way to winter and we spent the day reading and lounging around the fire. In the evening we listened to *A Prairie Home Companion* on National Public Radio and then to a lovely local folk music program from nearby Albany, *Hudson River Sampler*.

At ten I put our son to bed and at ten-thirty Anne and I went out to the hot tub together. The sky was now full of broken clouds, with an occasional star peeking out through one of the rushing gaps.

We had been in the tub for no more than five minutes when I saw a very peculiar light appear just above the tree line across the deck from the house. This object consisted of a bright central light with a noticeably rounded bottom that was glowing pink. Clustered close to it on one side was a brilliant blue light. On the other side was a white light strobing furiously, its intensity far greater than any aircraft strobe.

By this time I had not only become familiar with dozens of aircraft illumination configurations, I also knew all the various airways that could be seen from our house.

Thus I knew at once that if this was an airplane, it was displaying a radically nonstandard lighting configuration and must be a private plane as it was nowhere near a route an airliner would be using.

It was below the ceiling, which I later estimated at about eight hundred feet. A call the next morning to the nearest airport, which is thirty miles away, established their ceiling at eleven hundred feet at the hour of the observation. Allowing for our slightly higher elevation, I believe my eight-hundred-foot estimate for the bottom of the cloud cover was reasonable.

This meant that the lighted object was below eight hundred feet and probably no more than a thousand lateral feet from us. And yet there was absolutely no trace of a sound. A helicopter at that distance would have been clearly audible. An ultralight aircraft would have been easy to hear. A small private plane would have had to move faster that this object, which came forward very slowly.

I recognized that the object fitted no common pattern. My next thought was that I alone might be seeing it. I approached the matter obliquely with Anne. I did not even want to ask her if she could see something in the sky. That might be suggestion enough.

Instead I said how beautiful the line of trees was against the moving clouds.

She looked up and said, "What's that?"

So my question was answered. She could see it too. I replied, "I think it's them."

As soon as I said that the object stopped and moved back down below the tree line as if trying to keep itself hidden. A few moments later I saw it flickering past some trees in front of the house, so low at this point that it must have been coming up a draw behind the ridge we are on. It was perhaps two hundred feet from the ground.

The next thing I knew, a flash of blue-white light hit me in the face. Simultaneously Anne saw a brilliant bar of light suspended above the house.

A wave of exhaustion swept over me. I felt that I had to get out of the hot tub at once or risk drowning. I was about to lose consciousness.

We both got out of the tub and went in to bed. There was no question of my doing anything about the fact that I knew the visitors were here. It was all I could do to climb the stairs to the bedroom.

Although she said nothing about it later, we must have both been affected because I don't think we were awake for another five minutes.

In the wee hours of the night I abruptly woke up. There was somebody quite close to the bed, but the room seemed so unnaturally dark that I couldn't see much at all. I caught a glimpse of someone crouching just behind my bedside table. I could see by the huge, dark eyes who it was.

I felt an absolutely indescribable sense of menace. It was hell on earth to be there, and yet I couldn't move, couldn't cry out, couldn't get away. I lay as still as death, suffering inner agonies. Whatever was there seemed so monstrously ugly, so filthy and dark and sinister. Of course they were demons. They had to be. And they were here and I couldn't get away. I couldn't save my poor family.

I still remember that thing crouching there, so terribly ugly, its arms and legs like the limbs of a great insect, its eyes glaring at me.

And there was also the love. I felt mothered. Caressed. Then the terrible insect rose up beside the bed like some huge, predatory spider. The eyes glittered as it tilted its head from side to side.

Every muscle in my body was stiff to the point of breaking. I ached. My stomach felt as if it had been stuffed with molten lead. I could hardly breathe.

The next thing I knew, something had been laid against my forehead. I felt it there, a light electric pressure vibrating softly between my eyes.

Instantly I seemed to be transported to another place, a stone floor with a low stone table in the middle of it. The table was a bit more than waist high and on it there was a set of iron shackles. A man was led down some steps and attached to these shackles. He was right in front of my face, not two feet from me, looking directly at me with eyes so sad that I almost couldn't bear it.

He was a perfectly ordinary-looking human being. He had curly brown hair and he was naked. His body was muscular and normally formed in every respect. Behind him was a taller person wearing black. I was not able to see this individual clearly, as he was moving very quickly and the shadows were deep.

The next thing I knew, this person was beating the poor man with a terrible whip. Before my eyes this man was being almost torn to pieces by the fury of the beating.

I was shocked to my core when it started. I remember how the surprise undid me. The man's face collapsed into agony and he began straining at the cuffs around his wrists.

Somebody behind me said, "He failed to get you to obey him and now he must bear the consequences."

The horror went on and on. The man was getting desperate. His head would loll for a moment, then another terrible blow would bring him to his senses. Another voice, the old voice, the one I identified with the feminine being I had seen during the *Communion* experience, began to intone, "It isn't real, Whitty, it isn't real."

That didn't make me feel much better. My heart was sick for the poor man in front of me. I knew perfectly well that this whole business had to do with the eating of sweets, as stupid as that sounds.

Even as this little psychodrama proceeded, I felt myself getting furious with the visitors. The beating went on and on and the voice kept saying, "It isn't real, Whitty, it isn't real...." But I experienced it as if it was all quite real.

I went through hell watching that poor man suffer for me. I have never felt such raw humiliation and guilt. I would have done anything to trade places with him. But they beat him until he was a slumped, broken ruin.

And then I was back in bed again. The visitor was now standing beside the bed. I could see her face quite clearly. There was a sardonic expression there that I will never forget.

Our son started screaming. The shock that went through me this time was absolutely explosive. I tried to get out of bed but I felt as though I were tied down around my shoulders and waist and ankles. I couldn't move.

She said, "He is being punished for your transgression." His screaming filled my ears, my soul. Listening to it, I wanted to die. I tried to call out to him, to arouse Anne, to do anything at all to somehow regain some control over the situation.

I thought I was going to suffocate. My throat was closed, my eyes were swimming with tears. The sense of being *infested* was powerful and awful. It was as if the whole house were full of filthy, stinking insects the size of tigers.

Then it was over. He was silent. There was nobody in my room. The sense of menace was gone. I started to get up and go to my son. Somebody hit me. It was as if I had been slapped across the face. I fell back into the bed and I don't remember another thing until morning.

The instant I woke up I jumped out of bed and went straight to our son's room. He was sleeping with all of the covers off the bed. He looked cold. As I covered him he woke up. He seemed perfectly normal. Anne seemed perfectly normal.

I said to her, "They came last night." She answered, "I know." I asked her if she remembered anything. "Just the thing in the sky. And then we went to sleep."

Feeling like a zombie, I dressed and went to get the Sunday papers. A few minutes later I almost ran my car into a ditch. I was going much too fast for our narrow road.

I slowed down, stopped, pulled my car over. My eyes were streaming with tears. My hands were shaking so badly that I couldn't steer. My mind was thick with the visitors. They were so terrible, so ugly, so fierce, and I was so small and helpless. I could smell that odor of theirs like greasy smoke hanging in my nostrils.

Again, though, I felt love. Despite all the ugliness and the terrible things that had been done, I found myself longing for them, missing them! How was this possible? I wanted them to come back to me!

I was crying not only because I was scared but also because I was lonely. I felt as if I belonged more to the other world I had glimpsed last night than I did to this one. It seemed greater and more intensely real and far closer to the truth.

I regretted the contempt I had shown for its needs and its laws and felt a desperate desire to make amends.

I had tempted their rage, and now I knew what it meant.

There was something worse, though. I remembered a glimpse, no more than that, of another level of their being, and it was very, very distressing to recall. When that voice had been intoning "It isn't real, Whitty," I had felt a pain greater than the pain of punishment. It was the pain of their love. They had given up something for me, and I suspected that it was access to the full joy of a thing that I could not even name. I had the sense that they had on my behalf turned away from perfect love, and that they had done this to help me.

If they are an element of the divine, to come into our world would be like penetrating deepest darkness. I realized that I was isolated in myself, turned away from the light that surrounds us.

I suspected that the ugliness I had seen last night was not them, but *me.* I was so ashamed of myself that I almost retched.

When I got back with the papers I made some pancakes, going about my work like an automaton. As I worked, I kept hearing our son's voice howling down the night.

But he was happily reading the funnies. Obviously they hadn't hurt him, but they had served notice that he was vulnerable. He was *never* going to suffer for my weaknesses, not as far as I was concerned.

For the first time in my life, I refrained at that breakfast from putting syrup on my pancakes. I felt like an idiot for doing it, but I was damned if I was going to allow what had happened a few hours earlier to escalate. God only knew what the visitors might do next if I continued my experiment in defiance.

I stopped eating sweets on that day. I discovered how strong one must be to change a single innocuous habit. My renunciation has been far from perfect. I am a sugar addict and I will always be a sugar addict. Sometimes I fail. But then I begin the struggle again.

And that seems to be the point of the whole exercise, to engage in the struggle.

It is a small, humble thing. But I am a small being, so I suppose a humble struggle is appropriate.

By defying the visitors, I had learned a great deal more than I would have any other way. They did not often answer my requests unless they themselves had a need to fulfill.

When I defied them I found the limit of their tolerance of me. They waited for six months for me to do what they were asking, and then they expressed rage. So they can be frustrated and angered, and they can react in anger, although—at least in this case— with the restraint of reassuring me that it was all an illusion.

I sat eating my unsweetened pancakes and wondering if they realized just how hard this was going to be for me. And at once I felt like an idiot. Obviously that must be perfectly clear to them. That was the whole damned point, wasn't it?

Our son had finished his breakfast and was now playing happily.

The suggestion that he had been drawn into my punishment must have been intended as a reminder to me that the stakes were very high.

They were indeed. I could never have imagined how high. Nothing that had come before could compare to what now awaited me, now that I had faced the fury of the visitors and thus surrendered myself to whatever wisdom they possessed.

2026 Update

I believe this to be the most accurate description of what an interaction with the visitors is like that exists anywhere in my body of work. It begins with Anne and I both seeing an object in the sky close to the house. We are then hit with a flash of light that causes us to become extremely sleepy and we go to bed.

I must mention here that I have no memory of this incident now. However, Anne read every page of this book as it was being written, and if she had objected to anything in it, I certainly would have heard about this from her. What this means is that she definitely did see what I said she saw, and did experience the overwhelming need to go to sleep.

But what of what happened later? Looking back, I also have no memory of those events, and reading what I wrote doesn't jog a memory, either. I don't have those memories because of the trauma involved in the experiences. Had I not written this passage a few weeks after the incident happened, I doubt that I would have remembered any of it, not from the UFO sighting on. If Anne was still with me and I asked her now, I would not be at all surprised to find that she didn't remember the sighting either.

But why?

The first thing to understand about memory is that it is not fixed. Memories change over time. They are altered. They are forgotten. And, in the case of trauma, they may be suppressed.

Even if it seems passive, a close encounter with a UFO is traumatic. It is a penetration of the unknown into the sacred spaces of mind and heart, and, if the encounter is very close, there may also be physical effects, as I have discussed.

After I published *Communion*, story after story appeared in the press, some claiming that lie detectors were ineffective and others that hypnosis was not a valid means of recovering memory.

In the hands of professional operators, lie detectors are effective. They are routinely used by intelligence services around the world, as well as some police and investigative organizations. Similarly, a professionally trained hypnotist can uncover repressed memories.

In 1992, the False Memory Syndrome Foundation was created by Pamela and Peter Freyd after their daughter Jennifer accused her father of abusing her sexually when she was a child. It asserted the theory that there was no such thing as repressed memory and was regarded for some years as authoritative, until the actual mechanism of repression was discovered. It was dissolved in 2019.

Throughout this period, I followed memory research carefully. I have always suspected that the proliferation of news stories debunking lie detectors and hypnosis that appeared after I published *Communion* had to do with hidden social engineering, and were not valid or true. Similarly, I feel that the False Memory Syndrome Foundation's position had the effect of protecting abusers, and I do feel that it's possible that the founders knew this from the beginning, although I have no idea if Jennifer Freyd's accusations were true.

The foundation's original science advisor was Ralph Unterwager, who had published articles in the Dutch journal *Paedika* asserting that sexual contact between men and boys was healthy for the boys. That someone holding such an opinion was sought out to be the scientific advisor to the foundation discredited it in my eyes.

Nevertheless, I did believe many of the assertions of the false memory syndrome community, and feel that I was misled into doubting some of my own memories, including some in this book.

In fact, memories can be repressed, and I think that we are looking in this chapter at an incredibly valuable example of a memory that was traumatic from the beginning, and that, soon after it was committed to writing, sank into amnesia.

This is, to me, quite a precious example of the sort of thing that we probably do not remember about our encounters with the visitors, and I have to wonder how many people have such memories repressed in them right now.

Let's take a closer look at how memory repression actually works. The fact that I forgot this entire event and the way that happened speaks to many similar stories that appear throughout the close encounter narrative. I have long suspected that there may be hidden behind the wall of amnesia an entire level of human experience that we are not acknowledging. Perhaps the close encounter experience is not rare, but rather part of what it means to be human.

I am haunted by something my wife said when she reconnected with me after her passing. One of the first things, in fact: "Whitley, it's all a game."

If this is true, then this may indeed be a simulation, and behind that amnesia may lie another, entirely different vision of the human experience. If so, then we cannot progress much beyond where we are now, we cannot hope to expand into the cosmos, unless we understand what this means to and about us.

When impressions enter through the senses, most types are organized (except for scent) in the hippocampus. When it is turned off by the visitors, which they are clearly capable of doing, we experience what is known as "missing time." It can be so seamless that we never even notice that it has happened. If it is noticed, in some cases it can be penetrated by various mnemonic techniques, hypnosis being one of them.

But this type of interruption obviously did not happen here. Anne and I saw a UFO, then later I had an experience that I remembered, probably for a few days or weeks—long enough to get it into the manuscript I was working on.

The memory was encoded, so the hippocampus wasn't affected by the event. When traumatic amnesia occurs immediately after a violent experience, the amygdala can become hyperactive, in which case encoding will occur but without conscious retrieval. This is where the False Memory Syndrome Foundation made it's basic mistake. The assumption that nothing would ever prevent conscious retrieval of a memory was wrong. This does happen when trauma causes the amygdala to malfunction.

But that wouldn't be the case here. I did remember the events immediately after they happened, and for an unknown period thereafter, What I think did happen is that the parts of the brain that cause people to feel distanced from traumatic events, an effect called dissociation, gradually made me reject these memories. This happens in the right temporal lobe and the dorsal prefrontal cortex where this type of memory suppression can actually be measured.

When two people witness the same UFO or close encounter event, and then a few weeks later one of them has no memory of it, this is what has happened to that person, and it is what happened to me.

When you look at the experience, though, and, as a matter of fact at the terrifying flight as well, what you see is something very surprising. Facing death on that flight led to a freedom of a kind that I had never felt before. It was exactly like a near-death experience, and is probably part of why I have not, for years now, had a fear of death.

Anne didn't, either, but this was because she had an NDE after her October, 2004 stroke, and as happens in so many of these cases, lost her fear of death. When death did come to her in 2015, she passed away calmly and in great peace.

If one thinks deeply enough, it becomes clear that the visitors could have *known* that the flight would involve storms, and known this many months before it took place. The way I felt afterwards, the awakening to the preciousness of life and the beauty of life, was a gift.

So mark this carefully: what might look like acts of cruelty may often or even always be intended to free us from something. One cannot help but be reminded of the great medieval theologian Meister Eckhart's observation, as delivered so beautifully by Danny Aiello in "Jacob's Ladder," "The only thing that burns in Hell is the part of you that won't let go of life, your memories, your attachments. They burn them all away. But they're not punishing you, they're freeing your soul. So, if you're frightened of dying and you're holding on, you'll see devils tearing your life away. But if you've made your peace, then the devils are really angels, freeing you from the earth."

It is going to be very hard for us to understand the teachings of the visitors, and I think this is the first time the structure that they use has really been laid out. I hope that it is clear, for they are teachers of a higher order than we are used to. They do not instruct or force "downloads" down our throats, not the ones who care about us and want us to be free and strong. Theirs is a more dynamic and more difficult way of teaching, and to follow it despite the terrors that it will draw up from our depths, we must lead with the peace of the heart, and trust that what will look like a flood of demons swarming our world, is actually a flight of angels.

CHAPTER EIGHTEEN

A SOUL'S JOURNEY

I was lying down at about four o'clock in the afternoon of November 15, 1986, when something odd happened. We were at the cabin. I wasn't napping, but I had my eyes closed and was carefully moving my attention from place to place in my body in order to strengthen my sensory awareness. This was something I had been doing for many years, and I certainly didn't expect any unusual side effects. Suddenly, however, I heard a familiar group of young voices say in unison, "Oh, good. Now we'll show you something."

An instant later I appeared to be in two places at once. I was still lying on the bed, but a quite conscious and sensually alive "other" me was also standing beside what was quite clearly a new Cadillac. I put my hands on the roof and felt it. There were people I recognized but could not quite name standing around admiring the car. Then the peculiar sensation ended. I was confused. I am not likely to dream about cars. My interest in them goes no farther than taking care of the one I own.

The next day I was surprised to find that some acquaintances had bought a Cadillac. It had been delivered the day before, at about four o'clock. At that hour they had been showing it to some neighbors ... me included, apparently! As far as I could tell—and I wasn't about to ask them if they'd "sensed" my presence—they had no idea that I'd been around.

Was I really there? If not, then how did I know about the car? These people were not friends but acquaintances. I hadn't been in contact with them in a couple of months. The fact that they had gotten a new car was mentioned the next day by a mutual friend, apparently by pure chance.

After that I started asking other people who'd had visitors encounters if they'd ever had out-of-body experiences. It turned out to be a very common perception.

One of them recommended that I read Robert Monroe's book *Journeys Out of the Body.* I did so and was fascinated but not convinced. It seemed to me that what Mr. Monroe was describing was a dream state.

I read this book toward the end of November 1986. I began to try the methods for getting out of one's body that were described in the book. Almost immediately I discovered that a certain sensation reported by Mr. Monroe was readily available to me. He wrote of feeling a sort of pulsation traveling through his body when he was lying down and preparing for a journey. I found that this sensation would come so reliably that I was able to ask other people to observe me while it was taking place. Anne could detect no difference in my physical appearance when it was happening and it did not lead to any out-of-the-body travel.

On the night of November 27, however, I had an absolutely remarkable dream. It was the most awesome and beautiful dream I can remember. Its intensity was startling. Unlike the appalling perceptions I'd had of the moon exploding and the Chernobyl accident the previous April in Boulder, or the vision of the golden city, it was clearly a normal dream.

In it I found myself standing on the beach of a green sea. Little waves were sifting up the strand, and I had the impression that they represented human beings on their journeys through experience. Each tiny lapping movement was dense with wordless emotional impact, as if the whole transit of a life had been contained within it.

Above me there was a sky of clear blue so perfect that it made my heart ache to see it. And hanging in this sky was a large object that seemed to be made of clay. It was round on one side and square on the other, and was rotating slowly.

Even though it seemed old and was worn and cracked, it appeared to me as something of great beauty, a perfect object floating in a radiant sky.

Voices began to speak around me. I was aware that a group of children were approaching, and I told them to look up into the sky. Then the object changed in its rotation. The square and round parts separated and began circling one another. This motion was incredibly satisfying. It seemed to represent a reconciliation of opposite forces, a sort of "squaring the circle."

A very large emotion filled me as the children came closer. They were dressed in green and yellow and tan clothing, loose-fitting. Some of them said that they were Muslim and others that they were Christian.

This did not disturb me, but on the contrary seemed extraordinarily fortunate, because it meant that there would be friction, and out of the friction would come balance.

I began to feel a sense of inner balance. I walked a little way into the water, my feet touching the cool stones beneath the waves. On the far horizon there was a beautiful star, a huge white-blue radiance. It seemed like a living thing and

I wanted to call to it. I found myself producing a sound from deep within that seemed to carry far into the silence.

As the star faded I felt a long, long way from home.

Just a dream, but for me a deeply moving one.

I was interested to see that children were again involved. They were emerging as a subtle but important motif of my experience. I remembered the children's circle from my boyhood, the children running past me into the field of yellow flowers, the voices of children, and now this dream about holy children. It was also true that the visitors' admonition not to eat sweets was the sort of thing that one told a child. Both my response to it and their reaction were childlike as well.

I wondered if mind in its disembodied form is not wise and old but wise and young.

Perhaps we grow old and die quickly, but there is a superconscious level of being that matures much more slowly. Maybe, on this level, there is something very ancient that is also very young.

On the afternoon of November 28 we returned to the cabin after a short absence. As we left the highway and passed through the toll plaza we noticed that one of the cars beside us had quite an unusual-looking cat in it. It must have been a Siamese. It had a long, rather simian face and two glaring, black eyes. Our son noticed how strange it looked and pointed it out to me and Anne.

As I glanced at it I saw something really startling in the backseat of the car. The cat in front was bizarre-looking, but there was another one in the back that was impossible to believe. All I could see of it was the top of its head and two gigantic, pointed ears. These ears were easily bigger than a human hand. The animal was gray and looked a bit out of focus. Just at that moment my son said, "Dad! Look at that thing in the backseat." I had already seen it. I looked more closely. The car was a BMW about five years old. The driver was male, and he appeared to be in his mid-forties, normal in every way. The Siamese beside him was odd-looking, but not completely unacceptable.

The animal in the backseat was another matter. It still hadn't raised its head enough for us to see its eyes. I stared at it. The head must have been three feet across. Our son said, "Where's the rest of it?"

I had no idea how to explain what we were seeing. Something with such a huge head could not possibly fit into the backseat of a BMW unless there was no floor. I told Anne to look at it.

"At what?" she asked.

"The giant cat in the BMW."

"You guys are kidding me."

When I looked again the backseat was empty. My son and I were perplexed. We had both seen the thing, and there hadn't been a word spoken about it between us beforehand. We'd both seen it at virtually the same moment.

It was one of those experiences that we used to ignore before we became aware that such things often had a larger significance. Instead of ignoring it, I told myself the truth about it: Both my boy and I—independently and with no verbal communication between us—had seen a completely impossible animal in the backseat of a nearby car.

Could it have been a reflection on the window? Possibly, but it certainly appeared to have a form and substance of its own, and to be very definitely inside the car despite the fact that it was not noticed by either the driver or the other cat.

As we entered the tollbooth I was able to see down inside the car. The backseat was empty.

I recount this story not because I know what happened or why, but because it had a peculiar sequel a few hours later during one of the most fascinating experiences of my life.

That evening I saw two figures in the front yard. I only saw them for a moment and I could not make out any particular shape except that they appeared to be entirely human, moving through the yard. I recall that they were tall and wearing white uniforms. Although I went outside and looked around carefully, I saw nobody.

Later that evening there was a power failure lasting four minutes. It was confined only to our immediate area, as I called friends in the town and down the road and they were unaffected.

At about eleven-thirty I went walking in the woods, but found nothing unusual about my experience. I was quite nervous and practically jumped out of my skin when some deer snorted at me.

I went to bed with no inkling of what was to happen next. Until four-thirty I slept easily. I awoke as I often do at that hour, got up and took a drink of water. I then went to the window and looked out into the predawn stillness. After a time I lay back on the bed. The thought crossed my mind that I would like to try having an out-of-the-body episode. Robert Monroe had counseled in his book that this experience was most likely to be available when one was in a "mind awake/ body asleep" state, and I thought that this might be a good time to try for such a state.

My many years of meditation made it a familiar condition for me. I began attempting to roll out of my body.

An instant later I saw a strange image as if on a television screen about a foot from my face. It was the image of the long, gray hand of a visitor pointing at a box about two feet square on a gray floor. The hand was extremely long and thin, with four fingers. They had black, clawlike nails on them. The longest one was pointing down at the box.

For some reason this image had the effect of causing an explosive sexual reaction in me. My whole body was jolted by what I can only describe as a blast of pure sexual feeling. I have never known anything like it before or since. It was especially odd because the image was so completely asexual. In fact, the hand was actually repulsive looking, and one could hardly consider a plain gray box an object of sexual interest. The effect only lasted an instant, but it had an amazing effect on me, quite beyond anything that one would have thought.

What happened was that the blast of sexual energy seemed to loosen connections inside me. I rolled out of my body. It felt as if I had come unstuck from myself. The experience was strange in the extreme—almost beyond description.

For an instant, I was very confused and disoriented because the sheet I was lying on had just slid past my field of vision. Then I found myself in the air above my body. I was hanging there, floating effortlessly. I saw my face down below, the eyes partly opened, the lips parted. It did not look like me, not quite. Later I think I understood why: I had never before seen myself except in mirror-image.

I was not asleep. I had not had a chance even to enter a meditative state. On the contrary, I felt alert. Thus I was able to examine my situation carefully and to experiment with such things as observing my shape and moving about.

I was calm and collected and not at all afraid.

I looked around me. The first thing I noticed was that I could see the entire room at once. It was the same dimly lit bedroom it had been a moment before. Anne was sleeping in the bed, very much alive. By contrast, my body was still as a stone.

Between us on the blanket there lay a cat. This amazed me since our cats were in the city. The animal was aware of my presence, and looked up at me. It was a familiar face: It looked like Sadie, our Burmese. I would almost say it was Sadie, except that I knew for certain she was not there. The cat stood up and jumped off the bed. She slipped slowly and gracefully to the floor as if she were no heavier than the wings of a butterfly.

Then she began walking around, completely unconcerned with me.

I found that I could move about quite freely. I wanted to go to the foot of the bed and glided there easily. Parallel with the foot of our bed is a double set of windows. Outside one of these windows I could see the face of a being like the one on the cover of *Communion*. It was however, a uniform gray color. Its large, almond-shaped eyes were much less alive than I could remember seeing them before. I would almost have been willing to believe that this was a mask or picture of some sort. In any case, I took it as a warning not to go out that window.

There was no way, though, that I was going to cower in a bedroom considering the remarkable state in which I found myself. I moved toward the empty window.

Would I be able to open a window? Did I even have hands? I examined myself. I appeared to be a roughly spherical field. I had rather dulled sensation. I was neither breathing nor feeling a need to breathe. I tried closing my eyes, which was possible, but it felt more like I was willing myself not to see than like I had dropped my eyelids. There were absolutely no body sounds at all. The slight tinnitus or ringing that I have in my left ear was gone.

I moved toward the window and touched the sash—a light touch that felt normal in every way. But when I tried to raise it, my hand simply went through it. As a matter of fact, what I was calling a hand wasn't a hand at all, but a sort of gray, hazy probe that would move out from the center of my body when I wanted to touch something. The end of it was about as formed as a mitten.

I found that I could push through the glass of the window and the screen beyond. There is a hemlock right outside the window and I thought I would try to grab some of its needles and bring them inside with me. This would tell me if I was having real access to the physical world in this state.

As I passed through the glass and the screen, I could feel a slight difference in density, exactly as if I were moving through cool smoke. Once outside I could see that the world around me was very much the same as it had always been.

There was one striking exception. I noticed that the power lines coming into the house appeared fat because of a sort of gray, hairy substance that was adhering to them. The phone line was like this also, but the substance was much more sparse. It looked exactly like hair that has been raised by a static charge. I think that I may have been seeing the electro-magnetic field around the wires.

I touched the tree and took some of the needles between my "fingers." Although I could see the needles I had taken, I could also see that there were still needles on the tree. It was as if I had taken a sort of coating off the needles, something that paralleled their form but was made of another, more subtle substance.

When I attempted to return to the bedroom, I found myself impeded by the screen. For a moment I thought that I was not going to be able to get back inside. I thought to myself that I had died a really strange death ... unless death is always like this.

Then the screen seemed to give way and I popped through into the bedroom.

I tried to make a sound to arouse Anne. Although I found that I could sing and possibly even talk, she remained totally unaware of me.

I wondered, if she was awake and I had spoken in her ear, would my voice have sounded like a small radio? Had I just entered the state in which the visitors ordinarily live?

I looked around for the cat, but did not see it. Then I saw myself lying in the bed. I was so still. I looked dead.

Was I dead?

I felt no sense of uneasiness, but rather a quite calm and rational desire to see if I could get back into my body. I had read in Monroe's book that there is a connection between the physical body and the second body when one is in this state, but I couldn't see or perceive anything at all.

Looking at my body was eerie. It was as still as a stone. I thought I could see a little breathing, but it was hardly detectable. Anne, by contrast, pulsed with life. Her breast heaved, her face seemed full of a living presence.

My body appeared coarse. Going down into it again didn't appeal to me very much. I had the feeling that I could leave and never come back. Then I looked at Anne and there was no real question about where I belonged.

When I dropped down into myself, my body seemed to have an invisible opening in it that I went through. But I was terribly loose inside and found myself coming out again. I drifted like a leaf to the floor.

Suddenly my situation changed dramatically. I was no longer in the bedroom at all, but at our old house in San Antonio. Characteristically, my father was up at the crack of dawn mowing the lawn, a chore I was planning to do later. I was watching him from the front window of my bedroom. He glanced up at me and asked, "When are you going to come help me?"

Not soon, it seemed, because I shot back into my body like a frightened rabbit and this time I clung there. I had the feeling I'd touched death just then. A moment later I felt entirely normal. I sat up in bed. There was no sensation of having been asleep, or of any discontinuity of consciousness. I did not feel I had just awakened from a dream.

I also noticed that my body was quite cold. I felt chilled to the bone and yet the bed was comfortable and warm. My arms and legs were stiff, as if they hadn't moved for a long time. According to the clock, only about ten minutes had passed.

I moved my arms and legs. It was like manipulating a puppet. My own body seemed strange and unfamiliar. I stood up and walked around the room, examining the window, looking outside to see the hemlock. It was familiar, but also possessed of the mystery that I had sensed before from time to time, the mystery that I now feel is at the very core of life. I put on my slippers and robe and went downstairs.

The house was perfectly quiet. My son was asleep in his bed, the covers pulled up around him. How peaceful was his sleep.

I went out onto the deck. It was cold and extremely quiet. I had no fear at all. The woods seemed to bear great secrets in their silence, as if the trees knew all that had passed beneath them.

The coolness of the night crept in past my robe. I felt then the depth of the question that confronted me: What had just happened? Had I really gone out of my body?

Certainly it wasn't a conventional dream. It may have been a hallucinatory experience, but I did not believe that. The "answers" rang hollow. What I could say with conviction was what was true: Something wonderful and mysterious had happened. Not even in the literature of out-of-the-body travel have I often read of an experience so conscious or so completely grounded in the physical world.

I found some stories, though. While my experience was unusual, I certainly wasn't alone. The noted psychiatrist Dr. George Ritchie had a famous experience of this type while he was in the military in World War II. Dr. Ritchie died of pneumonia and his body was placed in the morgue at Camp Barkeley, Texas. Pneumonia is a disease that devastates the body, leaving it full of toxins.

Dr. Ritchie, however, came back to life after nine minutes of apparent complete death, where he was without respiration or any other vital sign. Dr. Donald G. Francy, chief medical officer at Camp Barkeley, described it as "the most amazing medical case I have ever encountered." Among other things, he signed a notarized statement that reads in part, "Private Ritchie's virtual call from death and return to vigorous health has to be explained in terms of other than natural means."

Dr. Ritchie came back with vivid memories of what had happened to him after he died. In his book *Return from To-morrow* he described in detail how he left his body, flew toward Richmond, Virginia, seeing the countryside below him, eventually going down into a city and attempting to get directions from a man who could neither see nor hear him! His book is eminently worth reading, because it may provide a very real glimpse into the initial stages of life after death.

What it offered me was the realization that I was not the only person to leave his body in a state of total consciousness. There was plenty of precedent, in this case in the experience of a prominent medical doctor.

With the exception of Robert Monroe, most of the other cases of separation taking place in an ordinary state of consciousness came from the literature of the near-death experience. I had not been ejected from my body by death. Rather, it was the strange vision of the box that had triggered my experience.

My ordinary dream life is hardly filled with images of dull gray boxes that produce explosive sexual excitement. I am not the only person with visitor experience to have been shown such a box, though. I've dreamed about boxes, and one of my most upsetting fragmentary memories is of the hand of one of the visitors sliding a box into its place in a stack. This memory is out of context, but I cannot evoke it without a shudder. Back in the early sixties I wrote a poem called "My Box."

"I will go when I must to the sentence of my box where I will seek the love behind life's black truth."

Does it refer to a place of painful and ecstatic contemplation, where the soul is left to cook after death in the juices of conscience? Is the real reason we fear death that we know we must then face the truth of our lives?

But I felt such extraordinary physical excitement when I saw that box. Is death really a secret ecstasy? Certainly the vision of the box drew me so powerfully that I literally left my body.

I could not prove that I had been out of my body, except to myself. In my own mind it wasn't—and isn't—possible for me to think otherwise. The experience was too overwhelmingly real in every detail to have been anything other than what it seemed ... or so I would have myself believe.

Out-of-the-body travel has been extensively documented. Many of the people who have experienced it, like Dr. Ritchie, have impeccable credentials and almost indisputable stories to tell. And yet our society persists in viewing the state as something strange and startling. In scientific circles it is generally assumed to be a dream or hallucinatory condition.

Why? Not because we lack proof that it is real. Not even because it flies in the face of accepted knowledge. Something with as much supporting evidence as this has would long since have become the subject of serious study unless some other factor were operating.

I think that we are afraid to face out-of-the-body experience for the same reason we are afraid to explore the idea of reincarnation. Both of these notions suggest that the soul has an independent existence.

This is what I believe we are having such a hard time facing. I think that the prospect of a postmortem review of life so frightens us, we would rather simply deny that the soul exists.

Our denial is not rational, in view of the implications of some of the scientific work that has been done in this area—and ignored. Dr. Ian Stevenson, Carlson Professor of Psychiatry at the University of Virginia Medical School, has published *five volumes* of case histories, mostly of children under the age of four who have detailed memories of past lives. Some of them even describe the process of dying and being reincarnated. The vivid detail of the best cases, all verified by Dr. Stevenson and his assistants, suggests strongly that reincarnation is a real process—and therefore, by implication, that the soul is real.

I cannot forget my memory of the visitors' claim, "We recycle souls." It had also been said to other participants. I thought of Jo Sharp's experience, of the whole tone of what was happening to me. It was becoming clear to me that the visitors were concerned with the life of the soul as well as the body.

Could it be that the soul is not only real, but the flux of souls between life and death is a process directed by consciousness and supported by artistry and technology?

Human cultural history is rich with references to the "second body," or soul. The Greeks called it *eidolon,* the Romans *umbra.* Similar references appear in every culture. In 1972, Dr. Harold Burr published *Blueprint for Immortality: The Electric Patterns of Life.* In this book, which was the outcome of many years of research, he demonstrated that each life form has an electric body which is present from birth to death, which does not change as the body grows, and which is different for each species.

I remembered the way the needles of the hemlock outside my window felt when I touched them while I was in my "electric body," separated from the physical. I could feel a sort of substance surrounding the needle, seeming to coat it, which fell away under my electric touch. Is this how it feels to touch one electric body with another?

We ignore the reality of the soul not because there is reason to do so, but because we just don't want to find out about it. I suspect that it can be detected, understood, and even affected by the proper instruments.

I also read more of Robert Monroe's work, a book entitled *Far Journeys,* and found it to be as interesting as the first volume. I spent a week at the Monroe Institute in West Virginia, where I learned the methods Monroe has developed for enter-

ing the "mind awake/body asleep" state that is most condu-
cive to the out-of-the-body experience. Monroe himself was
a delightful and brilliant man, and I found his techniques to
be highly effective in taking me into a state of mind where I
did access experiences that are very definitely not ordinarily
available.

The point of the Institute is not to enable people to induce
out-of-the-body travel so much as it is to teach them to reach
a state that is open to contact with more energetic levels of
being.

When I had my experience in November, I was not in an
altered state of mind at all, or at least I couldn't perceive it. I
retained not only my ordinary consciousness but also my perceptions of the world around me when I left my body.

I wondered about that cat, though. Was she a dream within a dream? Or was it that cats can also travel about in their
plasmic state? Maybe that was why the Egyptians were so obsessed with mummifying cats as well as human beings. Maybe
they knew something about cats that we have forgotten.

During my experience I had a definite but slight weight
and a sense of the limits of my "body." I could move by simply
wishing to do so. When I wished to touch something, a part
of me extended out of my body and I was able to feel just as
I normally feel, except that too hard a push would cause my
"finger" to go through the object I was touching.

When I tried to get back into my body but slipped out, I fell
like a leaf or a feather as I floated down beside the bed. Then
I saw my dead father. He was in a completely different place,
sunlit and landscaped. While my bedroom was dim, this place
was as bright as midday.

I know that my experience will be dismissed by many as
nothing but a dream. Such a dismissal must arise in part from

a failure to entertain the large body of evidence that such states are not dreams, and in part from fear of the implications of the soul.

Those implications are remarkable. First, there appears to me to be some part of ourselves that can live outside the body. Judging from my own movements and behavior in that state I would suggest that it must be some sort of plasma. It would seem that a being can exist in an energetic form that is in no direct way sustained by the brain/body system.

Does this mean that souls are all around us, able to see and hear everything? Dr. Ritchie reported that he saw souls tied to their sensual desires, wandering everywhere in the world. Suicides who have been resuscitated have reported following desperately those they had left behind. Dr. Ritchie himself observed that he could see the physical world clearly, but he could in no way affect it.

I had exactly the same impression.

But I also slipped into a very different reality, where I encountered my father reliving a moment that was the essence of the friction in our relationship. Can souls migrate back and forth to richer, more radiant worlds that lie in the same space as this one but bear a different connection to reality?

If this is all true, it means that we are not alone within ourselves, and that all our secrets are available for this other world to see. That we know this instinctively might be why we deny it consciously. For most of us it would be very hard to bear.

The Neoplatonist philosopher Plotinus speaks of the "light" of souls as being their primary reality. Perhaps when the visitors said that they had come here because they "saw a glow," it was not the glow of our cities that they were referring to but the glow of our souls.

In any case, I count that experience on a morning in November as another one that caused fundamental personal change. I began to try as never before to understand the wonderful mystery that had come into my life.

I thought again of the admonitions of the Virgin in her many appearances, always to pray, to seek guidance within, to give oneself to the good. And as well I contemplated the implications of my contact with the great feminine image of *Communion:* to deepen my inner search and also to take personal responsibility for the condition of my soul.

Our culture has gone about the denial of the soul with vicious eagerness. But I think it's all an illusion, a way we have of pretending to ourselves that we are not responsible and accountable for our lives.

I suspect that every instant of life literally freezes in memory, ready to play its part later in a rigorous self-examination that follows death.

The fire of hell may be kindled by seeing oneself as one really is. And heaven's balm emerges if there is reconciliation.

Of course, one can take the comfortable road and say that I am lying, that the descriptions in this book are hyperbole or hallucination. But they are not. I am telling the truth of what happened to me, and the implications are there for anybody to see. Not only are we not alone, we have a life in another form—and it is on that level of reality that the visitors are primarily present.

I call them visitors, but now I am beginning to think that is a misnomer. I have had the impression that they think of themselves as family, and perhaps that is exactly what they are.

I had the notion, standing in the perfect predawn silence, of a world balanced between the living and the dead.

Our civilization is addicted to its sins. We despoil the earth and corrupt the lives of millions of people without a qualm. We do not take responsibility for anything we do. Calumnies, lies, public character assassinations, theft, murder, and self-abuse of all kinds are routine among us. Every sin is glorified and committed until we choke ourselves with it. Because we have deluded ourselves into ignoring the reality of the soul, we imagine everything we do to be some kind of secret.

I suspect that we do not have any secrets at all. I may now understand those strange places of drama in the golden city. Under the ruthless lights the human world squirms in its folly.

Who watches us? It is a question that was once answered by the richness of mythology and faith. We have abandoned the mythology and lost the faith. The question must be addressed afresh, I suspect, if we are ever to understand our own true nature.

Should we ever do this, I suspect that we will also find the secret of the visitors.

2026 Update

This chapter begins with me doing the "sensing exercise" that we had learned when Anne and I started in the New York chapter of the Gurdjieff Foundation in 1969. Our leader, Joseph Stein, considered it part of the core of "the Work," second only to the esoteric dance practice Mr. Gurdjieff called "the Movements."

I did not know it then, and I still didn't know it in 1986 when this chapter begins, that this exercise—taught in the West, as far as I have been able to determine, only by Mr. Gurdjieff, would turn out to be the foundation of both my relationship with the visitors and with Anne after she died.

I have known since shortly after she passed that it is uniquely important, and that doing it in the early hours of the morning is particularly so. This is because, as I discussed in *Afterlife Revolution*, she communicated to me through a third party that she could perceive me when I was doing the exercise. Then I knew why the visitors had told me that they came into my life because "we saw a glow." It was the glow my body was giving off when I did the exercise. I think that my entire relationship with the nonhuman world and the nonphysical part of the human world would not exist if I hadn't been so devoted to this exercise.

Now, in 2026, the exercise permeates my life. I do it daily with friends, I do it at eleven in the evening and again in the early morning hours. I used to believe that the right hour was three, but I've learned that I will be waked up when the time is right.

I discovered, thanks to a friend, that the early morning meditation takes place during what is known as Brahma Muhurtha Time, roughly an hour and a half before sunrise. This is the time that the mind is supposed to be most quiet, and thus open to subtle influences from the outside.

In my case, the influences are hardly subtle. I have now written five books, starting with *Afterlife Revolution* using the rich exchange of ideas that I participate in during these early morning sessions. I clear my mind by taking my attention to my body. What sometimes feels like an entire committee forms, and there is give and take about what I am working on. Nothing is dictated to me. Instead, everyone in the group floats ideas and asks questions. In fact, it was during one of these sessions that the idea to create this book was born. I was working on *Reunion* and not getting much response. Then the idea of doing this floated into my mind. At first, I ignored it. I wanted to write something new. But when whoever is 'out there' wouldn't work on the new book, I thought I would take a break from it and do this—and immediately, the connection was back. My writing group was at my side again, and still is.

I don't care whether it's difficult to believe or not, because it's true. I am waked up, as I have reported in other books, in many different ways. They are physical, most of them. As time passes, when more people have understood that the visitors are real, the idea that beings who may not be part of reality in the same way that we are can still touch us physically will be more easily accepted.

It is to people who either already have this sort of experience, or are willing to seriously entertain the idea that it is real, that I am directing this chapter.

The visitors found me in the first place, in the summer of 1985 (months before they broke through into my consciousness by abducting me and roughing me the next December) because they noticed the glow that appears when the attention is used intentionally like this rather than being allowed to go wherever life happens to take it. I was alone in the countryside, living near an area that they frequent, apparently because it contains a huge seam of iron.

When they ranged the outer world at night, perhaps they noticed the little glow that appeared in the darkness when I did the meditation.

They did not first come into my life when they abducted me in January of '85, nor in the previous October when they woke up the household by shining a huge light down on us in the wee hours of the morning.

I think that they re-entered my life, after leaving it when I was 12 or 13, in the summer of 1985. We had bought our cabin the previous March. Soon after we moved up for the summer in June I began to have excruciating headaches every afternoon and to feel that there was somebody getting in the house at night. This was when I bought a shotgun and a pistol and installed an alarm system. I think that the headaches were coming because I was refusing to see what was there, and the defensive measures were an unconscious reaction to a presence I knew was there.

But why was I so resistant? Why couldn't I simply accept this presence back into my life? I was fine with it when I was a child, up until the moment when, at the age of eleven I found myself with my father and sister in a room with a gray who was attending a group of sleeping soldiers. I wasn't afraid and I explained to my father that it was all right. When he replied, "No, Whitty, it's not all right," an ice cold knife of fear went right through me, which I have been struggling with ever since.

This is not fear of the unknown or even fear of attack. As I have previously suggested, I think that it is something deeper. When our cats reacted to the nine knocks, they were experiencing this fear.

I think that it has to do with the fear that the soul, that eternal fragment, is somehow exposed to danger during contact.

When people are asked whether or not we are ready, they too often will say, "of course we are." But we are not ready and cannot be ready until we have understood the reason for this fear and know for certain whether or not it's justified. It is absolutely nothing like any normal fear that we know. What those two cats were going through that night was more than fear of death. I think it is a fear that is nameless among us. It is the fear of damage to the soul, or perhaps its capture, and we have no words for that. But I think we can name it and we must, because it is likely to emerge as a significant obstacle to mass contact.

I have been threatened often in my experience with something worse than death, that feels as if it might involve my soul, or essential and eternal self—some part of me that is greater than whom I know, anyway. Once I was shown that this essential part of consciousness was subject to confinement, and that this could last for eternity.

Was it a real threat? Is there a part of us that lasts forever? If so, can it be captured? Strange questions even to ask. Unanswerable, of course—which only intensifies the fear that accompanies the threat.

We are predators. If they are, too, then perhaps we have that in common, especially if neither is the prey of the other. On the foundation of shared instincts and needs, we can form a relationship. It is likely to be dangerous for both sides, but we can still find our way together, I feel sure. If we couldn't, how could I possibly have lived as I have with them all these years?

Admittedly, it has not been easy. They have threatened me and terrorized me many times, but never beyond my capacity to learn and grow from it. When they are being themselves, they come across as negative, hostile and ferocious. I respect that. It's when they start to do things like project images of things like beautiful goddesses into the minds of the innocent that I worry.

For example, when Jake Barber commented on Ross Coultart's show that something he perceived as a beautiful female presence had come out of a crashed UAP he was attempting to collect and possessed him, he said that he had gone beyond ontological shock and entered a state of "ontological relief."

I am familiar with this sort of thing. In my opinion, our visitors have a capability to alter emotional states at a distance, apparently using some sort of energy that affects the brain. One form generates a dopamine rush in the brain which makes the target cease to be aggressive and become passive. The lion becomes the lamb. Threat removed. Another form triggers a flood of adrenaline, which causes a rush of fear. Another involves the use of light to affect emotions. I am aware of an application of this in the summer of 2025 when the woman working with me on the creative project was abducted. When she wished that the sun would come up, the huge light that shone into her house had the effect of suppressing her fear. This would seem to also be, in effect, a weapon designed to make a target more compliant and easier to handle.

Yet another such weapon intrudes into the mind telepathically, and can also affect dreams. Memories can be altered and even false ones created. There is another—the only really dangerous one—that affects the brain physically by stripping away the myelin sheath around neurons, thus killing them. It can be used to destroy parts of the brain, and to cause death.

The first six are all control mechanisms, intended for use on people who don't present an immediate threat. The physically violent one will be used against, say, a pilot who is on combat air patrol and arms his missiles. I don't think it is too likely to be used if he just locks onto a UAP, but only if he engages in an actual, aggressive move. (I discuss this particular weapon more extensively in *Them*. I believe that Havana Syndrome is caused by application of this weapon, or one derived from it, but by whom I don't know.)

I have had both the one that generates fear and the one that intrudes into the mind telepathically used on me. The one that utilizes light to allay fear was used in May of 2025 on a friend who is working with me on a creative project. I will return to this in a moment, but first I would like to discuss the way emotions can be activated by affecting the brain.

Anne and I were walking in the wee hours of the morning when we lived in Texas when we experienced the weapon that projects fear. In those days, we would walk between two and three in the morning in the summers because it was too hot to go out earlier. On this particular night, we were coming over a hill when we saw a shadowy figure standing on the sidewalk in a little strip mall across the street. Almost before we could register his presence, we were hit by a literal wall of fear. Then we saw him, a shadowy presence.

I said to Anne, "are you feeling scared?" She replied, "Whitley, let's go another way." So we did. We got home without incident.

Talking about it, we both felt sure that he had done something to us. As Anne put it, "it felt like being hit in the face by a fear-ray." But there is no such thing. Or is there? Something that could somehow activate the amygdala, which controls the fear response, could have triggered our reaction. When we got home, we were both shaking, meaning that the hypothalamus had released adrenaline and noradrenaline from the adrenal medulla.

The experience was far from mild unease, but it should have been no more than that, and probably should have been less, probably no more than a momentary, uncommented awareness of an old man out walking in the early hours to avoid the heat.

I suspect that people directly connected to the visitors probably lived in the area, and this was one of them. Which gets me to another thing that we will experience if the visitors ever enter the public space, which is the emergence of such people into ordinary life. They are unvoiced and fluently telepathic, and most of the ones I have encountered seem to be profoundly autistic. I discussed their probable genetic issues in *The Fourth Mind*. If they do become part of public life along with the grays, we can expect that they will be provided with defensive weapons—or perhaps I should say skills—like the one Anne and I encountered.

The gray that abducted the woman who was working with us appeared with three smaller guardians, which is typical of what happens when one of the taller ones approaches. She stood in my associate's living room looking through into her bedroom. The guardians rushed back and forth nearby making gasping sounds.

When my co-worker thought to herself that she was terribly frightened and wished it was dawn, a gigantic light immediately flooded the room. As her fear inexplicably melted away, she was grabbed by the wrist and lifted toward the ceiling. She remembers moving up right through the ceiling. Her next memory is of finding herself in a heap on the floor of the bedroom, and the light of the actual dawn just coming in the windows.

In another case, a friend who was coming home from a meeting about funding for a UAP related project heard a voice in her head say, "Don't believe Whitley. Whitley is wrong." This is a type of telepathy, a projected thought, that as often as not remains subliminal. I believe that it is used extensively in social control to manage how people regard things like the close encounter experience, in order to keep them ignorant and therefore helpless, and there may be human groups who have access to the ability and/or technology involved.

Countering it will be difficult, especially if it can emerge into the mind of the victim as their own thought—a decision that they think they have made, that has actually been imposed on them from an unknown outside source.

As the visitors come close to us—if they do—we are going to need to be aware of all of these weapons and capabilities, and learn to insist that any demands they make be negotiated, and not allow them to be imposed on us. As they wouldn't be here if they didn't want something, we are not powerless. Once we understand what that is, we will have a basis for negotiation. If we are careful and clever, we are likely to find a great deal on offer—in fact, a whole new world.

Let's take it.

CHAPTER NINETEEN

DECEMBER 23, 1986

We had been in New York for a time, and returned to the country for Christmas on December 23. I spent the evening hiding in the bedroom attempting to assemble Christmas toys. We went to bed at about ten-thirty. Earlier in the evening I had seen a flash of light on the abandoned road behind our house. It was sufficiently bright to induce me to go down and investigate, thinking maybe somebody had come in with a snowmobile.

Everything was normal. At five-fifteen I had been talking on the phone when I saw what looked like a very bright star move across the sky outside the window. It was too slow to be a meteor, and seemingly too bright and close to be a plane.

We went to bed that night quite normally. At 3:30 A.M. by the clock I woke up and went to the bathroom. When I lay back down in the bed a strange thing began to happen. I began to feel a tingling, pulsating energy running up and down my body. I shuddered. Then I had the feeling that somebody had just come into the room, somebody moving with graceful, quick strides.

A feeling came over me of being watched. It was so strong that it fascinated me. I'd felt it once or twice before. I would characterize it as a sensation of having another consciousness inside my mind. It was like being watched from the inside.

An instant later I must have blacked out, because the next thing I knew somebody was slapping me on the shoulder.

I woke up and saw one of the visitors beside the bed. Under normal circumstances it is easy to see in the dark in our bedroom because the burglar alarm is lit by a number of bright diodes and functions as a night-light.

At first I could hardly bear to look. I wanted it to be an ordinary person there. But my sense of recognition was so strong that I feel it must have been the one I remembered from December 26, 1985. She still seemed feminine, even though I was now aware that I couldn't possibly tell the sex, if there was any, of someone so differently constructed.

Then she darted her head toward me with the jerking suddenness of an insect. I was just plain horrified. But her other motions, gracefully gesturing at me to get up, made me want to touch her, to cherish her.

Even so, there was a tremendously powerful feeling of what I can only describe as pure menace coming from her. Could it be that they are also afraid? Is coming into contact with us frightening to them?

Were we *both* frightened, she and I?

I had been waiting a year for this moment. I was fully prepared—or so I thought. On the bedside table there was a totally automatic camera fully loaded with film. Even though my body felt distinctly strange, I was able to sit up quite normally. I reached toward the camera.

I then saw my hands move away from it, entirely on their own! I didn't move them. I had nothing to do with it. Their motion was completely normal. However, it did not originate in my mind. I was telling my hands to pick up the camera. They were moving elsewhere without my participation.

Next I found myself standing up. I loomed over the visitor, but not as much as I'd imagined I would. She was actually about five feet tall, not nearly as short as I'd thought.

Seeing her move in her smooth and then sudden manner, I could hardly believe that she was not some sort of a machine. But she was also totally alive. There was consciousness there, all right. I knew it well. She was now radiating what I can only describe as sardonic humor.

She was clearly visible to me. As I had not activated it, the lights on our burglar alarm were all shining green instead of red. And there was a light on in the bathroom downstairs as well as I could see clearly. Why hadn't I turned on the burglar alarm? I'd completely forgotten, which I suspect was their doing.

She went around behind me. Suddenly I found myself moving toward the bedroom door. I made a grab for a tape recorder that was on the desk near my bed, but I missed that as well.

If I walked, everything was normal. But if I stopped, I began to float along. I could feel her pushing me from behind, her hands against my buttocks. In addition to pressure, her touch produced a mild sort of electrical tingling in my body.

I had no control at all over my direction. I was not moving, I was being moved.

In view of the fact that I had been prevented from taking the camera and tape recorder, I was really desperate for something that would test the reality of this experience. As before, it *seemed* like something that was happening in the physical world. But, if so, why was I doing this dreamlike floating whenever I stopped trying to walk? My body appeared to be functioning normally. I could see and hear. I could feel myself moving. I was passing through a normal and completely real version of my own house.

As a matter of fact, I was now passing behind the living-room couch. We had brought the cats up during Christmas vacation because it was too cold for them to beg to go outside, where they would be threatened by dogs or coons. The Burmese cat, Sadie, was on the back of the couch, crouching as if ready to jump and run.

I grabbed her and took her with me. My reasoning was that I knew how she looked and acted, and if she continued to appear normal I could assume that my other perceptions weren't being distorted either.

We approached the door to the deck, which was standing open.

The visitor paused and we both stopped. I turned around and saw that she was working back the little washer that keeps the screen door from closing automatically.

She carefully pushed it closed.

We moved again, and this time I entered a profoundly different situation. No longer could I see normally. There was a glittering blackness before me. I could still feel Sadie in my arms, and I was very glad for her companionship.

The next thing I knew I was standing in a room. It was an ordinary room. I was in front of a big, plainly designed desk. Behind it was a wall of bookcases stacked with books. There was a volume of Bruce Catton's work on the Civil War, a biography of Madame de Stael, a number of vaguely familiar novels of forties and fifties vintage, a volume of Kafka, some books on mathematics, and, pulled partway out of a shelf as if to draw attention to it, Thomas Wolfe's *You Can't Go Home Again*.

In this room with me were four other beings. The visitor who had come to get me was standing behind me. Sitting behind the desk was what looked to me like a man with a very, very long face, round, black eyes, and a ridiculous excuse for a curly black toupee on his head. He was wearing a green plaid flannel shirt and leaning so far back in his chair that I could see he had on baggy khaki pants and a wide belt. He looked like something from another world wearing the clothes of the forties.

Standing to my left was a tall man in a tan jumpsuit with many pockets and flaps on it. He was very blond and had a rather flat face. He was easily six feet six and might have been taller. Behind him was an ordinary wooden door. I got the impression that it was not intended that I go through that door. I do not wish to suggest that there was anything menacing about this man. On the contrary, when our eyes met his expression was gentle and touching and full of pity. He reminded me of a son looking with forlorn love at his senile parent. I have since had other encounters with similar tall, fair beings.

Immediately to my right there was a woman. She appeared to be entirely normal, about five feet five, and she was wearing a blue jumpsuit under a white body-length apron. She had a small black case in her left hand. Her hair was brown and pulled back into a bun behind her head. I was no more than a foot from her. When I turned to her we were face-to-face. I looked directly into her eyes and saw there concern, a little pity, and considerable wariness. I was also aware of the presence of what it seems best to describe as an acute sense of attention or concentration. Something about this young woman communicated a startling consciousness. She had fair skin and regular features. Overall, she was conventionally pleasant-looking. I could easily recognize her today if I saw her in the street.

The being behind me thrust a stool under me and I sat down rather abruptly.

The one at the desk asked, speaking in normal English, "Why did you bring the cat?"

Sadie, in my arms, was looking around. Her eyes were wide.

"I'm reality-testing," I replied.

There followed a scene of the most frank and total confusion that I have ever witnessed. They literally looked at each other as if I were completely crazy. At this point I noticed a change in the ambience of the room. It was like a sort of mental pressure being exerted on me. It became very powerful. It seemed to be something that would compel me to speak the truth. I suddenly felt a need to *really* explain that cat!

"I've made the cats a part of the family," I heard myself saying. It felt like this was a deep, deep truth. "They have to be taken when we're taken. They have to participate in the life of the family. It's their right."

The one behind the desk glared at me. "We'll have to put the cat to sleep."

Now I felt a sense of being a co-conspirator, and I was aware that I had felt this way with the visitors before, but I had no idea when this might have been. I replied, "We can't do that. It's my son's cat. How will I explain it to him?"

There was a short silence. Finally the one behind the desk said, "No, put to sleep for now."

At that the young woman beside me stepped forward, removing from her case a small object made of what looked like two triangular pieces of brass with rounded edges. She placed a flat side of this against Sadie's thigh and the cat at once sank into unconsciousness. Her breast heaved twice and then she was more than asleep, she was as still as death.

I understood perfectly well that they could bring her back to life. At that moment I remembered having seen this done to people many dozens of times.

The one who seemed to be doing all the talking asked me, "What can we do to help you?"

The sensation of my mind being under pressure got stronger. It was as if I had been entered by an overwhelmingly powerful force that would not allow me to say anything except the absolute, deepest truth. It felt like an actual, physical pressure, as if some disembodied awareness had gone inside me and there acquired mass, form, and force.

I could have asked for some physical proof of the visitors' existence. I could have asked them to enter my world with me instead of hanging back in this half-reality. But I did not care about those things, not down deep. At the deepest level of myself I knew at that moment exactly what I wanted and needed. If a coherent and useful relationship was ever to develop between me and the visitors, I had to reduce my fear.

I replied, "You could help me fear you less."

There was a long, silent moment. Then an answer seemed to emerge from all of them. "We will try, but it will be very hard,"

After that the young woman stepped behind me and applied her little brass device to my neck for a moment. The next morning there was a small raised knot with a red spot where she had touched me. The next thing I knew I was being taken by the being who had come to get me in the first place to a small, dark room. As she maneuvered me along, again pushing me from behind, I could sense that she took an almost proprietary interest in me. I'd had the feeling earlier that she was rather pleased about something.

I'd glimpsed a sort of crooked smile on her face as I sat down in the chair.

She suddenly seemed little and vulnerable and old and I felt a cherishing feeling toward her. No longer did she seem all-powerful. I could imagine carrying her in my arms.

From behind me there was what I can only describe as a sardonic snort full of power and derision. I was with a proud old warrior.

I recalled that Robert Monroe had said in his book that one could ask spirits for things. One could demand that only what was most needed be given. One could insist that no harm be done.

My mind went back to the extraordinary dream I'd had a few weeks before, of the beautiful star approaching the strange, mystic sea.

At that moment we arrived back at the house and I had a glimpse of it twirling around below me, looking like a toy in the night, and then we were suddenly on the deck, the two of us and Sadie in my arms.

Something happened to me at that point, but all I can remember is a jumble of disconnected images.

I have thought that my difficulty in determining where we went might have had to do with the fact that I was not taken to some craft in the sky or a hidden base of some kind, but to a perfectly ordinary building, a place I could have returned had I known where it was.

Then we went back into the house. I still had Sadie. We went into my son's room, where he was sleeping normally. The other cat, Coe, went scrabbling wildly away, making a strange noise. I thought he would wake my son, but he didn't. Then I put Sadie in the bed. She was as limp as a sodden leaf.

I realized that I had only a few more moments with the visitor. Again my dream came to mind. I asked, mentally, to be taken to the place where I had seen that star.

The answer was another burst of sardonic contempt.

The next thing I knew I was being pushed somewhere. I ended up in a strange wooden room. I couldn't understand it. Was this the place where I had seen the star? I saw a bed with a very vulnerable-looking woman asleep on it. I thought to myself, *How can that woman sleep when these people are here?*

Then I was absolutely thunderstruck to realize that I knew the woman. It was Anne, and the room was familiar too. It was our bedroom.

All sense of otherness then left my body. I felt perfectly normal. I turned around and saw the visitor standing in the doorway. When I took a step toward her, she did something that made me no longer want to walk toward her. Was it a gesture, a sound, a mental image? I cannot remember.

Then she turned and stepped into the shadows beyond the door. I felt extraordinarily tired—a sensation that I was expecting from the previous experiences.

For a moment or two I fought it, but there was no hope. I collapsed onto the bed. I managed to shake Anne and tell her, "I was just with the visitors." She murmured concern for our son. I said he was fine. As I was dozing off I heard people moving noisily around in the house. A low voice may have laughed softly. That was the last thing I remembered until morning.

The moment I woke up I went to check Sadie, for fear that she might actually be dead. I did not want our son to wake up and find her like that.

She was sleeping on the pillow beside his head, curled up in a ball. She remained like that until after supper. When she woke up she drank an enormous amount of water. Until the next morning she seemed to have a stiff thigh where the brass object had been applied, but I couldn't find a mark. A month later when we were back in the city, people were still noticing that she was not herself. She would sit staring for hours and she appeared uneasy. I would work all day with her sitting in my lap. A friend, Canadian filmmaker David Cherniack, commented five weeks after the incident that she seemed like "a shocked cat." Eventually she got over it and has returned to her usual open, curious self. But I will never take her with me again, because it was obviously very hard on her.

When he got up that morning, our son was full of questions about the visitors. I was unaware of anything happening to him during the night, but Anne's sleepy question made me wonder if she was not subliminally aware that he had also been involved.

We never discuss them with him unless he brings them up, and it was unusual for him to do so. He complained about them, saying, "They're strict with me." He never volunteered what was meant by that, and we didn't ask him. I did ask him if he thought the visitors were real. "They can be," he said, and went on eating his breakfast. I thought that was a healthy response and took it no further.

2026 Update

This chapter begins with a description of something that I hardly understood at the time, but is now the center of my life and, as I have come to believe, will be an important, even crucial, aspect of any relationship we may develop with the visitors. These few words were the beginning of the rest of my life: "I would characterize it as a sensation of having anoth-er consciousness inside my mind. It was like being watched from the inside." When I wrote them, I had no idea that I was talking about is what I now understand as the "Communion experience."

It is not possession. In fact, very much the opposite. If my experience is any example, they are not here to control us, but rather to share our experience of life.

I also note another reference here to the "vibrations" that take place when they touch you. Other people at the cabin also noticed this when touched by them. They are often as-sociated with altered states of various kinds across a broad range of literature.

Some associate them with kundalini energy and I know of one incident where a person who had levitated in front of a group of six people including a psychiatrist and a priest, emit-ted them when she was gently pushed back down into the chair in which she had been sitting by one of the assistants present.

We don't know what they are, but I think that we should make an effort to learn more. The reasons nobody is likely to do that are two: first, they are not part of our current under-standing of reality; second, they cannot be replicated on de-mand.

These two issues, taken together, mean that they cannot be successfully addressed and measured by our current sci-entific method.

Personally, I theorize that such sensations are a form of conscious energy, and given that our visitors seem able to materialize and dematerialize at will, I think that, in their non-physical form they may actually *be* this energy. As, indeed, would be our own dead. Borders between species may not even exist at this level, only different memories that have emerged out of different physical configurations. A gray's perceptual system is going to create different memories than ours, which may be the only real difference between us at the nonphysical level.

The experience that I described of going to the house and taking Sadie with me would normally have been one that I would doubt. Even the next morning, I would have suspected that it had been some sort of dream. But there was one thing that made me sure that it had happened, which was that Sadie had drunk so much water the next morning. I still remember her standing over the bowl in the kitchen lapping and lapping. Anne also noticed how unusual it was.

Thirst is part of the syndrome that develops after acute radiation poisoning, but it isn't generally associated with milder forms, and Sadie didn't exhibit any other symptoms. It can also be a stress response, and given that Sadie continued to be in a very uneasy state for the next few weeks, I think that this was the cause.

It means that, whatever it actually was that happened, it was definitely a real event and one that she found extremely difficult to experience. This gets me back to the night of the nine knocks, and the obvious stress that the cats endured then, much more intense and raw than my own.

I believe that what my dear cats have left us is a warning, and it's serious. There is something about the visitors that animals sense and we do not. They have no intellectual filters and cannot be under any illusions because their minds are not complex enough to do things like cushion fear with hope. They can react to what's in front of them, and that's it.

Unlike us, they can never see the visitors through the eyes of illusion. No gods, no angels, no demons. They can see only what is there.

As the visitors draw closer to us, as best we can, we must try to see what is actually there. No beautiful ladies possessing us and curing our shock, no gods, no saints, no demons, none of that. Rather, we must try to see them more as they probably are: scared, far from home, needy and in possession of powers of mind and technology that can enable them to disguise themselves as all sorts of things that they are not.

I now understand more about who was in that house. The tall, pale man was what is known as a "tall white." I would meet two of these people again, and be introduced, at my request, to one of their children. This was done by a Defense Department specialist whom I knew somewhat and a gray who I assume worked with him.

I described this event in the original text of *Transformation*, and it is in the early editions, but it has since disappeared from the text. It is not present, for example, in the Kindle edition that was available from Crossroads Press: However, the story does appear in the manuscript of the book:

"Another month or so passed, and I found myself in the baggage claim area at Stapleton Airport in Denver. Suddenly three people walked in front of me. One was a heavily disguised gray wearing a shabby dress. The other was a man I had met before, whom I believe was a US government operator who 'interfaced' with aliens. The third person was a startlingly large little boy. He had a child's face, but the deep-set eyes of the "nordics," and he was well over five feet tall. They were all carrying cheap golf gear. The boy and the disguised gray proceeded to play patty-cake. In seconds, a loud, rapid-fire clapping filled the air and their hands started going so fast you could hardly see them. And, understand, this was in a public place. There were people all around us. And they reacted. A crowd formed, watching this amazing display. People started clapping."

Looking back from 2026, I recall the incident vividly.

I don't want to trample through sensitive territory willy-nilly, but I think this suggests that the connection between some element of the DoD and non-human entities may be more extensive than anyone on the outside has yet realized. So far, none of the whistleblowers I have seen testifying before congress seem to have an inkling of this level of contact, but I am quite certain of my ground here. I would argue that it suggests that there could be a direct interface between individuals in the U.S. Defense Department and the visitors.

Despite the sense of threat and the disturbing feeling of invasion that contact may bring, I am living proof that, after an intense, years-long period of acclimatization, living in intimate contact can be fruitful. For example, on a recent morning at 4:35 I awakened to what I think was a work of art. It was hanging in my window where the hieroglyphs often appear. I saw it as an image of a gray made of thousands of what appeared to be tiny glyphs, each one no bigger than a dot, which overall formed the face. It radiated a shocking sense of presence. I knew I was looking at a portrait, but it seemed to exude the actual, living presence of the individual it represented. It was quite wonderful to see, the sort of thing that satisfies the eye like a great Rembrandt does or a dancing, joyous Picasso.

It was the second piece of art I have seen from them. The first was a week before, and it consisted of elegant, curving geometries that seemed to convey a taste of the personality of the artist. It was beautiful in the same graceful and precise way that crop circles are beautiful.

For all the dangers contact threatens, it also promises enrichment. What if our artists could learn the techniques that resulted in the images I have been seeing? It would be the next step in the evolution of art, more important, I would think, even than Brunelleschi's discovery of perspective in the 14th Century, or the new ways of capturing light that came to the impressionists.

What will emerge with the visitors into the public space—if they do emerge—will be at once a deeper threat than we have ever known and the promise of a new renaissance.

I have already made my choice. I've been through many dangers and toils and snares. But I have also found grace in my life with them, and I have made a choice that they cannot deny me: I have chosen that grace.

CHAPTER TWENTY

THE RAZOR'S EDGE

The visitors almost immediately set about making good on their promise to help me deal with my fear of them. They did not do this by giving me a reassuring pat on the back. Rather, they created conditions that would force me to have a direct taste of my fear so that I could see it and know it. What I did with this knowledge they left up to me.

Unless they are simply by nature terrifying to us, it must have taken a lot of determination to do what was done, so much so that there must have been love behind it.

On December 27 and 28, Anne and I saw a number of magnificent owls around the house during daylight hours. I observed a great gray owl and we both saw another owl, but it flew away too quickly for us to identify it.

At that time I was already aware of the association of owls as an apparent screen memory for the visitors. But these owls were not screen memories. They were simply ordinary owls, though their presence during daylight hours was unusual.

On the morning of December 29 our closest neighbors called to say that a beautiful owl had just flown off into the woods toward our place. We looked out and saw it in a tree a few feet from the window. I was astonished; it looked to me like a hawk owl, which would be a very unusual sighting in our area. My neighbor thought that it was a great gray.

It left the tree and attacked what I assumed was a field mouse on the ground and began to feed. Again, this was a classic hawk-owl feeding pattern. At that moment I could not help but think of how apt the image was of the silent, all-seeing creature of the night swooping down upon the helpless surface dweller to feed off his blood and bones.

Observing nature, one soon learns that there is much to the prey-predator relationship that we have forgotten. There are levels of love that we barely touch in our lives. When one observes the whole violence of the attack, the high drama of the death, the strangely humdrum quality of feeding, one sees that there is a deep mystery there, a wild, urgent love that seems to contain the whole relationship.

And one wonders how the survivors feel—the moose that has defeated the wolves, the mouse that has reached the bracken before the owl's talons could rend him. Because they threaten life, the wolf and the owl also reveal its sweetness.

I thought to myself that a relationship with the visitors could be dangerous and sweet at the same time.

Later that day we were driving through a nearby town when a voice told me to stop at the house of a friend, glass artist Gilda Strutz. Another car, driven by a tall and imposing bearded man of about thirty, pulled up at the same time. We all went in to see Gilda together. The man turned out to be another friend of hers, Barry Maddock. *Communion* hadn't been published and neither of them knew anything at all about it.

We chatted for a while and I soon found myself talking about the owls we had been seeing.

Barry was surprised to hear this because he had had a very unusual dream about an owl the night before. He proceeded to describe what sounded to me like a screen memory for a visitor experience. He had been asleep in a house where he was housesitting until the new owners moved in. Suddenly he was awakened by what sounded like somebody kicking a baseboard heater. He got up because the house was new and he'd helped build it. He knew that the heating system shouldn't be doing that.

He walked into the living room. The first thing he saw was a pair of huge, dark eyes. When he later saw the cover of *Communion* he was amazed by the similarity. At the time, he had the bizarre impression that an enormous gray owl with big, black eyes was in the room. The owl took him into a large, vaulted chamber that reminded him of the Sydney Opera House. There it turned into a bird of paradise.

He remembered sitting beside a small man who seemed to him like a gnome or a gremlin. His impression was that this man was good-natured. He didn't remember anything about the man's appearance, except that he was "dark."

The next morning Barry had what he said was an extremely strange feeling. He seemed "loose" in his body. He was also suffering from "missing time" in that he could remember getting up and going into the living room, then having the vivid dream. The trouble was, he could not recall going back to bed before he had the dream. The sort of confusion that Barry described fitted very well with my own initial conscious reactions to the visitors. He also noticed a small raised mark on his neck. He didn't think to mention it at the time, and I didn't see it, but his description, given later, suggested that it was similar to the one I had found on my own neck on the morning of December 24.

The dream had frightened him badly.

I resolved to get to know him better to find out if anything more would emerge from his mind. On the morning of December 30 we went hiking together deep into the woods and we talked. He turned out to be one of the most fearless people I had ever met. He was well traveled and had had some remarkable confrontations in his life. He'd been stalked by a jaguar at night in the jungles of Central America—and could tell that as an "interesting" story!

The more he spoke about his dream, however, the more he revealed deep fear. It seemed to me that he was aching to say he thought the dream was real, but dared not do so because of its content.

I found that the house at which he was sitting was quite near my own place. It belonged to a couple that was just moving in. I introduced myself to them a few weeks later, and it turned out that the woman had seen a strange light outside the kitchen window a couple of nights before I arrived. She was quite curious about it because she did not understand what it could have been. The house is on a bluff and the kitchen window is a considerable distance from the ground.

In January 1988—a year later—I discovered by chance that a local resident had seen a huge lighted object hanging a few hundred feet above a road about two miles from our houses. This sighting took place at approximately five o'clock on the morning of January 1, 1987. It was not on the exact night that I'd had my experience or Barry his dream, but it suggested a presence during that same week. Similarly, I have received a letter from a *Communion* reader saying that he and his family saw a huge object over their town on the night of December 26, 1985, when I had my first consciously remembered visitor experience. What my correspondent did not know was that his town was only a few miles from my house. Another correspondent wrote of a series of dreams of a female being who spoke to him of an "age of sisterhood" long ago and looked very much like the being on the cover of *Communion*. His dreams, which he had in the 1970s, took place on a very specific road. Unknown to him, it is the road to my house from his town.

But Barry's case was special to me, because he seemed to have experienced some sort of face-to-face interaction that could be connected to my situation.

To me, the lesson of his encounter was clear. If as fearless a man as Barry could be afraid over a dream that appeared connected to the visitors, then I could accept my own fear. I did not need to think of it as a weakness. The content of Barry's dream suggested that the visitors might be revealing, in the transformation from a predatory owl into a bird of paradise, an aspect of their nature that I had suspected but had been unable to prove to myself.

It was a valuable lesson, but it would take me nearly a year to assimilate it. I was more interested then in quelling my fear. It had not yet occurred to me to simply accept it for what it was, a very natural reaction to the unknown.

The events of the past few days, starting with the incredible experience of December 23, had caused all the fear I had stifled to come back, and to get even worse.

My memory of the night of December 23 was vivid. It was totally real. Those people had *been* there. That being with those huge eyes and that fearsome and sardonic attitude had touched me, controlled me, taken me through the night. My relationship with the visitors was now more than close. It was intimate.

I kept thinking that they were going to lash out at me, kill me, steal me, do something to my family. This wasn't rational.

It was because they seemed so furious and had so much control.

Facing the woods became hard again—even harder than before.

I tried unsuccessfully on the night of January 2. The following night I tried again. I was desperate with fear. When I went outside there was such an atmosphere of menace that I almost couldn't bear it. I took a few steps but found that the darkness was profound. Then I noticed that the lights in the house seemed unnaturally bright, almost as if the air were somehow darker than it should be. But there was no fog, no smoke. Light just didn't work as well as it should.

In all the times I had taken this walk before, things had never looked like this. The woods were as dark as a cave. I went back inside, deciding that I must be spooking myself.

The visitors had said that they would "help me" work with my fear. Had what happened to Barry been induced by the visitors in such a way that it impacted me as well? Had they somehow drawn all those owls to my place, thus ensuring that Barry and I would start talking about them when we met?

Or was I so frightened that I was beginning to invent connections where none existed? I did not think so, any more than I thought that what had happened to Jo Sharp was a coincidence. Calling these events accidents was just another way of denying the fact that there was a controlling intelligence behind them—powerful, incredibly observant, and concerned with the fate of human beings.

On the night of January 3 I challenged the woods again.

As I left the house I made sure that the door that opens onto the deck was unlocked. Anne had gone up to have her shower and I didn't want to be locked out. I crossed the deck and headed for the woods, determined this time to walk no matter what happened.

What happened was that I heard the most terrible howling that I have ever heard in my life come out of the woods. I know a good deal about North American birds and mammals, and there isn't anything that can howl like that. I'm not even sure that a human being could produce such a sound.

It rose up like the shriek of a banshee, hideously savage. It echoed amid the trees ... and it began moving. Whatever was doing that was coming swiftly closer—*above* the woods.

Then it stopped. I thought it must be an owl. *Must* be. But every dog up and down the valley was absolutely screaming with terror. The desperate, wailing barks filled the air. And then the howling came back, this time farther down in the woods.

There was no way on earth I was going to take my walk.

Later, I researched bird sounds very thoroughly, and I satisfied myself that the terrible noise I had heard was no common thing.

Right there on the spot I started going blind. It got darker and darker and darker. I looked down and could not see my own feet. Frantically I turned toward the house. The howling started up again, rapidly coming closer. In the distance the dogs were now beside themselves.

Paradoxically, the lights in the house seemed a thousand times brighter than normal. And I saw, in one of the windows, a visitor. It was standing there in the full light staring at me. But before I could get more than a glimpse, it jumped out of sight.

The howling had come down out of the sky and was now moving toward me on the path. I found myself with the howling behind me in the woods and the visitors in my house with my wife and son. And I was three-quarters blind.

I stumbled across the deck and pulled at the door. To my horror it was locked!

Then I heard the shower start. I pounded on the door but Anne couldn't hear me. I wanted to give up, to sink down and just scream, but I couldn't do that. My little boy was in there and he might wake up and he mustn't see his dad like this.

I ran around the house and found the basement door open. I rushed in, took the stairs three at a time—only to discover that the door at the top of the stairs had been locked as well.

There was no doubt at all in my mind now. The visitors were inside the house with my family and they had locked me out with the howling.

I thought about running to a neighbor's house, but I was afraid that there wouldn't be enough time and I was still having trouble seeing. Terrible fears raced through me: They were predators and they were going to eat our souls; they were demons and they were going to drag me off to hell; they were vicious aliens and they were going to steal us all for some kind of experiment; they were crazy and to amuse themselves they had unleashed some kind of preternatural monster in my woods.

I went to the side of the house. I could hear the shower running in the upstairs bathroom. I had an idea. I would throw stones at the window. Anne would hear and let me in and at least we'd be together.

I threw a couple of stones and they hit the wall. I heard Anne say, "All right, very funny." I threw one at the window and the next thing I knew she was screaming too. "God help me," she cried. "Whitley, please come home! Whitley!"

"I'm here," I shouted. "I'm here."

Finally she heard me. She put a towel around her and came down and let me in and we hugged each other. It was over. The howling was gone. I could see again. The night was normal.

It developed that she'd thought I was knocking on the door when I was throwing the stones against the wall. When they started hitting the window she thought the visitors were coming in and she panicked. "I felt them all around me while I was in the shower," she said. "It was like they were right there."

I then told her that I had seen one of them in the house. For the first time, Anne that night acknowledged that she was afraid of the visitors. And now that she had touched her fear it was less. The next day our son said to me, "Guess what. I'm not scared of the visitors anymore, at least not much." He had no memory of the disturbances we had experienced.

The next night I challenged the woods again.

I really had to sweat blood to get myself to go out there. It was like walking into the enormous, dark body of some dire phantom.

As I went down the path, deeper and deeper into the darkness, I remembered the howling. A predator, something that would tear my soul out of my body and steal it away. I felt small and alone.

I realized at that moment that I could not bear to go on like this. I could not live with this fear, and I did not know how to live without it unless I lied to myself and arbitrarily decided on my own to believe that the visitors were benevolent.

I absolutely refused to, in effect, make them my religion. Instead I just kept walking, not knowing what I was moving toward. I was crying, I couldn't help it.

Then I found that there was something else in me, something besides the fear. It was not a false belief. Rather it was acceptance, the same kind of acceptance I had felt on that airplane when I thought it was crashing.

I could balance my feelings. On the one hand was the desperate fear of a man alone in the dark with an unknown menace. On the other hand was this enormous, silent, and beautiful thing, the peace that lives deep within.

I held my peace in one hand, my fear in the other. Believing in nothing but the strength of my own two hands, I walked out of the woods into the silent, frozen meadow.

The ancient light of the stars was shining on every icy limb and strand of grass.

I looked around me. I had entered a garden of snows. I raised my face to the radiant abyss.

I remained there, balancing between the light and the dark. Slow shadows approached, hung like smoke at the edge of my vision.

My fear came crackling up in me, a thing of bones. Beside it there was the acceptance: I was me, I was here, I was not going to run.

The shadows started to move closer. I took deep, calm breaths, preparing myself as best I could. Then some deer walked out into the starlight, four does behind a fine young buck. He stopped and turned toward me, his antlers glittering with frost.

Eye to eye we regarded one another. The moment extended, deepened. We were impossibly close, each of us as still as the laden trees. He seemed like a friend, a fellow sufferer of sorts, this wary, nervous creature.

Then, with a soft snort and a flick of his tail, the buck led his family past me, to a sapling whose bark they had been eating before my approach had disturbed the ordinary course of their night.

2026 Update

This chapter is a prime example of just how careful the visitors are to make sure that our independence is preserved as they draw closer to us.

If they had wished to, they could have come to me directly and reassured me. That would have worked, certainly, but it also would have deprived me of a level of autonomy. When I wrote *Transformation*, I did not understand how important that was to them. Since then, I have seen by how extensively their actions both toward me, toward others and toward the society as a whole are intended to preserve our free will. This is an absolute core motive.

You don't preserve anybody's autonomy by stifling their fears under a blanket of kindness. Because it disdains the value of their free will, it is an act of indifference, even contempt. But if you create situations in which they are forced to face their fear of you, two things happen. First, their independence is preserved. Second, they get a chance to explore their own deepest selves, and come away from it not with their fears suppressed, but rather with them understood.

They were willing to risk me turning against them, jumping in the car, selling the cabin and washing my hands of the whole affair—that is to say, to risk the whole relationship rather than compromise my free will.

I did not understand how important this was to them, so when I realized that I could not overcome my fear, I asked them to help me. I assumed that I would be given reassurances. But, as you have seen, the results were the exact opposite. I still remember that howling in the woods as being among the most terrifying things I have ever known. Looking back, I cannot imagine how I continued to go out there.

They frequently touch the edges of my life. But never forget that when I say a word like "they," I do not know, even yet, exactly who they are. One of the things that is slowing down real contact is our tendency to decide that things un-proven are facts. When we are left with a void, we want to fill it, and if we do not have good information, we will fill it with bad. Thus you can find all sorts of speculation about non-human intelligence in books and online, all based on assumptions but presented as fact.

I do not have direct physical contact with them like I might with another person, but it is very close to that, and it takes place both day and night. Because of the way it intensified after Anne passed, and so clearly involves her, I am more certain than ever that our own dead are part of the overall phenomenon. Stripping away all the theories and assumptions, I think what we are actually in the process of discovering is the fact that reality extends beyond the limits of what we think of as the physical, and consciousness does, too. After all, the limits of the physical have been expanding steadily for generations. We have gone from thinking that all celestial objects revolved around our planet to understanding that planets are more numerous in the universe than grains of sand are on Earth.

It is this reality that dips into my life and touches me and communicates with me, and that I once feared so greatly, but now simply accept as part of my daily experience.

I am not going to go into detail about what happens, not because I want to hide anything but rather because I don't know how to describe it in such a way that it would make sense to another person. Suffice to say that the physical part unfolds extremely quickly but also richly, in the sense that a great deal of information might be exchanged during the brief moments of companionship that are involved.

In spite of this, it doesn't take much to evoke the old fear. In October of 2024, when I was challenged by some friends who were with me at the old cabin to go back into the woods by myself, I found it extremely hard. Just a few minutes before, a group of us had been walking in the same woods when one of the little gray people swept past us. I saw the slight shaking of the brush as it dashed along. Others glimpsed it, and one or two saw it more clearly.

So the challenge to go back out there alone was quite serious for me. In the days prior, I had found myself imagining what it would be like to get lost in the tunnels I believe they have carved in the seam of iron that runs under the ridge behind the house. In this fantasy—if that's what it is—I find myself entering the maze of narrow tunnels from an opening I have stumbled upon by accident. I have not gone six inches before I am hopelessly lost. I can't understand the topography of the place. Its twists and turns make no sense to me. I am lost.

Finally, they come and get me out.

Given the struggle I have had to separate memory from imagination, I can't tell which this is. But it certainly made it harder for me to go back into the woods alone—as, I am sure, it was meant to.

The lesson from all this is clear: we are not necessarily expected to overcome our fear, and there are compelling reasons why they do not wish to help us do that. Instead, they stand ready to help us learn to live with it.

I would like to return briefly to the discussion of the woman who is working with me on a writing project and found herself abducted. When she felt afraid, she was calmed down by a huge light. It is also true that the being who was confronting her was afraid.

The night before the incident, she had heard someone shuffling around on her roof. From the description, I felt that it was probably the visitors, some of whom are short and stocky and kind of scrape along when they walk.

She had called me and I had gone over to her house. I could see that, even though it was in the city, its isolated location and wide view made it an ideal spot for the visitors to make contact.

On the second night, when the taller one came close to her, they were accompanied, as was often true at our cabin, by what seem to have been guards. There were three of them. While the taller one peered through the curtains that separated the bedroom from the living room, the three short ones rushed back and forth in the living room making the sound that I have heard many times. It is a mix between a snort and a gasp and it conveys an equal mixture of fear and menace. It is unmistakably the sound of somebody who is agitated and afraid and ready for a fight.

There are three things revealed by this event. First, they feel vulnerable around us. Second, their fear response is similar to our own.

Their unusual abilities, such as the use of telepathy, the ability to levitate at least a short distance above the ground, and, most remarkably, the ability to move through solid objects such as walls and to take us with them if they wish, mark them as either having evolved differently from us or being in possession of extraordinary technologies or, which I think is probably the case, having a mixture of both. Add to that the different brain structures and sensory organs that I discussed in *The Fourth Mind*, and the challenge is obvious: both sides have to find ways of engaging with each other, not by suppressing our mutual fear, but by understanding that we are going to have to live with it.

When I was originally writing this book, I was trying to control my fear. I did not understand that this cannot work, not for either side, not yet.

The reason is that we don't know each other well enough. They are unable to tell when we might lash out; we don't understand what they want with us. I remember how hard I found it in December of '86 when I woke up in their ship or wherever I was. I recall their automatic voice repeating again and again "what can we do to help you stop screaming."

I was trapped in a small room with beings who had a menacing appearance. I did not know what they were or where I was. I could not move a muscle—and then they began an intimate invasion of my body with frightening looking instruments.

There was another level of effort to calm me: they showed me the instruments before they put them to use. So they were making two different efforts—generating a voice that would reach my mind and showing me what they were doing.

These are not the actions of somebody who doesn't care about the feelings of their subject. They are the actions of somebody who does understand that the subject is terrified and would like to calm them down, but does not understand them well enough to succeed in doing that.

Given that I am hardly the only person who has had experiences like this with them, I think it is reasonable to conclude that at least some of the ones who did the abductions did not know us all that well and therefore had not been here for a particularly long time, or if here for a longer time, had not had much contact with us.

Official disclosure is one thing. Whether it happens or not, it will not necessarily be accompanied by the appearance of our visitors. If that happens, it will be because enough of us have understood how to respond, not with a kneel, but with an independent curiosity that seeks to understand more, and know more, and is willing to try to make this relationship happen, fear or no fear.

There—right there in our minds and hearts and their minds and hearts—is the beginning. Two brilliant species, each terrified of the other, but willing to try to build a relationship anyway.

CHAPTER TWENTY-ONE

THE VISITORS EMERGE

Absolutely incredible things began to happen after I published *Communion*. The first of these took place in late January 1987 in a bookstore on Manhattan's Upper East Side. Morrow senior editor Bruce Lee and his wife walked into this store on a cold, windy Saturday afternoon. Mr. Lee showed his wife the display for my book, which was facing toward the front of the shop in the fifth or sixth rack behind the store's entrance. They commented on the good display and separated, moving to different parts of the store. Mr. Lee was reading the flap copy of a book of fiction when he noticed two people enter the store and move without hesitation directly to the display of *Communion*. He was fascinated. The book had barely appeared in the stores and this couple went right to it, which suggested that people were beginning to hear about the book very early in its career.

Mr. Lee moved closer to the couple. They were both short, perhaps five feet tall, and were wearing scarves pulled up to cover their chins, large dark glasses, and winter hats pulled low over their foreheads. They were paging through the book and making such comments as, "Oh, he's got that wrong!" and, "It wasn't like that." There was gentleness and humor in their demeanor—at least for the moment. Mr. Lee also noticed that they were turning—and apparently speed-reading—the pages at a remarkable rate. He went up to the couple, introduced himself as being associated with the publisher, and asked them what they found wrong with the book. The couple looked up at him and said nothing. It was then that Mr. Lee noticed that behind their dark glasses both the man and the woman had large, black, almond-shaped eyes. "You know the look you get from a dog when it's going to bite?" Mr. Lee told me. "That was the feeling I got from their eyes. I didn't want to get bitten, so I moved away."

It was not the usual response Mr. Lee would have had in a more normal situation. A former reporter and correspondent for *Newsweek* and *Reader's Digest,* he had covered the White House, the Hill, the Pentagon, and the State Department. He was used to confronting tough people. But in this instance he felt decidedly uneasy, deeply shocked. He went over to his wife, pointed out the couple while mentioning the similarity of their eyes to those on the *Communion* jacket, and urged her to leave the store.

Nobody, least of all myself and the Lees, knows what to make of this experience. Was it an example of the visitors' odd sense of humor? By simultaneously confirming their existence by appearing to a man of high credibility and reputation but also saying that *Communion* was full of perceptual errors (a revelation that certainly didn't surprise me), they proved me right and wrong at the same time.

I must say that I wondered about the small, fierce woman Bruce had encountered. Was it she? And how did *he* determine the sex of the two beings? "They seemed to be man and woman" was his only explanation.

The two visitors had obviously been almost mad with fear themselves, to have communicated such a powerful impression to Mr. Lee.

This appearance was, I believe, as close to public and physical confirmation of their existence as the visitors have yet come.

A telling detail was Mr. Lee's description of the two visitors as wearing mufflers that concealed their chins. I recalled that the correspondent who had provided such an accurate description of the visitors who entered her home in the middle of the day had described the tallest one as having "an elongated face." Mr. Lee and my correspondent do not know one another; in fact they live in different countries. The concurrence of subtle details such as these is strongly suggestive that something real was seen by both people.

Certainly there will be those who will dismiss Mr. Lee's testimony because of his association with my publishing company. But others will be able to see that the man is not lying. The event happened. Because I feared that his testimony would seem selfserving, I did not mention it while promoting *Communion,* except in one minor case where I more or less tripped up. Now, though, with public interest already so well established, the argument that Mr. Lee is merely serving the interest of his employer is thin. Morrow does not need his testimony to sell books, and Mr. Lee feels that the event has brought him nothing but unwelcome exposure.

In any case, the next event did not concern my publisher. In fact, the witness hadn't even heard of *Communion* when it took place.

Two months after Bruce Lee's encounter, a completely unrelated but oddly similar event took place in Chicago. In this case a well-established psychoanalyst, Dr. Lee Zahner-Roloff, was walking through a bookstore when a very strange thing happened to him.

He wrote me, "While wandering in the aisles, I passed a tall woman in a beige suit; I cannot recall her face. This interesting fact emerged only after I was describing to a fellow analyst how I came to purchase the book. The beige-suited woman was carrying *Communion* cradled in her arms, the cover picture forward. In passing her I was overwhelmed with a sudden urge to *pick up that book*. Why would I pick up that book, about which I knew nothing, and seemed to have a loss of control regarding the purchase of? This is most unusual behavior for me, I assure you." In a postscript Dr. Roloff added, "I must repeat that I *lost* personal volition completely."

He continued, "That night I began reading the book, became drowsy, fell off to sleep. *Never* have I had such a tumultuous night of dreaming. I recall nothing of the dreams. Repeat for the next night, save that the dreams were more chaotic. The following morning I told one of my colleagues that she *must read this book* and even at one point advised all of my colleagues to read it. When I was asked what it was about I experienced the most terrifying stares of rebuke and doubt.... After the meeting I took my one sympathetic colleague to the bookstore and bought her the book and asked her to begin it that evening, please! The next morning my first analysand brought a dream about being invaded by aliens, the first such dream in my personal analytical career. My colleague met me for lunch and reported, excitedly, that two analysands had brought outer space dreams, invasion dreams. What did I think? Two days before I had been a *naif*; now I was studying three alien dreams...

"Every once in a while I think about that tall woman in the beige suit carrying your book face forward through the aisles.

One not easily subjected to an impulse purchase of a book, let alone one that I never encountered in any publication and, especially, one that deals with the subject of abductions. I smiled at my colleague over lunch and asked her what she thought of the woman in beige. Incredible, was the response. I concur."

The experiences of Mr. Lee and Dr. Roloff were extraordinary. What neither man could have known was that the filmmaker I mentioned earlier who was my houseguest at the cabin the previous August had stated that the briefing paper he had read told of small gray beings with large eyes not too dissimilar from what Bruce Lee had seen, and that he had been told about tall blond beings such as the one encountered by Dr. Roloff. In addition to this, I had seen a tall blond man in a beige jumpsuit on the night of December 23, 1986. He was well over six feet and clearly very much a part of the group in that room. My impression was that he was guarding the door, presumably to prevent me from making a run for it.

What's more, the grays were thought to be an essentially negative force in conflict with the blond beings. The two that Mr. Lee encountered exuded the same sort of "mad dog" energy that I have observed in them, and were in part negative about *Communion*—although their negativity communicated priceless knowledge to me at the same time. It told me that they were physically real and capable of entering the human environment. It also told me that *some* parts of *Communion* are wrong. To me, this also means that some parts of it are right. Typically, they did not mention which parts were which, but it was still extremely valuable information.

By contrast, the blond woman literally forced Dr. Zahner-Roloff to buy the book.

It would be an oversimplification, however, to conclude that the gray beings were therefore evil and the blond ones benevolent. People have had hair-raising encounters with the blond beings and pleasant ones with the grays, so the picture is mixed.

What is clear to me, however, is the way I react to the two different types of being. The gray ones almost make me jump out of my skin. I don't think I will ever completely lose my fear of them. My reaction to the others is exactly the opposite. They seem much more reassuring. Maybe it's only because of the way they look.

Their looks, by the way, were quite a surprise to me. I never would have believed that anything looking that human could be extraterrestrial in origin. It reminded me forcefully that the true nature of the visitor experience remains very much an unknown.

All of these beings—"grays" and "blonds" alike—fit the ancient notions of demons, angels, and "little people." I reflected that the greater part of my knowledge had come from the gray beings. The word *demon* is derived from the Greek *daimon,* which is roughly synonymous with *soul.* The daimon was the part of a person that could gain knowledge and become transformed. Traditionally, the daimon transformed would return to earth to give knowledge to others. In the Middle Ages knowledge and evil became synonymous and the daimon became the demon, the servant of darkness. In ancient esoteric thought, knowledge was considered an outcome of negative energy because its acquisition came only at the penalty of growing old and dying.

This led me back to something else I had noticed about the visitor experience. From the experiences of people like Mrs. Sharp and from dozens of the letters that were pouring in, it was clear that the soul was very much at issue. People experienced feeling as if their souls were being dragged from their bodies. I'd had an incident of total separation of soul and body. More than one person had seen the visitors in the context of a near-death experience.

"We recycle souls," they had said.

I no longer doubted the existence of the soul. I couldn't; I had been outside my body in a state of total and complete consciousness. This brief but so very clear experience of the soul had inspired me to an intense effort to achieve a conscious connection with it that would last more than a few minutes. I wanted to feel my soul, to participate in its life.

I practiced by constantly trying to leave my body and go to people I knew in such a way that they would be able to perceive me. My method was to use the technique I had learned at the Monroe Institute to reach the "mind awake/ body asleep" state, then attempt to leave my body and reach the target individual. Among the people I attempted to reach in this way were Dora Ruffner, John Gliedman, and Linda Moulton Howe.

I never managed to reach Dora or John.

In February 1987, Linda, (who has since spoken publicly about the incident) called me to report an odd experience. She had awakened and seen the outline of my face across the room from her. Later she wrote me, "What I saw exactly was the impression of your face wearing the glasses you wear amid the leaves of a plant hanging near the door of my bedroom for about 3 seconds in the dark. I turned on the light and nothing was there."

I cannot say that I was trying to reach her on the night that she saw me, because we could not establish the exact date. But her experience took place during the period when I was making the attempt.

I probably would not have mentioned the incident had it not kept happening.

Chicago radio personality Roy Leonard—who does not know any of the other people involved and had heard nothing whatsoever of the episode I just described— awakened on the night of June 7, 1987, to find my presence in his bedroom. He reported that he could "almost" see me. On the same night that this took place—perhaps even at the same hour—I was in a small town near Madison, Wisconsin, having a very unusual experience along with Dora Ruffner and Selena Fox, a leader of Circle Sanctuary, as witnesses and participants.

Circle is the primary networking organization of the Wiccan religion. Wicca is also known as Witchcraft, but it has no relationship to Satanism and other such perversions. It is recognized by the United States government as a legitimate religion, and many of its ministers, such as Ms. Fox, can perform marriages and carry out all the other legally recognized functions of the clergy. Dora and Anne and I were interested in Wicca because, when all the superstitious nonsense that surrounds it is cleared away, it emerges as an ancient Western expression of shamanism, which is the oldest of all human religious traditions. In this it is very similar to Native American and African religions. Like the other nature religions, it has an important lesson to teach us about love for the earth.

The Circle Sanctuary is located in beautiful, rolling Wisconsin land. Dora and I took our families there to meet the members of the group and learn more about the traditions they were trying to restore. We arrived on a warm June afternoon with both of our families—four adults and three children—for a weekend at Circle.

We learned a great deal over that weekend, about Circle's work and its problems communicating its ideas to the many people who are confused about the real nature and goals of Wicca.

Sunday night was windy and moonlit. Selena, Dora, and I went out through a meadow of chest-high grass and flowers, up the side of a hill to Selena's ceremonial stone circle, which is located in a grove of ancient oaks. The wind was tossing the trees, making wild blue shadows on the ground. It was a beautiful moment.

The three of us entered the circle and stood facing one another at its center. Selena was about to begin the ceremony when we heard the footsteps of a fourth person approaching. These footsteps came close to the north point of the circle and stopped for a moment. I was disturbed, because they came right into a patch of moonlight and I couldn't see anyone. Assuming that it must be another person, we called out a greeting, all three of us. Selena walked to the spot where the sounds had come from. She saw nobody, but sensed a very definite presence.

I began to become uneasy. Circle Sanctuary is the object of harassment by the local town board, county zoning officials, and a pressure group of local citizens. Local fundamentalist churches had shown a film about Satanism and falsely claimed that it described Wicca and the practices of Circle Sanctuary. Legal maneuvers were under way to prevent Wiccan religious activities from taking place on Circle Sanctuary land. The American Civil Liberties Union had become involved on the Sanctuary's behalf.

I was afraid that we were about to be attacked by superstitious townspeople. The darkness was now silent. I felt exposed and helpless.

Then the footsteps resumed, this time walking off into the underbrush and apparently over a cliff. We waited, but there was no crash below. Two other people had seen odd manifestations earlier that evening, one a lighted disk sailing along beneath cloud cover, the other a ball of fire bouncing through a meadow.

Selena began the ritual. Despite my fears that either a posse or the visitors were about to come marching out of the dark, I managed to stay throughout to the end. There were stealthy footfalls all around us, even inside the circle. I heard some a couple of feet away from me, but saw nothing at all. As the three of us meditated on behalf of planetary healing, the sounds subsided.

That night I had an extremely strange dream of moving like a ghost through an endless, dark woods and entering a little room that was so dark I couldn't see a thing. How Roy Leonard ended up on the receiving end of that dream I do not presently understand.

A month later I tried consciously to project myself to somebody else. I chose a man I have known for years. At the time, he was going through a number of life changes, and I wanted very much to help him. I lay down on my bed in the city at about ten at night. I waited, conscious of him. Suddenly I saw him. He was sitting with a group of people. He was wearing white clothes. A strange, gray fog seemed to rush out of him and into me. Then the experience ended.

The next morning he called me. I receive perhaps three calls a year from him, so this was a rare occasion. His girlfriend had insisted that he call because she'd had a powerful dream about me the night before. I asked him what he'd been doing at ten, and what he was wearing. "We'd just finished dinner, and we were with friends. I was wearing white jeans and a white shirt." He went on to say that he felt like a fog had lifted from his mind that night, and he was beginning another attempt to reconstruct his life.

In the ensuing months I became better at projecting myself or doing whatever it was that I was doing. I began to be able to intentionally take these journeys from time to time. I will not report on any that did not result in conscious awareness on the part of the individual I visited, because such a journey is considered so extremely improbable in our culture that the narrative of those experiences would serve no useful purpose.

Usually the approach is not noticed by the object individual. Sometimes they appear entirely aware of my presence, but in later conversation they never mention it. Since it would defeat my purpose to bring it up myself, I remain in the dark about whether people I have visited in this manner thought they were dreaming or simply remembered nothing. I have been unable even to approach anybody on an unconscious level when they were awake during the day. In ordinary consciousness people seem literally to be functioning like robots. It is as if they are running on automatic pilot. The effect is astonishing, weird, frightening. One is left with the feeling that human society is a giant machine, and we are all just cogs in it, capable of arousal into higher consciousness only from a state of physical sleep, when the habits of personality do not have us in their snare.

On the night of March 14, 1988, I was talking to writer Barbara Clayman when I realized that she could give a certain man a type of information that he appeared to me to need very badly. I realized that I had to go to Barbara on the nonphysical level in order to prepare her for her encounter with this individual. I told her nothing of my thoughts, and concluded our conversation lest I even subliminally reveal my plan to her.

At four-thirty in the morning I found myself at her bedside. She lives about a thousand miles from New York. I saw her lying there, saw her husband beside her, and felt the enormous tenderness, the anguish of love, that I always experience on such journeys. I feel this even when I am with people who despise me. I suspect that many of us—maybe all of us—make such trips, but that we cannot consciously remember what we do. It takes a long time to be able to allow oneself to feel really consuming, ecstatic love for others. I feel that the visitors have enabled me to see this level of reality by reducing my fear. I am not afraid of overwhelmingly powerful feelings.

I projected my voice into Barbara's ear. I do not hear myself when I do this. It is a form of thought. My experience is that it sounds to the listener like a small speaker or radio in his or her ear. I said, "It's me, Whitley. Barbara, it's Whitley." Her eyes flew open. A flush of fear went through her and she appeared to me to start yelling. This startled me and I told her rather frantically to quiet down. I am a leaf in the wind at moments like that, and if her husband woke up, I would not be able to maintain my presence.

Barbara then became silent and I felt myself give her the material that she needed about the man, who is involved in making a policy decision of fundamental importance.

My next memory is of being deep in soft air, in a blue morning sky.

The next evening Barbara called. She left a message that it was "important." I did not allow myself even to hope that she had remembered our meeting.

To my everlasting delight, when I returned her call I found her full of amazement.

She had remembered our encounter vividly and in detail, right down to the words I had "said" to her. Like the woman in Denver, she recalled seeing my face hanging before her, also complete with the little wire-framed glasses. Lest it be assumed that the touch of the glasses is accidental or even incidental, I would refer readers to the tradition of magical spectacles, which were in olden times thought to enable the wearer to see that which ordinarily remains unseen. In the sixteenth century, *Labyrinth of the World* spectacles were described that possessed the power to reveal an unseen world.

I suspect that experiences such as those reported in this chapter are the outcomes of a fundamental shift of mind. They are what happens when people begin to abandon the old, false belief that each of us is isolated and trapped in our body, that the soul is an abstraction of no real consequence, and that such questions as those posed by the visitors are unworthy of serious consideration. The ability to migrate out of the body may well be a right possessed by all but almost universally ignored.

During the summer of 1987 a number of people who came to our cabin had visitor experiences. Some of these seemed quite genuine. The most extraordinary one happened to Philippe Mora, who was to be the director of the *Communion* film. Since the lunch we'd had the previous year he and I had redeveloped our friendship of twenty years before. It seemed natural and right that he direct *Communion,* especially in view of the beautiful work he'd done with such films as *Mad Dog Morgan* and *Death of a Soldier.*

He came up to get the flavor of the location, walk the woods, see the cabin.

He stayed in the same guest room where Jacques Sandulescu and Annie Gottlieb had encountered the visitors in October 1985.

On the evening of Philippe's visit there had been a spectacular display in the sky. At one point there were three simultaneous meteors and four apparent satellites sailing around. One of the satellites was pulsating. A star left the center of the sky and shot off to the south. The darkness where it had been flickered twice. I made careful note of the time, 9:40.

The following night I went out at the same time and observed the sky for half an hour. While it was similarly clear, it remained quiet. The "satellites" did not reappear, nor have they done so subsequently.

After the heavenly display, Philippe and I walked the woods together. Later he and Anne and I chatted for a while and then we all went to bed. Anne and I went upstairs and he closed himself up in the small guest room on the first floor. I heard the door lock. Futile, I thought.

When we were in bed Anne said, "They're coming tonight." She's usually right in her assessments of the visitors, I've found. Her increasing sensitivity was beginning to combine with her practical good sense and steadfast insistence on reporting only and exactly what she herself saw, heard, and felt to give her words great impact for me.

I did not tell Philippe what she had said. As a matter of fact, I went to sleep only with difficulty and slept lightly, expecting that the family was again to confront them.

At one A.M. I was still just dozing. I remember hearing the clock strike. But I must have been more deeply asleep later, because the next few hours are a blank.

Sometime between two and five I half awoke when I heard a woman downstairs say, "Don't scream or you'll wake up the boy." Instead of jumping out of bed upon hearing a stranger say such a thing in my home in the middle of the night, I just went back to sleep! I slept like a log until morning. When I got up I had no sense at all that the visitors had been near me. Anne was fine. Interestingly, when I asked her if she thought they'd come, she looked at me and sort of laughed.

Philippe was rather distant at breakfast. He spent a good deal of time staring off into space. Finally he said, "Look, I think something happened last night. I woke up and there were lights shining in the window of my room. I was scared. Then I got up and the next thing I knew I found myself in the kitchen. Anne said to me 'Don't scream or you'll wake up the whole house.'"

Anne told him that she hadn't been downstairs. Later she *insisted* to me that this was true. I must admit that the voice I heard didn't sound familiar to me. It was a young, pleasant female voice, average in tone and timbre. It sounded calm and gentle.

Philippe went on to describe seeing a huge object outside hanging over the pool, and lights swarming past all the windows of the house. Later he remembered seeing "a face trying to smile that didn't look like it was made to smile." He also saw a thin being standing and moving its hands as though it were signaling. And somebody showed him little tubs with what appeared to be strange, nonhuman arms and legs growing out of them.

What happened to him? A vivid dream because of where he was sleeping? I wouldn't deny the possibility. But I would also think it foolish to consider that the *only* possibility.

It could also be that he was literally visited by beings who showed him how they looked and even attempted to indicate their friendliness with an inept smile. If they emerge from a reality sufficiently different from our own, their halting and confused contact with Philippe might actually turn out to have been the outcome of many years of effort at learning to communicate with us.

On August 16, 1987, we elected to celebrate the Harmonic Convergence at our home. We did this not because we were certain of the accuracy of the calendrical predictions that led to the observance, but because it represented a coming together of many people throughout the world for a good purpose and because it recognized the validity and— above all—the intellectual potency of Native American thought as expressed in the Mayan calendar.

At our celebration were Dora Ruffner, her friend Peter Frohe, psychologists John Gliedman, Kenneth Ring, and Barbara Sanders, Omega Foundation director Alise Agar, and two people who have had the visitor experience. On the morning of August 16, both I and one of these two people had visitor experiences. Just before dawn this woman was taken from her room down to a meditation circle I'd built the month before. She remembered being talked to by somebody she described as "a man" who held a wand in his hand.

She was exhausted and disturbed by this, and I was concerned for her. A wand was used in October 1985 to strike three blows against my forehead, which forced me to begin the process of encounter.

She spent the rest of the day in bed and had the peculiar experience of forgetting where she had been when she went home on the train later that afternoon. By the time she got to Grand Central Station she could not remember where she had come from. It took her some time to reconstruct her day. It was as if she'd experienced a traumatic amnesia that included her entire visit to our cabin.

Just before dawn I was sitting in the living room waiting for the others to go down to the circle when a voice spoke quite clearly to me from across the room. It said, simply, "Whitley." It was an authoritative but immensely sad male voice. There followed an idea that something was about to happen, and that I should be calm so that I could see it.

The voice prepared me very well for what happened a short time later. A group of us went down to the circle. We sat together, quietly speaking about our reasons for being there— our hope that man will persist in the world and that our insults to the environment will not lead to our destruction but to the awakening of new respect for the needs of the earth.

I expressed my hope that the world would come to see Native Americans, Australians, Africans, and other ancient peoples as the precious and threatened sources of wisdom and guidance that they really are. We offer our wise old peoples the same indifference that we give our wise old parents.

Then we began to look into each other's eyes from around the circle. I had shared this sort of moment with Dora many times before. Suddenly the circle was literally filled with light. I could see Dora through a golden haze. This continued for as long as a minute, and then faded like the fading of bells, leaving me filled with explosive energy and an almost overwhelming desire to get on with my work.

After we left the circle, I asked each person individually what their experience had been. Ken Ring noticed nothing. John Gliedman got a fierce headache. When the light came into the circle, I saw him frown and then seem to inwardly turn away, and I wondered if the headache was not an outcome of an effort to ignore what he had seen. Dora had seen the golden light as clearly as I had. Anne had seen it too. She said, "It was like the sunlight had become incredibly beautiful and clear." The others had not perceived it.

All three of us, especially Anne, date fundamental changes in ourselves from that moment.

Whatever the visitors are, I suspect that they have been responsible for much paranormal phenomena, ranging from the appearance of gods, angels, fairies, ghosts, and miraculous beings to the landing of UFOs in the backyards of America. It may be that what happened to Mohammed in his cave and to Christ in Egypt, to Buddha in his youth and to all of our great prophets and seers, was an exalted version of the same humble experience that causes a flying saucer to traverse the sky or a visitor to appear in a bedroom or light to fill a circle of friends.

It should not be forgotten that the visitors—if I am right about them—represent the most powerful of all forces acting in human culture. They may *be* extraterrestrials managing the evolution of the human mind. Or they may represent the presence of mind on another level of being. Perhaps our fate is eventually to leave the physical world altogether and join them in that strange hyper-reality from which they seem to emerge.

What is interesting to me now is how to develop effective techniques to call them into one's life and make use of what they have to offer. I have described gross versions of such techniques, such as developing real questions and being willing to be taken on a journey through one's fears. The most effective technique seems to be simply to open oneself, asking for what one needs the most without placing any conditions at all on what that might be.

I hope that my book is fair warning of just how hard this journey can be. The few simple techniques I have found are only a beginning. If we choose to deepen our relationship with the visitors, I have no doubt that much more fruitful interaction can be accomplished. This would represent a complete change in man's relationship with this enigma. We would no longer be passive participants. Rather, we would be to some small degree in co-equal control of the relationship.

There can be only one reason that the nature of the visitor experience is changing. They seem more realistic, more *possible,* than ever before. Conceived of as extraterrestrials, they become almost understandable. Perhaps the prevalence of this concept is our way of admitting to ourselves that we *can* now begin to understand.

The "visitor experience" is old. Two hundred years ago a farmer might have come in from his plowing and said, "I saw fairies dancing in the glen." A thousand years ago he might have seen angels flying. Two thousand years ago it would have been Dionysus leaping in the fields. Four thousand years ago he might have seen the goddess Earth herself walking those old hills, her starry robe sparkling with the pure light of magic.

That we could even conceive of having an objective relationship with this force is what is new about the visitor experience in modern times.

Always we have been passive. We have knelt before the gods, been abducted by the fairies and the UFO occupants. But we have never, ever tried to explore a real relationship. This is why we know nothing about them. In a relationship, both partners seek to know and serve the other. So far all we have done, in all of our history, is to be submissive to this force, or try like the fearful, debunkers of today to ignore it. More even than repression of sex, repression of relationship with this level of reality is characteristic of what is most inhumane about modern culture. It is ironic that the West, with its relentless interest in the physical world, would fail to see that the soul also has reference to physical reality, emerges from it, depends on it, indeed is at once its progeny and its source.

Thankfully, the very way we think and perceive our universe may be changing. We may be in the process of achieving a more sane and objective view of something that has been a source of confusion since the beginning of time.

The temptation *not* to question, or to say, "I have the answer," is enormous. I agonized over it. I longed to decide that the visitors were part of my mind. As an intellectual I felt terribly threatened by the idea of extraterrestrial or "other" intelligence. I did not like it and I did not want it to be true.

One of the most difficult things I've had to face is the frank prospect that it is true.

We hide from the visitors. We hide in beliefs. They're the gods. They're gentry, dwarfs, elves. They're demons or angels. Aliens. The unconscious. The oversoul. Hallucinations. Mass hysteria. Lies. You name it. But what they never are, what we never allow ourselves to face, is the truth.

We can face the reality of the visitors. The first step is to admit that they exist but that we do not know what they are. We can then make a tentative beginning, seeking to understand what they may mean to us.

We can do this by developing our side of the relationship with calmness, objectivity, and determination, seeking to find what we can extract from their presence, and what we might be able to give in return. To continue to refuse to entertain the possibility of relationship would be tragic.

If we do that we will deny ourselves the flowering of understanding that seems now to lie just within our grasp.

We have been denying this terrifying, provocative reality for a long time, because to acknowledge it is to face what is smallest and weakest in ourselves.

But to look at it squarely, to accept that it is all one great, big, glorious question about something that is very real—that is at last to raise one's eyes and encounter the sky.

2026 Update

The concentration of named witnesses in this chapter and the extraordinary experiences they describe are a reminder of just how badly it was received on publication. The *Los Angeles Times* even went so far as to place it on its fiction bestseller list. But all they had to do to confirm that it was not fiction was to contact some of these witnesses. Bruce Lee of William Morrow & Company was a highly regarded editor with a distinguished career in military intelligence behind him. Dr. Roloff was also distinguished in his profession. He had a long career at Northwestern University and in 1973 had published *The Perception and Evocation of Literature*.

These and all the other witnesses were readily accessible. Instead of contacting them, some elements of the media attacked the book with striking brutality, with the LA *Times* leading the way: "A sloppy amalgam of… mysticism, psychobabble and shrill self-justification."

There were positive reviews, but not all that many overall, and in those days reviews mattered much more than they do now. The result was that *Transformation* died, and the only detailed account of day-to-day life with the visitors that had ever been published sank into oblivion. The next volume, *Breakthrough*, which marked the final book in the *Communion* trilogy, continued this chronicle. Having already killed *Transformation*, the media received it mostly with silence, fatal in those days to a book.

There is an obvious question here: why? Part of it, as has been discussed previously, seems to have involved a concerted effort on the part of unseen players to make certain that I remained an outlier and—above all—that the abduction experience not be taken seriously. Understandable, given that the U.S. government either allowed it or could not prevent it. As I have already pointed out, Dr. Webb clearly knew a great deal about it, and the fact that his professional credentials were removed from his Wikipedia entry in 2025 by editor "Mayfair" means that these forces are still out there, still dangerous, and still servicing the lie.

For the most part, the intellectual community has decided to ignore the claims not only of close encounter witnesses, but also the many whistleblowers who have come forward from within the government.

To understand this, I want to refer back to the brief mention of Dr. John Gliedman's headache, which occurred after he looked straight at but could not allow himself to see the shaft of golden light that came down into the meditation circle when he was present. To this day, I recall the way he almost shrank into himself.

He did not dare see what was there because, if he had, then his entire understanding of reality would have been undermined, just as mine had been starting in the summer of 1985 when I first started suppressing experiences I could not face and suffered headaches of my own. If it hadn't been for the pain of the rape, I probably would have either continued to ignore them or dismissed the experience as an exceptionally vivid nightmare.

There is a known mechanism that causes this type of memory suppression. When an individual is face-to-face with something they dare not see, the prefrontal cortex can send a signal to the hippocampus to ignore the input. This is why two people witnessing the same event may have entirely different memories of it, or one may remember it and somebody standing right beside them won't.

But it takes energy to do this, and a headache is a classic symptom of what is known as the "think-no think" reaction.

(Anderson, M. C., & Green, C. (2001). *Suppressing unwanted memories by executive control. Nature*, 410, 366–369.)

Denial is another symptom, and is the primary reason that the more intellectual news outlets such as the *New York Times*, the BBC, the Guardian and others do not report the congressional UAP hearings in much detail, if at all.

This denial is a symptom—the core symptom—of the same kind of ontological shock that drives the 'think-no think' response discovered by Anderson et al.

The reason for their unwillingness to face this reality is that doing so seems to endanger the secular paradigm that has evolved since the Enlightenment and which has freed us from the religious dictatorship that suppressed intellectual progress from the fifth through the fourteenth centuries. This is because the way the visitors function suggests that there are elements of consciousness that lie outside of the body. The fear is that recognition of this may bring back the old religions and the enforced beliefs that come with them. However, the fact that there are elements of consciousness that are not connected to our bodies doesn't mean that they aren't part of the physical world. They are, but part of it that we have not yet learned to detect. Instead of denying that it is there what we need to do is try to understand it.

There is so much in this chapter, including veiled references to meeting with "Nordics." One, in particular, was much in my mind at the time, although I did not report it directly in this text. In it, a Nordic had said to me, "if you start a war with the grays, they will never let you win and they will never let you stop fighting."

In *A New World*, I showed from press reports at the time that the U.S. Air Force had been shooting at UFOs as early as the 1950s. We still are. In a hearing on September 9, 2025. Eric Burlison (R. Missouri) showed a tape of a failed attempt to destroy a UFO using a Hellfire Missile off the coast of Yemen.

So we are making the foolish mistake of shooting at something before we understand it, and risking war with an advanced extraterrestrial presence, exactly what was warned against.

All of this—the hysterical denial, the misguided military response and the fact that the public has been kept in ignorance for so long—could have been avoided if in 1947 President Truman had given the problem to social scientists, scholars of myth and religion and neurologists instead of soldiers, weapons designers and physicists. We would never have ended up where we are, locked into a futile military response and a desperate secret effort to develop effective weapons against something that we are not even close to understanding, not its motives, not its capabilities, not its nature.

As unfortunate as the situation is, I don't think that there is really anybody to blame, not our politicians or soldiers or weapons specialists, not even our bizarre and secretive visitors.

I understood this a long time ago, which is why I have consciously and intentionally devoted my life to reducing ontological shock by putting on display every detail of what is, in fact, the only life that has ever been lived with the visitors not as mythological figures but as people. For that's what they are—people who are different from us. They are not gods, sacred beings, demons or any part of our supernatural pantheon. As to their motives for being here, they may be opaque to us but they are powerful enough to keep them here...for better or for worse.

For our part, 'better' is the byword. We can do better. I am not going to advocate for disclosure here, because I don't think that the U.S. government dares to disclose the fantastic magnitude of its failure. This includes not only the mistakes of shooting at the visitors before we understand even whether or not they have hostile intent, but also concealing the abductions, and possibly ceding agency in the matter of contact to powers like Russia and China, should it prove true that they did not shoot, but rather sought and have achieved relationship.

The United States has much to repair, clearly. If it is still possible, we urgently need to stop the fight with the grays. We need to open the door to the broad academic and scientific cultures and they, in turn, need to face the truth: the material world is not bordered by what we know. Rather, the border of reality lies somewhere beyond, and it is out of that beyond that our visitors have come.

It is time that we step out of the house we live in, just as I did when I first left my cabin for the dark of the woods. I began a new life then. When our cultural, political and military leadership faces the dark both within and without, then the same sort of new life that I have chronicled here—and so much more than the little bit I have known—awaits us all.

CHAPTER TWENTY-TWO

BEYOND NIGHTMARE

I hope that I have made a case for more general acceptance of the reality of the visitor phenomenon as something external to the minds of those perceiving it, and communicated what I feel is the critical importance of keeping it in question.

Because of the effort to dismiss the phenomenon, which has been carried out by government and echoed throughout the scientific and intellectual communities, we remain in ignorance about it.

I believe that the visitors themselves have compelled this ignorance. I have three reasons for my opinion.

First, when he resigned from NICAP, CIA Director Hillenkoetter remarked that the air force had done all it could and that further disclosures were up to the visitors. Second, they keep themselves secret when they obviously could do otherwise. Third, in my personal experience, they have defeated my every effort to photograph them and have continued to come to me only late at night or in the predawn hours, when there is the smallest likelihood of detection by others.

The effect of the secrecy has been to keep us ignorant, and thus to deliver us into their hands in a completely helpless state. From my own experience, I see the wisdom of this policy. Had they not surprised me and shattered all of my preconceptions in the process, I would never have learned anything really new from my encounters.

I feel that it is up to each one of us to seek our own contact, develop it if it occurs, and challenge ourselves to use it for intellectual, emotional, and spiritual growth instead of letting our fears overwhelm us.

To do this, we must learn to live with the question.

I know from experience how hard this is. But if we are ever to develop meaningful insight, we must do just that. Dr. Donald Klein's advice to me when we concluded our work together was of absolutely fundamental importance: Learn to live at a high level of uncertainty. Only by doing this will we begin to gain the rigorously clear and objective outlook we need to perceive what is happening correctly.

I will not assert anything final about the visitors. But I will say—indeed, am clearly obligated to say—what I suspect may be true. I have learned a number of important things from my experience.

1. The visitors are physically real. They also function on a nonphysical level, and this may be their primary reality.

2. They have either been here a long time or they are trying to create this impression. So far, our perceptions of them have been conditioned by our own cultural background.

3. They are an objective reality that is almost always perceived in a highly subjective manner.

4. They have the ability to enter the mind and affect thought, and can accomplish amazing feats with this skill.

5. They have taught me by demonstration that I have a soul separate from my body. My own observations while detached from my body suggest that the soul is some form of conscious energy, possibly electromagnetic in nature.

6. They can affect the soul, even draw it out of the body, with technology that may possibly involve the use of high-intensity magnetic fields.

7. They used few words to communicate with me. Their primary method was a sort of theatrical demonstration, richly endowed with symbolic meaning.

8. When I challenged my own fear of them they responded by taking me on a journey deep into my unconscious terrors. From this I learned that suppressing and denying fear are useless. I discovered how to accept my fear and not be surprised by it.

I suspect that the visitors may have been here for a long time. It has even crossed my mind, given their apparent interest in human genetics, that they may have had something to do with our evolution.

I cannot speculate why we are beginning to see them as a demythologized reality— if indeed we are. It is possible, though, that we are in the process of evolving past the level of superstition and confusion that has in the past blocked us from perceiving the visitors correctly.

The small gray beings that I encountered carried a tremendous load of negativity. In his letter to me describing his encounter in the bookstore, Bruce Lee added the following personal comment: "I was brought up on a farm. I know what it is to look into the eyes of a mad dog. I have had to kill rabid dogs and foxes. That mad-dog look was there...."

But, like so many things about the visitors, there is more to all this than meets the eye. It may be that we are also encountering our own secret savagery when we face them.

I think that the most terrible thing I have ever seen was my face reflected in the eyes of a visitor. I looked like a mad dog.

To the degree that I learned to use their fearsome onslaught as a means of gaining insight into my own fears, I acquired an effective coping tool: The more frightening they got, the stronger I became.

At first they assaulted me without regard to my strengths and weaknesses. My reaction, once I had recovered from my initial panic, was to try to face them. I did this because I got tired of running away; and my wife and I also found the possibility that they might be real tremendously exciting and interesting, though I cannot deny that they may also be dangerous.

I feel that the potential for gain outweighs the risks of contact.

As our relationship developed, the visitors began to tune it very carefully, leading me step by step through my fears. They always seemed ready with the hardest challenge I could manage. They never sought to destroy me with an assault beyond my strength. Thus they can hardly be called evil. Based on the actual outcome of what they did to me, they must be counted the allies of our growth.

I have emerged from my experience a thousand times stronger than I had ever been before it. I am not at all afraid, not even of death. Rather it has become another rich potential in my life, a challenge to be met with a peaceful heart and an interested mind.

I have been in my soul separate from my body. My own experience thus tells me that the soul has a separate life, and the work of people like Dr. Ian Stevenson suggests that it persists beyond death, and that reincarnation is apparently a very real possibility. The visitors have said, "We recycle souls," and—of the earth—that "this is a school." It may be exactly that—a place where souls are growing and evolving toward some form that we can scarcely begin to imagine. I can conceive that the fate of souls may be one of the great universal questions. It may be that we have emerged as a means of at once creating and answering this question.

My own struggle has made me realize that our lives are, at least potentially, a place of reconciliation between positive and negative energies. My encounters with the visitors were at their most satisfactory when I was actively struggling against my fears and hungers. It was friction that gave me strength.

I do not now find the small, gray beings terrible. I find them useful, as work with them is an efficient way to assault the dark battlements of fear and acquire the wisdom beyond.

Throughout our history we have rejected the negative and sought the positive. There is another way, I feel, that involves balancing between the two. It is up to us to forge in the deepest heart of mankind the place of reconciliation. We must learn to walk the razor's edge between fear and ecstasy—in other words, to begin finally to seek the full flowering and potential of our humanity.

I have learned much about the value and sense of communion with the visitors. The whole point of it seems to me to involve strengthening the soul. Certainly this has been central to my relationship with them.

They made me face death, face them, face my weaknesses and my buried terrors. At the same time, they kept demonstrating to me that I was more than a body, and even that my body could enter extraordinary states such as physical levitation.

In order to transform the visitor experience into something that is useful to us, we must, each of us, face the fact that they evoke fear—and realize that we possess a peace within ourselves that cannot be assailed even by the most powerful negative force.

Really facing the visitors means accepting that one may also endure great fear ... and become free of all fear.

I have been in anguish many, many times, immersed in the fury of their malevolence, feeling them as a kind of tremendous, overwhelming superconsciousness that saps all sense of self-control.

If we can strike an effective inner pose of balance instead of confronting the visitors with the irrationality of cornered animals, I feel that we will begin to extract a measure of value from our exposure to them.

Should we seek to expand the relationship, we will have to face some very, very difficult things. The journey will be almost inconceivably hard, but also rich with marvels and full of hope. We will walk a narrow way between dangers. To our left there will be a sick planet and all the social discord and economic misery that must accompany its suffering. To our right there will be the rigorous, demanding, and wise unknown that is the visitors.

We will discover truths about ourselves, truths that will change each of us—and all of us—forever. We will pierce the fog that has for so many long years obscured our vision.

At last, we will see.

2026 Update

And now, nearly forty years later, we have seen a lot. Assertions have been made in congressional hearings and video revealed that make it difficult for even people in deepest ontological shock to deny that something unexplained is happening. But they still do deny, of course, largely by ignoring the story. It remains risky to address the issue in academy and the scientific community, but it can now be done in such a way that one's career is not necessarily going the be undermined. Some elements of the intellectual press are at least a bit open to the idea that the UAP might be a genuine unknown. But the close encounter experience remains an outlier in all of these communities. Not, though, among the public, which increasingly understands that if UAP are real, then there must be somebody controlling them, and therefore that people who claim to be in contact with this presence deserve a hearing.

Someone still works to undermine the claims of close encounter witnesses or "Mayfair" would never have removed Dr. Webb's professional credentials from his Wikipedia entry.

Something that is touched on in this chapter but not fully explored is a question that was too large for me to really see at that time. It is whether or not we are living in a naturally occurring solar system or in something that has been designed, and, if it is designed, are we also?

Earth, the moon and the sun are so perfectly positioned that solar total eclipses are possible. As the moon passes in front of the sun, the two disks merge precisely. In addition, Earth is in the narrow goldilocks zone, and not only is it shielded from strikes by large objects by the presence of the moon, the huge gas giants that populate the outer solar system provide even more protection. So life has been allowed to thrive and evolve here over a period of many billions of years.

Did someone long ago come here and devise this as a sort of life-creating machine? And if so, are we ourselves in some way designed? If so, then who are these so-called "visitors," really? They may not be visitors at all. Perhaps this place is their property and we are their creation.

I'm not going to make a complex argument on behalf of these ideas, but I can say now with an assurance that I certainly didn't possess in 1986 that the grays do have some proficiency when it comes to genetic engineering, which I discussed in *The Fourth Mind*.

They also have a proficiency in drawing the consciousness out of the body. I suppose it's fair to call this "the soul," but that word carries with it so much baggage that I prefer to refer to it as "second body."

While I was working on this book and for some time prior, I had both been trying to get out of my body and they had been taking me out. It hasn't happened in years, but I remember those days very fondly. It was quite a thrill to realize that people could actually see me when I was in their presence in a nonphysical state.

Then there was the incident in Petaluma, described here earlier. I would like to add that I was removed from my body by the application of that strange vibration I have referred to here and in *The Fourth Mind*, that I think is some sort of conscious energy.

It was applied just above the atlas (C-1) vertebra that connects the spine to the neck. Then the whole, wonderful event unfolded.

When, during my abduction, one of the visitors called me "the luckiest of the lucky," I did not have the slightest idea what that might mean. As I mentioned above, later I began to understand.

Among the many things that it means is that I have been granted the blessing of certain knowledge that there is a non-physical level of consciousness, and that the identity remains intact even when we are not in our bodies. There is so much more, though. I know that the dead persist, as Anne demonstrated to me after she died, and which I described in *Afterlife Revolution*. I also know that the visitors have both a physical and a nonphysical presence, and that they can move between them with proficiency.

Above all, the greatest blessings that have been conferred on me are two: the continued presence of Anne in my life; and the intimate, ever-deepening relationship I have with the grays. It has been very hard and I know, in detail, many of the dangers involved, but I intend to persist in developing it as long as I can and as deeply as I can. They appear to have a predatory nature, but that may only be because they want us to build our side of the relationship as an independent species, and not become supplicants. I doubt that a little planet full of beggars would be of much interest to anybody, and if I know anything about them, they are not patient. And yet, they wait for us. They keep the pressure up, but not too much.

Insofar as the new world that is on offer promises things, like an ability to move among the stars and to understand the true nature of consciousness, it is the best thing that we have had the chance to take and to make our own.

Can we?

My answer is, "yes, of course." So join me, why don't you? Let's take a walk together tonight, a walk in the woods.

2026

We have now arrived at the end of the first quarter of the twenty-first century, a time that, when the *Transformation* events took place, seemed almost inconceivably distant. Had you asked me then to predict what our relationship with the visitors would be like now, I would have said that it would be far more evolved than it actually is.

If you had told the Whitley of 1988 that less progress than he was expecting had been made, he would have been disappointed. But I am not disappointed. Far from it. The Whitley of 2026 knows a great deal more about what it happening, how it is happening and what it means than did that younger man.

He did not understand just how difficult everything was going to be, or how important ontological shock really is. Had the visitors come marching into our lives in 1989, our world would without doubt have descended into a chaos from which it had, at best, a very limited chance of recovering. We would have been forever locked out of the relationship with the world around us that we have now, and which seems so fundamental and so impossible to change.

As was seen in the discussion of the quiet walk to the pecan trees, we would find ourselves seeing our surroundings in subtle but important new ways. We would, *en masse,* be forced to accept that we no longer understood what our everyday world really was. And what of our lives?

So contact for which we have not properly prepared is a danger. Of course it is.

This is something I have known for a long time. Getting past the shock of contact is what this book is about. We did it. I live in contact and I live in *this* world. This is because I understand the points of divergence between our vision of reality and theirs. I know that they see the world differently, and when I am with them, I expect there to be a problem of focus.

Back at the beginning, I didn't understand this, but the visitors did. This was fortunate, because in 1989, I was far from being able to handle interaction with them in any useful way. Because most of us have been forcibly kept in ignorance, we still are, far more so than I would have believed possible in 1989. But here we are. The government, the scientific and academic communities, the intellectual media and social control, perhaps even the visitors themselves, working through our own social institutions, have continued to enforce ignorance.

No matter who is doing it, my ambition is to fight it with every ounce of my being. We can achieve contact. We can make it work for us. Because of the trajectory of my own life, I am convinced that this is the case.

I see real, meaningful interaction with them as leading to the collapse of the barriers not only between us and them, but also between us and our own true powers of being. On one side of contact, we are as we are now. On the other, we are something entirely new, and very much more in touch with reality as it actually is, and adventuring beyond the constricted dream that comprises our current understanding.

To make progress, we must—absolutely *must*—face the fact that we cannot detect a substantial part of the world around us, that we now dismiss as the "supernatural" or the "paranormal," but which is actually part of the normal world that we do not yet understand.

It exists, therefore we can find a way to understand it on terms that make sense to us, and flow naturally out of the techniques of discovery that are established in our scientific and academic disciplines.

It was clear to me back then that our planet is a school for souls. For some of us, it can also become a prison. After *Transformation* was written, I was accorded the fantastic privilege of knowing through the medium of physical proof that there is an afterlife, a series of experiences that begin to be described in the final book in the *Communion* series, *Breakthrough*. I also know that not everybody graduates from this school. My wife Anne knew, though. In fact, there was a hidden master behind the whole process of contact we were undergoing together in those days. It was not the visitors. It was her.

On one level, she was a kid from Ann Arbor, Michigan, smart as hell and attractive as she could be, but—well—like me, just an ordinary American kid. On another level, she was an absolute master of contact. After *Communion* was published, letters poured in from other witnesses. 3,400 of those letters are now housed in the Archives of the Impossible at Rice University in Houston, and will be one of the key tools that we will use to overcome the shock of the tremendous change that the emergence of the visitors will cause. She saved those letters because she knew that they would one day form the basis of a new and deeper understanding of our relationship with the visitors. They would provide a path out of the shock and confusion that surrounds the experience.

She also edited *Communion* and played a huge role in managing the tumultuous relationship with the visitors described in this book and in *Breakthrough*. Nine months before she died, this amazing and deeply sacred person began the process of creating the avatar that would appear after her death, a process described in *The Afterlife Revolution*. To my knowledge, she is the only person to have created an identifiable avatar like this, in her case a white moth, which appeared many times to many people, often simply disappearing before their eyes after the contact was made. She created her avatar as a teaching tool, and many thousands of people have engaged with it, learning in the process what she considered to be essential to contact: that we are not just bodies, but also souls, and it is our souls that are the primary focus of our relationship with the visitors.

In 1988, I was only just becoming aware of the fact that the dead were involved in contact. Actually, I was then just beginning to really understand that the soul not only exists, but is a more important part of us than the body. She did understand this, and was the one who showed me that our visitors and our dead inhabit the world in the same way. In fact, the chief difference between us is that they appear to be able to put on and take off their bodies at will, while we are so welded to our bodies that most of us live as if the greater part of us doesn't even exist.

In 1988, I did not fully understand the consequences of our being soul blind. I do now, though, and the primary consequence is that, until enough of us have a clear and objective awareness of this inner presence, absent imagination, absent myth, absent religion, contact is not going to happen.

But it *will* happen. Of this I am quite certain. The reason I am certain of this is that I can see a clear development, starting as far back as 1933 with the Italian UAP crash near the town of Magenta, then expanding dramatically after the end of World War II until now, when UAP sightings are a commonplace of life.

This means only one thing, and it is why I made the unusual decision to reprise a book this book. *Transformation* and *Breakthrough* are the only accounts in the world that describe, clearly and accurately, what it is like to live with the visitors as *people*. There are no magical beings here, no demons, no ladies from above, no gods and goddesses—but rather only this: immensely knowledgeable and extremely complex beings who are, in the end, also people, often tired, often scared, blundering along trying to make sense of us just as we are of them.

And the miracle of it is that both sides are succeeding. Slowly, with many twists and turns, setbacks and triumphs, we are beginning to understand what we have to offer one another, and—more slowly—how to navigate the fear that is at the heart of the relationship. For they are scared, too. Just last June, when the friend who is working with me on a creative project was abducted, the visitors who approached her were clearly as scared as they could be, but doing it anyway.

Anyway. That was always Anne's approach: even if we don't have the understanding, don't have the right tools, don't know where we stand—let's try anyway.

So, let's do just that. Let's follow the lead of that extraordinary woman, the first person to really understand the hidden meaning of contact, that it was not just about coming together in the physical, but also in the greater world of which we are all a part.

Over the next few years, the world is going to change very dramatically. Artificial intelligence will morph into quantum computing and digital minds of essentially infinite power will be born among us. At the same time, the planet's overstressed resources will lead to food and water shortages worldwide and increasingly desperate populations.

At some point in this perfect storm of change something incredible, complex, disruptive and in the end, I hope, beautiful is going to happen: the visitors are going to begin to make themselves available to more of us. They will come as both teachers and students. There will be conflict: the U.S. Defense Department has apparently been at war with them for some time. A mistake? Only time and more knowledge will tell.

In any case, no matter what our visitors think of us and what they may wish to do to us, it is absolutely inevitable that some of us will figure this out and will make contact, and will find ways to rise out of the shadowy depths of our planet's gravity well, and adventure into a cosmos more vast than we can presently imagine, to find a new and deeper human truth there than we know now, in the dark and the vastness of mind and universe.

HEALTH

I t is important to me that I not participate in the creation of a false unknown. I have thus been eager to explore all possible prosaic answers to the question of what happened to me.

There are a number of diseases of the brain and disorders of the mind that can lead to hallucinations. The most prominent disease is temporal lobe epilepsy, which is a transient disturbance to the temporal lobe of the brain. It causes vivid hallucinations that are often associated with powerful odors. Less frequently, sounds can be mixed with visions and smells in this disease. People with temporal lobe epilepsy tend to be verbal and philosophical and to lack a sense of humor.

Paranoia and schizophrenia are also associated with delusional states and hallucinations.

How my having such a disease could have caused total strangers like Bruce Lee, Dr. Zahner-Roloff, and so many others to encounter the visitors in so many different ways I do not know. Certainly these encounters cannot be dismissed as hysteria. Dr. Zahner Roloff had never heard of me and my book; nor had Jo Sharp or Barry Maddock. In addition, the great majority of my encounters used to occur in a specific place, my cabin. None of these diseases is recorded as being in the least geographically specific. We have also had the water tested for all manner of pollutants, including pesticides and metals, and nothing unusual was found. The air in the basement of the cabin was tested for gas content, and nothing unusual was detected. Nevertheless, a vapor detector was installed. Our water-purification system uses chlorine, a filter to remove metals, and activated charcoal to remove pollutants. There are no gases or substances in the water that might distort perception.

I was tested for temporal lobe epilepsy on December 6, 1986, and no abnormalities were found. This test was conducted by Columbia-Presbyterian Medical Associates. It included the use of nasopharyngeal leads and induced sleep and is the most sensitive test for this disease that is available. The conclusion of the examining physician was: "This EEG, which includes nasopharyngeal leads, is normal with the patient awake and asleep."

TLE, however, is an elusive disease, and I have continued to have myself tested for it.

I undertook another test series beginning on March 14, 1988. An EEG (without nasopharyngeal leads but with sleep), a CAT scan of my brain, and an MRI (a supersensitive brain scan) were performed by a different facility (New York University Hospital) from the one that did the TLE exam. They were evaluated by a different neurologist. Either the MRI (Magnetic Resonance Imaging) or the CAT (Computer Axial Tomography) scan would have located epileptic areas in the brain of an adult with longstanding (two years or more) disease. No such areas were observed.

There was an interesting finding from the MRI scan. This is a new type of brain scan, providing a more detailed image than the CAT scan. It works by placing the brain in a high-intensity magnetic field and allowing a computer to generate patterns from protons emitted by affected molecules in the tissue being examined. The image that it provides is remarkably fine, showing even very small details.

The findings were described by the examining physician as follows: "The ventricles and sulci are normal. There are no masses, shifts or displacements. Occasional punctate foci of high signal intensity are located in the cerebral white matter of the frontal lobes bilaterally as well as the left temporoparietal region." The neurologist explained to me that these extra structures were so-called "unknown bright objects" that are occasionally seen with this test in normal brains.

Such objects are associated with multiple sclerosis, trauma, microvascular disease, and, very rarely, healed scars from an unusual parasitic disease. I do not have MS and have never had any episodes of weakness or any other symptom that would suggest this disease. Even if I did have it, it does not cause hallucinations; nor do any of the other diseases that might be associated with unknown bright objects found in the brain areas where they were located in me. I have never had any trauma to the head worth mentioning, certainly no parasitic disease, and, as the parts of the vascular system of my brain that were visible were in exceptionally good shape, microvascular disease is unlikely.

I do recall, as I reported in *Communion,* a number of occasions when needles appeared to be inserted into my head by the visitors. One such intrusion took place on December 26, 1985, behind my right ear, and another in March 1986, up my left nostril. Are the unknown objects in my brain an outcome of such intrusions? There is presently no way to determine this, but if a test sensitive enough to reveal them in even greater detail is ever devised, I will certainly take it. In the meantime, I have no intention of attempting to have them excised, nor can I imagine that any reputable neurosurgeon would perform such an operation, given that the objects are of no neurologic consequence and similar structures have occasionally been observed in other normal brains.

However, I do think it would be most interesting if other people who recall similar intrusions to the cranium taking place during visitor experiences also undertake the MRI. It is an easy test. Unlike the CAT scan, it does not require the infusion of iodine into the blood, and it does not introduce radiation into the brain. Should a substantial number of such people display similar objects in their brains, it would be suggestive that the recalled intrusions could be leaving a physical trace that we can now detect.

I have also taken a number of psychological tests. Among these was the MMPI, a standard test designed to detect personality abnormalities. I have also taken the Bender Gestalt test, the WAIS-R adult intelligence test, the House-Tree-Person test, the Rorschach test, the Thematic Apperception test, and the Human Figure Drawing test. When I took this test group on March 7, 1986, I appeared to the testing psychologist to be "under a good deal of stress," and to suffer from "fatigue" and "inner turmoil." The overall finding was that I suffered from a great deal of fear, which was consistent with my state at that time. The tests were taken during the time when I was most terrified of the visitors.

I have also been interviewed at great length by a number of psychiatrists and neurologists, and none of them has ever discovered the least sign that I am anything except what I appear to be: a normally integrated man of above-average intelligence, with highly developed verbal skills.

At the moment that is the status of my case.

Should any psychophysical condition be discovered to have caused my experiences, I will certainly make it known. I have not the least intention of creating or in any way supporting a false unknown. Indeed, I would be the first to suggest that any and all of our present interpretations of the visitor experience may be wrong.

Most of the physicians involved in my case have requested confidentiality. I will not release their names. What I have done instead is to turn over all of their findings to Dr. John Gliedman, and I have given them all permission to discuss my case fully with him. While also respecting their confidentiality, he has agreed to correspond with licensed medical and mental-health professionals and concerned scientists about my case. We will not respond to "investigators" without scientific, medical, or mental-health credentials, or to "debunkers" intent on twisting the facts to serve their own emotional needs, and not to get at the truth.

I do believe, and strongly, that behind all the strange experiences and perceptions, behind the lights in the sky and the beings in the bedroom, there lies a very important, valuable, and genuine unknown. My hope is that we will eventually face the fact that it is there, and begin a calm, objective, and intellectually sound effort to understand it.

2026 Update

In recent years, there have been two important changes in my medical record insofar as it involves the close encounter experience. The implant that was placed in the outside edge of my left ear in 1989 has been imaged, and an MRI of my brain done in 2019 has been examined, and there are new findings.

The implant was imaged on September 24, 2019, and shows the object lodged in the pina (upper part of the external ear). It can also easily be felt with a finger. In addition, the video of the removal attempt shows both Anne and the doctor observing it move away from its location in the pina when the attempt to remove it was made. It moved down into the earlobe, remained there for two days, then returned to its present position.

After many years of inactivity, in late 2015 or early 2016, as I have reported, it began to function. It is now my constant companion, working whenever I write and when I am in interviews.

This leads me to mention the realization that has grown steadily in me over the years of how profoundly our own dead are involved in the entire close encounter experience. It is as much about contact with nonhuman intelligence as it is with them.

We have an awfully long way to go, though. It takes many years of patient inner work doing neutral meditations such as the sensing exercise that I learned in the Gurdjieff Foundation in 1969 before you can gain even a slight feeling of this hidden part of us. There exists within us an intelligence, a memory, an emotional life that is hidden from the outer person. This person—the personality attached to the name we were given at birth—has to be connected to the inner person. We have been in the past, but never in the way that now seems possible.

If you look across the past, you see a great army of gods, demons, ghosts, angels, enlightened beings, saints—an enormous, ghostly assemblage of sacred beings.

I was afraid one night out in the woods, alone with the dark and the wind and the sense of somebody nearby, and I began to pray. One of the visitors said in my echoing mind where their voice is found, "listen to him, calling on his gods."

And there you have it—why this juncture in the human adventure is so profound. We are not going to lose our gods, but rather the way we now imagine them. Our future is to see them in the light of that city I flew across in those days, the city where the truth is known. That is our city now, our new home. We are all going to enter it and live in it, and there will be our gods as they really are and our beliefs in their true meaning.

I wish I could say that I knew what our gods will be like then, and what our beliefs will mean in the blistering light of truth, but that is for the future and the children, not for me here on the crumbling shore of what is already the past.

Anne never wanted me to have the implant removed, and I am certainly glad now that it is still a part of me! She knew so much, my wife, just a kid from Michigan—but so much more…just like every one of us.

On June 18, 2014 I had an MRI scan consequent to persistent headaches. This was the first scan I'd had since the one immediately post the Communion experience in 1986, so MRI technology was much more advanced and more was made visible.

A doctor who examined the scan in February of 2022 reported that the striatum/caudate/putamen white matter connections "are unique in my experience: they're very distinct, more than I have ever seen. And they are highly non-striatal, not running parallel in any plane. And while in upper normal in density, they are tortuous and irregular in path." He goes on to explain that this does not mean that they are evidence of pathology, but that they are unique.

I have discussed this in *The Fourth Mind*, but did not discuss the two needle insertions into my brain that are mentioned in this book. The first one occurred during the December 26, 1985 event and left a distinct mark which was observed by my doctor, who thought it might be a spider bite. The second one took the form of the insertion of a needle into my left nostril. An otolaryngologist noted a swelling shortly after the event, but an MRI of the area revealed no sign that a needle had ever been pressed up into the skull through the nostril.

If someone wished to insert a needle into the region of the caudate-putamen, they would typically insert the needle along the midline of the scalp, but the insertion that took place during the encounter involved the left temple. While I cannot say that the white matter wasn't affected, normally a needle penetrating that area would have been directed at the temporal lobe or possibly the hippocampus. As to the insertion up the nostril, the idea horrified the neurosurgeon I consulted because any needle in that area that penetrated into the brain would bring with it debris from the nasal cavity. No human surgeon would do it. If it was done, the prefrontal cortex would be the target.

As to the mental health tests, I remain the same mentally normal individual I was then. Since my wild and wonderfully fun college days, I have led a quiet life, married once for life, fathered just the one child, who has grown up into a fine man with children of his own. My life is lived in moderation. I am healthy and robust. My moral stance and religious beliefs can be found in my book *Jesus: A New Vision.*

I am happy living this wonderful, complicated and often extremely challenging life with the visitors. I do not know who they are and I cannot tell the difference between human and nonhuman aspects of the presence. For all I know, there is no difference. But in any case, I take on all comers. Whatever emerges into my life out of the vibrant shadows is welcome.

My door is open.

TRUTH

In *Communion* I reported the results of a lie-detector test performed on me before publishing the book. I passed this test. I have always tried to tell the truth about my perceptions. Even Philip J. Klass, a vociferous and skeptical UFO researcher, has written me a letter permitting me to state publicly that he doesn't think I am lying. On December 17, 1987, he wrote me, "I believe that Whitley Strieber honestly believes he experienced the weird encounters described in his book *Communion* and that he is not knowingly, intentionally falsifying same." He added that he thought a "prosaic" explanation would be found for my encounters and has asserted elsewhere that he believes me to be a temporal lobe epileptic. In view of the fact that no evidence of this disease—or any other intrusive abnormality—has been found, even with extensive testing, that is a theory that is now very hard to maintain.

On May 18, 1987 I was given another lie-detector test. It was administered by

Polygraph Security Services of London at the request of the British Broadcasting Corporation, and paid for by the BBC. I also passed this test. Among the questions asked were:

Are the visitors about whom you write in your book *Communion* a physical reality?

Whilst in the presence of your visitors, have you actually felt them touch you?

I answered these questions in the affirmative and was found to be telling the truth.

I was also asked if I had invented them for personal gain. My denial was evaluated as true.

I was retested at my own request for *Transformation*. The polygraphist (Nat Laurendi, who originally tested me for *Communion)* was extremely skeptical, but I once again passed the test. It is worth noting that on questions where I was directed to lie, my blood pressure and rate of sweating increased, allowing the tester to determine easily that I had lied. The fact that these two automatic functions were what changed when I lied suggests that I am not a person who could defeat a lie-detector test easily, if at all.

Among the questions asked in this test were the following:

Do you honestly believe that *Transformation* is a true account of your encounters with the visitors between April 1986 and March 1988?

Are the witnesses named and unnamed in the book real people?

Do you honestly believe that the visitors are physically real?

Have you encountered the visitors at least four times while totally and fully conscious?

I answered yes to all these questions, and my answers were evaluated as true.

I have now been tested three times by polygraph experts, and asked direct, plain questions.

It must be concluded that I am neither insane nor a liar. There is truth in my strange story. Indeed, it may be that its very strangeness is its strongest proof.

On March 31, 1988, Bruce Lee of William Morrow and Company was also polygraphed by Mr. Laurendi. He was asked if he thought the two beings he saw in the bookstore were visitors, and if he spoke to them. He replied "yes" to both questions and his answers were evaluated to be true. He was asked if I had offered him anything of value to tell his story. He answered "no" and this answer was evaluated as true.

GAELIC

One of the most interesting and unusual findings in *Transformation* is Leonard Keane's discovery that the star language spoken by Betty Andreasson Luca when she was under hypnosis might have been Gaelic. This is especially remarkable as Mrs. Luca is the daughter of a French immigrant and a native New Englander. Mrs. Luca's experience is reported in detail in Raymond Fowler's excellent book on the subject, *The Andreasson Affair.* This book stands as a classic account of visitor experience, and is especially noteworthy for its candid revelation of the stunning mystical and religious overtones of Mrs. Luca's experience.

After reading Mr. Keane's translation of her Gaelic words, Mrs. Luca wrote me as follows: "I must tell you when I read the first two lines of Mr. Keane's translation, uncontrollable tears washed down my face for at least five minutes.... Finally someone is bringing out the truth of the messages."

With Mr. Keane's permission, I record here his glossary of the "star language." All phonetic renderings are taken from *The Andreasson Affair* and were created by Mr. Fowler. I have listened to the original tapes and found that he did a careful and accurate job of transcription.

Star Language Gaelic Equivalent English Translation oh-tookurah ua-tuaisceartach descendants of Northern peoples *bohututahmaw beo t-utamail* living groping *hulah uile* all *duh dubh* darkness *duwa dubhach* mournful *maher mathair* mother *Duh Dubh* Dark *okaht ocaid* occasion *turaht tuartha* forebode *nuwrlahah nuair lagachar* when weakness *tutrah t-uachtarach* in high places *aw hoe-hoe athbheoite* revives *marikoto maireachtala-costas* cost of living *tutrah t-uachtarach* high *etrah eatramh* interval *meekohtutrah me-ancog t-uachtarach* mistakes in high places *etro eatramh* interval *indra ukreeahlah indeacrachlach* fit for distressing

The translation therefore reads:

"The living descendants of the Northern peoples are groping in universal darkness. Their mother mourns. A dark occasion forebodes when weakness in high places will revive a high cost of living; an interval of mistakes in high places; an interval fit for distressing events."

2026 Update

The time that was being referred to back in the 1970s is upon us. It is *now*.